Complexity and Institutions

This is IEA conference volume no. 150-II

Complexity and Institutions: Markets, Norms and Corporations

Edited by

Masahiko Aoki
Stanford University, USA

Ken Binmore
University College London, UK

Simon Deakin
University of Cambridge, UK

Herbert Gintis
Santa Fe Institute USA and Central European University, Hungary

palgrave
macmillan

First published 2012 by
PALGRAVE MACMILLAN

Palgrave Macmillan in the UK is an imprint of Macmillan Publishers Limited, registered in England, company number 785998, of Houndmills, Basingstoke, Hampshire RG21 6XS.

Palgrave Macmillan in the US is a division of St Martin's Press LLC, 175 Fifth Avenue, New York, NY 10010.

Palgrave Macmillan is the global academic imprint of the above companies and has companies and representatives throughout the world.

Palgrave® and Macmillan® are registered trademarks in the United States, the United Kingdom, Europe and other countries

ISBN: 978–1–137–03419–9 hardback
ISBN: 978–1–137–03420–5 paperback

This book is printed on paper suitable for recycling and made from fully managed and sustained forest sources. Logging, pulping and manufacturing processes are expected to conform to the environmental regulations of the country of origin.

A catalogue record for this book is available from the British Library.

A catalog record for this book is available from the Library of Congress.

10 9 8 7 6 5 4 3 2 1
21 20 19 18 17 16 15 14 13 12

Printed and bound in Great Britain by
CPI Antony Rowe, Chippenham and Eastbourne

Contents

List of Tables

List of Figures

Notes on Contributors

Masahiko Aoki is Henri and Tomoye Takahashi Professor Emeritus in the Department of Economics and a senior fellow of Stanford Institute of Economic Policy Research and Freeman Spolgi Institute of International Studies at Stanford University. He is also a fellow of the Econometric Society and former President of the International Economic Association (2008–11).

Svetlana Andrianova is Reader in Economics at the University of Leicester.

Ken Binmore is Emeritus Professor of Economics at University College London. He is a Commander of the British Empire. He is also a fellow of British Academy and an honorary member of the American Academy of Arts and Sciences. He is an Honorary Fellow of London School of Economics.

Silvana Cincotti is Professor of Economic and Financial Engineering at the University of Genoa, head of the Center for Interdisciplinary Research on Economics and Financial Engineering (CINEF) and coordinator of the EU IST-FET Strep Project EURACE.

Simon Deakin is Professor of Law at the University of Cambridge and director of the corporate governance programme at the Centre for Business Research, and the interdisciplinary research unit based at the Judge Business School in Cambridge.

Panicos O. Demetriades is Professor of Financial Economics at the University of Leicester and Academician of the Academy of Social Sciences in the UK.

Corrado di Guilmi is Post Doctoral Research Fellow at the University of Technology, Sydney. He earned his PhD in Political Economics at the Università Politecnica delle Marche (Italy).

Mauro Gallegati is Professor of Economics at the Polytechnic University of Marche.

Herbert Gintis is External Professor at the Santa Fe Institute (Santa Fe, NM) and Professor of Economics, Central European University (Budapest, Hungary).

Michihiro Kandori is Professor in the Faculty of Economics, University of Tokyo. He is a fellow of the Econometric Society.

Simone Landini has a PhD in Mathematics for the Analysis of Financial Markets at Bicocca University in Milan (Italy). He is a researcher in Political Economics at IRES Piemonte (Socioeconomic Rearch Instiute of Piedmont, Italy).

YBP Library Services

INTERNATIONAL ECONOMIC ASSOCIATION. WORLD
CONGRESS (16TH: 2011: BEIJING, CHINA)
COMPLEXITY AND INSTITUTIONS: MARKETS, NORMS AND
CORPORATIONS; ED. BY MASAHIKO AOKI.

Paper   247 P.

BASINGSTOKE: PALGRAVE MACMILLAN, 2012
SER: IEA CONFERENCE VOLUME; 150-II.

ED: STANFORD UNIVERSITY. PROCEEDINGS.

ISBN 1137034203   **Library PO#** GENERAL APPROVAL

	List	35.00	USD
5461 UNIV OF TEXAS/SAN ANTONIO	**Disc**	10.0%	
App. Date 4/17/13 ECO.APR 6108-11	**Net**	31.50	USD

SUBJ: INSTITUTIONAL ECONOMICS.

CLASS HB99.5   DEWEY# 330.   LEVEL ADV-AC

YBP Library Services

INTERNATIONAL ECONOMIC ASSOCIATION. WORLD
CONGRESS (16TH: 2011: BEIJING, CHINA)
COMPLEXITY AND INSTITUTIONS: MARKETS, NORMS AND
CORPORATIONS; ED. BY MASAHIKO AOKI.

Paper   247 P.

BASINGSTOKE: PALGRAVE MACMILLAN, 2012
SER: IEA CONFERENCE VOLUME; 150-II.

ED: STANFORD UNIVERSITY. PROCEEDINGS.

ISBN 1137034203   **Library PO#** GENERAL APPROVAL

	List	35.00	USD
5461 UNIV OF TEXAS/SAN ANTONIO	**Disc**	10.0%	
App. Date 4/17/13 ECO.APR 6108-11	**Net**	31.50	USD

SUBJ: INSTITUTIONAL ECONOMICS.

CLASS HB99.5   DEWEY# 330.   LEVEL ADV-AC

Katharina Pistor is Michael I. Sovern Professor of Law at Columbia Law School, a member of the Committee on Global Thought at Columbia University, fellow at the CEPR and a board member of the European Corporate Governance Institute.

Marco Raberto is Assistant Professor of Economic and Management Engineering at the University of Genoa, and Principal Investigator of the Iceland Rannis ICEACE project.

Prabirjit Sarkar is Professor of Economics at Jadavpur University, Kolkata, and a research associate of the Centre for Business Research, University of Cambridge.

Anja Shortland is Senior Lecturer in Economics at Brunel University, London.

Ajit Singh is Professor Emeritus of Economics at the University of Cambridge and a research associate of the Centre for Business Research, University of Cambridge.

Brian Skyrms is Distinguished Professor of Social Science, Logic and Philosophy of Science at University of California at Irvine and Professor of Philosophy at Stanford University. He is a member of the National Academy of Sciences and the American Academy of Arts and Sciences.

Joseph E. Stiglitz is University Professor at Columbia University. In 2001, he was awarded the Nobel Prize in economics for his analyses of markets with asymmetric information. He is currently the President of the International Economioc Association (2011–14).

Robert Sugden is Professor of Economics at the University of East Anglia and is a fellow of the British Academy.

Andrea Teglio is Visiting Professor at the Department of Economics of the Jaume I University at Castellon, Spain.

Foreword

The International Economic Association (IEA), the association of national economic associations/societies, held its 16th Triennial World Congress in Beijing, China, from July 4–8, 2011. This four-volume IEA publication, IEA Conference Volume No. 150–I~IV, comprises 55 papers selected from those presented at the Congress and, in many cases, revised afterwards incorporating discussions that took place at the event.

The Congress was organized in the aftermath of the financial crisis, the prolonged economic consequences of which continued to cast shadows over the global economic landscape. At the same time significant changes in economic structure, mechanisms and institutions were taking place globally – albeit in uncertain directions. It was thus a particularly appropriate time for economists from around the world to gather together in order to present their ongoing analyses about the evolving economic situations and to offer their prescriptions for the future orientation of economic policies. Further, the shared sense of uncertainty about the transformation of the world economy seems to impel economists to reflect on and debate the fundamental premises and focus of their discipline, and to seek advancements in methodology, conceptual terms and so on so that economics can once again become relevant, insightful and constructive.

Dynamic China provided a felicitous meeting place for economists from across the world to engage in this academic enterprise, and more than 1,000 papers were submitted in response to the Call for Papers by the Program Committee. From these submissions the academic program committee selected some 400 papers for presentation. In addition, the Committee organized five Lectures, four Plenary Panels and 22 invited sessions on various subject matters, inviting about 90 leading scholars to participate in them. The contributions to this IEA conference series are comprised mostly of invited papers, selected and organized into four volumes according to the following themes.

Volume I, Institutions and Comparative Economic Development (IEA Conference Volume No. 150–I), edited by Masahiko Aoki, Timur Kuran and Gérard Roland, contains 16 chapters. In the process of the rapid globalization of economies over the course of the past few decades, the landscape of the world economy as divided into developed, developing and underdeveloped terrains is being reshaped. Some of the economies that had stagnated for a number of years are now emerging as fast-growing economies; by contrast, developed economies are now facing unprecedented challenges to sustain growth under the rapidly evolving environmental, demographic and global market conditions. Will these changes lead to a new convergence of economic structure and performance across economies? Or will the differences in structure and institutional framework remain in spite of global market integration, entailing differentiated developmental performances? A plausible prediction about these issues would require, among other things, a deep understanding of the nature of the long-term developmental processes of economies from both a comparative and a historical perspective. Accordingly, the chapters in this volume consider themes such as: Why did divergences in development performance occur in the past across different regions: the West, Asia, the Islamic world, sub-Saharan Africa and so on? What role did institutional, political and cultural factors play in these divergences? Will differences in these factors persist, or will they become malleable in response to emergent global conditions? Whichever is the case, what will be the consequences for development? Why and how is the issue of food security still a matter of concern for some parts of the world economy? This volume presents a host of original contributions to these and related topics of development economics with historical, comparative and institutional underpinnings.

Volume II, Complexity and Institutions: Markets, Norms and Corporations (IEA Conference Volume No. 150–II), edited by Masahiko Aoki, Ken Binmore, Simon Deakin and Herbert Gintis contains 11 chapters. The totality of economic exchanges among agents in the society is complex, leading economists to grapple with questions such as: How do the agents in society deal with the complex reality in order to pursue their own materialistic and other possible preferences? How could economists construct a good theoretical explanation of complex reality and predict its future performance? According to one view, institutions may be identified with salient features of stable states of play of the societal game that are publicly represented in such forms as norms, laws, markets, organizations, political and corporate governance structures and so on. As such, institutions can provide an order to economic and other types of social exchange, helping agents to cope with the complexity of the real world. However, how can such an order, or an equilibrium state of play, be chosen from among the many possible, and in turn recognized and observed by agents? What are the relationships between such social orders and individual rationality? How do institutional forms, as mentioned above, mediate between the two and how do they evolve? Does the complexity of real life refute the traditional economists' premise of rationality? The contributions in this volume adopt a variety of perspectives to consider these and other related questions.

Volume III, The Global Macro Economy and Finance (IEA Conference Volume No. 150–III), edited by Franklin Allen, Masahiko Aoki, Jean-Paul Fitoussi, Nobuhiro Kiyotaki, Roger Gordon and Joseph E. Stiglitz, comprises 16 chapters. The financial crisis and the resulting persistent shortfall between the level of production in the USA, Europe and Japan and potential output indicates that macroeconomic mechanisms, theory and policy are not well tuned to, or in step with, rapidly changing global economic environments. Important advances in microeconomics over the past three decades have shown that whenever information is imperfect and asymmetric and markets are incomplete – that is, always – markets are not even constrained Pareto-efficient. These advances have created a presumption that markets are inefficient, but, unfortunately, these insights have not been built into most of the standard macroeconomic models. This may help explain their poor performance, in terms of predicting major downturns, and in providing coherent interpretations of the downturns and their persistence. Similarly, they have offered little of practical use in terms of providing advice about how to respond to crises such as the current global one, how to foster a robust recovery, and how to prevent a recurrence of such events. The chapters in this volume confront issues such as: Can the traditional measurement of GDP be a good measure for gauging and promoting social progress and global welfare? What was wrong with the financial mechanism that had been thought of as promoting economic development prior to the crisis? Is there a way to reconnect the financial and real sectors in a more stable and sustainable way? Alternatively, is it right to presume that the current economic crisis is essentially a financial crisis? Is there not a more fundamental structural problem in the real sector that caused the economic crisis on a global scale? If so, what is it? What kinds of prudent financial regulations, financial institution reforms, macroeconomic performance measures, and taxation on global activities are desirable for ever-interconnected but nevertheless diverse national economies to be stabilized and develop together?

Volume IV, The Chinese Economy: A New Transition (IEA Conference Volume No. 150–IV), edited by Masahiko Aoki and Jinglian Wu, contains 12 chapters. The rise of industrialized China and her resurgence as an economic powerhouse is a transformative event in the history of the world economy. However, there now appears to be an emergent consensus that the Chinese economy is facing a turning point, that is to say, another transition after the thirty years of successful transition from the command economy to the market economy. The nature of this new transition may be understood to some extent within a recent conceptual and analytical framework that unifies development economics and demography in a long-term perspective. After a rather long transition out of the Malthusian state (1911–the late 1940s) and then the phase of government-mediated initial industrialization (the early 1950s–the late 1970s), the era of high growth ensued, driven by favorable demographic factors such as the demographic dividend (an increase in the ratio of working-age population in the total population) and the massive domestic migration of labor from the rural agricultural sector to the industrial sector. However, this phase of development is now about to end. Simply put, improvements in the quality of human resources rather than a mere expansion of their quantity, as well as an increase in consumption relative to investment in physical capital, needs to become a major driving force of further development. This transition to the phase of human capital-based, market-oriented development is the key for China to sustain per capita income growth, albeit at a slower rate than in the past three decades, and to avoid a stall referred to as the 'middle-income trap' in the policy arena of development economics. As argued by authors of almost all the chapters included in this volume, this transition would call for a further deepening of the market mechanism driven by private incentives, governed by the rule of law and complemented by sustainable public policy. More specifically, the chapters ask and attempt to answer questions such as: How has modern economic science helped guide the Reform and Open Policy of China in the past and what suggestions can it offer for China's future direction? How does the Chinese (state) market economy operate in the areas of labor markets, social welfare systems, banking and corporate governance, foreign exchange and capital account controls, environmental control, and also in the area of relations between central and local governments? What kinds of future policy agenda and institutional reforms may be needed in these areas to make the transition to the new phase of development smooth and effective?

As noted, the papers compiled in this IEA World Conference series are selected not only for their academic merit but also on the basis of the selected themes. It is therefore regrettable that many excellent papers presented and discussed at the Congress have not been included in this series, especially those in the fields of experimental economics (both field and laboratory), international trade and foreign exchange, income and wealth inequality, environment and energy, econometric methods (especially those dealing with unobserved heterogeneity), country-specific empirical studies and so on. The whole program of the Congress may be accessed by visiting the Congress website: www.iea-congress-2011.org/Homepage.html.

The Program Committee responsible for the design and implementation of the program was comprised of leading economists from all over the world and from broad fields of economics. Their wisdom, academic expertise and leadership, organizing competence and generous sharing of time made the World Congress an enormously successful academic event. As the Chairman of the Program Committee *ex officio*, I would like to express sincere gratitude to them by listing their names below in alphabetical order with their institutional affiliations at the time of the Congress (those with an asterisk have also made additional contributions to the compilation of these IEA conference Volumes).

* Agarwal, Bina, India (Delhi University)
* Allen, Franklin, USA (University of Pennsylvania)
* Aoki, Masahiko, Japan (Stanford University)
  Araujo, Aloisio, Brazil (Instituto Nacional de Matematica)
  Ayogu, Melvin, Nigeria (Standard Bank Group, Johannesburg)
* Bai, Chong-En, China (Tsinghua University)
  Bardhan, Pranab, India (University of California, Berkeley)
  Basu, Kaushik, India (Cornell University/Indian Government)
  Berglof, Erik, Sweden (European Bank for Reconstruction and
  Development)
  Binmore, Ken, UK (University College London)
* Cai, Fang, China (Chinese Academy of Social Sciences)
  Calvo, Guillermo, Argentina (Columbia University)
  de Cecco, Marcello, Italy (Scuola Normale Superiore – Pisa)
* Deakin, Simon, UK (University of Cambridge)
  Englund, Peter, Sweden (Stockholm School of Economics)
  Esteban, Joan, Spain (Universitat Autonoma Barcelona)
* Fang, Hanming, China (University of Pennsylvania)
* Fitoussi, Jean-Paul, France (Sciences Po – Paris)
  Freeman, Richard, USA (Harvard University)
* Gintis, Herbert, USA (Santa Fe Institute)
  Goulder, Lawrence, USA (Stanford University)
* Gordon, Roger, USA (University of California at San Diego)
  Greif, Avner, Israel (Stanford University)
  Hong, Han, China (Stanford University)
  Ito, Takatoshi, Japan (University of Tokyo)
* Jorgenson, Dale, USA (Harvard University)
  Kandori, Michihiro, Japan (University of Tokyo)
* Kiyotaki, Nobuhiro, Japan (Princeton University)
  Kornai, Janos, Hungary (Harvard University/Hungary Academy)
* Kuran, Timur, Turkey (Duke University)
  Lau, Lawrence, China (Chinese University – Hong Kong)
  Lee, Joung-wha, Korea (Asian Development Bank)
  Li, Yang, China (Chinese Academy of Social Sciences)
* Lin, Justin Yifu, China (World Bank)
  Ndikumana, Leonce, USA (African Development Bank)
  Paganetto, Luigi, Italy (Università Roma 'Tor Vergata')
  Papademos, Lucas, Greece (European Central Bank)
  Piketty, Thomas, France (Ecole d'Economie de Paris)
  Polterovich, Victor, Russia (Central Economics and Mathematics
  Institute (CEMI), Russian Academy of Sciences)
* Qian, Ying-yi, China (Tsinghua University)

* Roland, Gérard, Belgium (University of California, Berkeley)
  Sheshinski, Eytan, Israel (Hebrew University)
* Stiglitz, Joseph, USA (Columbia University)
* Svejnar, Jan, Czech Rep. (University of Michigan)
  Tommasi, Mariano, Argentina (Universidad de San Andrés)
  Uygur, Ercan, Turkey (Ankara University)
  Vilamill, Winfred, Philippines (De La Salle University-Manila)
  Wei, Shang-Jin, China (Columbia University)
* Wu, Jinglian, China (Development Research Center)
  Xu, Chenggang, China (University of Hong Kong)
  Zhou, Lin, China (Shanghai Jiaotong University)

The meeting of the Congress was held in the excellent academic and historical atmosphere of Qinghua University which was simultaneously celebrating its centenary. The collegial academic discussions that took place in this ambience certainly marked one of highlights of the 50-year history of the IEA. The Association would like to express sincere gratitude to the university, headed by then-President Gu Binglin, for providing an amiable environment, excellent facilities, efficient administrative help and warm hospitality. The IEA also owes a great debt of gratitude to those who organized the Congress on site: Executive Vice President Xie Weihe of Tsinghua University, Chairman of the Local Organizing Committee, Professor Bai Chong-En of Tsinghua University, its Secretary General, and all the other members of the Local Organizing Committee:

Cai, Hongbin (Peking University)
Che, Jiahua (Chinese University of Hong Kong)
Ju, Jiandong (Tsinghua/University of Oklahoma)
Li, Hongbin (Tsinghua University)
Li, David (Tsinghua University)
Qian, Ying-yi (Tsinghua University)
Wen, Yi (Tsinghua University/Federal Reserve Bank at St Louis)
Xiao, Meng (Bijiao)
Xue, Lan (Tsinghua University)
Zhao, Yaohui (Peking University)
Zhou, Lian (Peking University)

In addition, the hard work of the administrative staff and student assistants at Tsinghua University coordinated by Mr Yu Jiang, ensured that the logistic operations of the Congress ran in an impeccably smooth manner, something for which the executive committee of the IEA would like to express great thanks.

The Congress was financially supported by CITIC Group, the China Investment Corporation, the China Construction Bank and the China International

Capital Corporation. The IEA would like to express deep gratitude to these donors for their generous support.

And finally, we are deeply indebted to Nick Brock and Rick Bouwman for their careful editing of the entire manuscripts, and to all the staff at Palgrave Macmillan for their great help in shepherding the volumes from the contracting through the production process.

July 27, 2012

Masahiko Aoki
General Editor, IEA Conference Volume No. 150: I–IV
President (2008–11), the International Economic Association

Introduction

Masahiko Aoki
Stanford University, USA

Ken Binmore
University College of London, UK

Simon Deakin
University of Cambridge, UK

Herbert Gintis
Santa Fe Institute, USA and Central European University, Hungary

The totality of economic exchanges among agents in the society is complex, which posits a number of questions for researchers in this field, including: How do the agents in society deal with the complex reality in order to pursue their own materialistic and other possible preferences? How could economists construct a good theoretical explanation of complex reality and predict its future performance?

In one view, institutions may be identified with salient features of stable states of play of the game that are publicly represented in such forms as norms, laws, markets, organizations, political and corporate governance structure (Aoki 2001, 2010; Greif 2006; Gintis 2009). As such, institutions can provide an order to economic and other social exchanges, helping agents to cope with potential complexity. However, how can such an order, or an equilibrium, be chosen from the many equilibria which are possible in the complex world, and in turn recognized and observed by agents? What are the relationships between such social orders and individual rationality? How do institutional elements as mentioned above mediate between the two and, if so, what does this process imply and how does it evolve? Or, does the complex reality of society refute the traditional economist's premise of rationality? The contributions in this volume adopt a variety of perspectives to consider these and other related questions.

Complex reality and theory

The volume begins with Michihiro Kandori's contribution entitled 'Theory and Reality in Economics: Insights from Three Allegories'. Given the complexity of economic environments, behaviors and phenomena, a variety of experimental

data have been generated by behavioral economists that deviate from the predictions of well-developed body of (neoclassical) economic theory. In this paper
Kandori asks how we should interpret such deviations of reality from theory that
are called anomalies. Do they imply that the traditional theory does not offer a
good explanation of complex reality? Should we propose a theory based only on
experimental data/experiments? Is there really no economic problem for which
theory provides a non-trivial prediction and field, experimental, and/or computational data repeatedly confirm it? Using three allegories from cases in natural
sciences where the causes of the anomalies are well understood, Kandori lucidly
sorts out the issues involved and suggests that an appropriate response to them
could be 'it depends'.

Agent-based models of complex market exchange

In Walras' model, market clearing was effected by a central authority, the auctioneer. It is well known that the resulting dynamic is not necessarily stable.
Nor has anyone developed a plausible decentralized dynamical model of market
exchange. This suggests that we lack understanding of one or more fundamental properties of market exchange. It follows that contemporary macroeconomic
models, which are highly aggregated versions of the Walrasian system, have no
plausible dynamical properties. In particular, these models do not deal with
interactions among many heterogeneous agents. The three papers in this part
of the volume assume that the market economy is a complex dynamical system
that is best modelled as a network of interacting firms and traders.

In the first paper in this section, 'The Dynamics of Pure Market Exchange',
Herbert Gintis models the multi-agent Walrasian system as a Markov process in
which each agent has a set of private prices that are updated through trading experience and networked information exchange. He shows that under
a large space of parameters, the economy moves to quasi-public prices, in
which the standard error of private prices across agents becomes very small,
and markets are close to clearing. These findings suggest that the Markov
process is an appropriate analytical tool for modelling the dynamics of a
Walrasian market economy. However, such models are far too large to solve
analytically, so solutions must be found through computer simulation. A
major goal for future research is to provide analytical conditions under which
the stationary distribution of the Markov economy approximates a Walrasian
equilibrium.

In the second paper in this part, 'Analytical Solution for Agent-Based Models', Corrado Di Guilmi, Mauro Gallegati, Simone Landini and Joseph E. Stiglitz
present an institutionally realistic model of the credit market. Their paper uses
standard procedures from statistical mechanics to aggregate over a large population of heterogeneous firms. They derive a system of coupled equations that

governs the dynamics of growth and output. These equations capture the basic features of a credit network economy, including critical nodes in the network and capacity of the system to amplify rather than damp disturbances. The model also exhibits all the systemic risk measures identified by the European Central Bank – the degree of connectivity; the degree of concentration; and the size of exposures – and models the causal relationships among them. By handling the adequacy ratio requirement, they show that policymakers can influence systemic risk. The model also illustrates that the exposure size limit is also a limit on the interconnectivity, linking the concepts of 'too big to fail' and 'too interconnected to fail.'

In the third and final paper in this part, 'The EURACE Macroeconomic Model and Simulators', Silvano Cincotti, Marco Raberto and Andrea Teglio describe the EURACE agent-based macroeconomic framework, which simulates a fully integrated macroeconomy consisting of the real economy, the financial sector and the public sector. EURACE agents have limited information and, like the Markov economy developed in Gintis's paper, exhibit adaptive behavior, interacting directly in decentralized markets. They use a balance sheet approach with stock and flow consistency checks, presenting computations that show the real effects of fluctuations in the aggregate credit supplied by commercial banks and in the money supply caused by open market operations. Their model shows that highly leveraged commercial banks lead to financial fragility, and that quantitative easing has negligible effects. In the EURACE framework, business cycles emerge endogenously from the interplay between the real and financial sectors.

Social norms as coordinating devices

The next part is concerned with social norms that may be considered as one of important societal artefacts that deal with complex social exchange. The study of social norms as devices for selecting one of the many equilibria in coordination games goes back at least as far as David Hume's (1975) *Enquiries,* where he describes some of the norms that had evolved for the very complicated version of the Driving Game that operated in the narrow streets of Edinburgh during the time of the Scottish Enlightenment. The torch was taken up again in modern times by Tom Schelling in his famous *Strategy of Conflict* (1960), for which he was awarded a Nobel Prize. David Lewis (1969) spread the word among philosophers, but game theorists were slow to recognize that rationality considerations alone cannot solve the equilibrium selection problem that is endemic in real-life games, because there is necessarily an arbitrary element in such matters as whether a country chooses to drive on the right or on the left. One cannot discuss such arbitrary elements in social norms without appealing to historical or evolutionary considerations.

This part of the volume contains three papers on the evolution of social norms by authors with game theory credentials. The paper by Brian Skyrms, 'Aspects of Naturalizing the Social Contract', focuses on the evolutionary dynamics by means of which social norms first become established as equilibrium selection devices. The literature on this subject is often obscured by biological jargon and impenetrable mathematical equations but Skyrms succeeds in putting his three points across using only simple examples. His first point is that nothing guarantees that evolutionary dynamics will converge at all. His second point concerns the evolution of altruism, which continues to be a rather controversial subject. However, as Skyrms points out, all sides to the controversy agree that for altruism to get off the ground there has to be some kind of correlation between the players. So why should we care whether the outcome of the correlation is called group selection or kin selection or something else? Finally, Skyrms introduces us to the dynamic signaling models he has been working on in recent years in which the number of signals may increase over time (Skyrms 2010).

The paper by Bob Sugden, 'The Role of Salience in the Emergence and Reproduction of Norms', looks in close detail at a particular traffic game that he calls the Right Turn Problem (which would be the Left Turn Problem in countries that drive on the right). In the absence of any road markings, who has effective priority when two cars going in opposite directions approach an intersection with a major road when one car plans to turn right and the other to continue straight on? Sugden's aim is to explore how the notion of *salience* can be founded on similarity considerations derived from better established social norms used elsewhere – so he differs from Skyrms in not confining attention to social norms that evolve from scratch. Sugden's purpose is not so much to reduce the incidence of traffic accidents, as to follow the lead of David Hume in using traffic coordination problems as examples that do not carry an emotional charge but which have the same strategic structure as those that do – notably the social norms that form part of our moral codes.

In the third of the three papers on social norms, 'Fairness as an Equilibrium Selection Device', Ken Binmore reviews his evolutionary theory of fairness. Traditional moral philosophers have no time for a theory that sees fairness as an equilibrium selection device no different, as they see it, from traffic signals or table manners. However, Binmore's theory endorses some of the intuitions proposed by John Rawls (1972) in his famous *Theory of Justice*, by offering an evolutionary origin for Rawls's original position, which he sees as providing the deep structure of the fairness norms that ordinary people use in solving the equilibrium selection problems that arise in the myriad of coordination games of which everyday social life largely consists.

Corporate organization and governance

The next part turns to another social device that copes with the complexity of the economy: corporate organization and governance, which is itself a complex micro entity. In order for such a complex entity to evolve and be sustained in a variety of form, social norms play a crucial embedding role.

Since the 1980s, corporate governance arrangements across the world have been increasingly influenced by the belief that listed companies should be run in the financial interests of their shareholders, with the concerns of other stakeholders, not to mention more general objectives such as the long-term growth of firms, seen as means to this end (Hansmann and Kraakman, 2001). The global financial crisis, which originated in those national contexts most influenced by the logic of shareholder value, has posed in stark terms the question of whether policymakers and corporate actors in the years prior to the crisis were misled by the simple shareholder primacy model, which, it turns out, is far from being the last word on the essential features of the modern corporation. The contributions in this part of the volume deal with how corporations evolve in tandem with social and legal norms, technology, and collective cognitive capacities.

In chapter 8, 'A Shapley-Value Parable of Corporations as Systems of Associational Cognition', Masahiko Aoki focuses on a view of the corporation as incorporating a system of associational cognition, building on his earlier work on this theme (Aoki, 2010). He argues, in line with recent developments in neuroscience but somewhat in opposition to the 'hidden information' premise of orthodox theory, that human cognition can take place at the group level and that this is a generic common property of corporations originating even before the emergence of the modern business form of corporations. Then, relying on a recent development in potential game theory, he argues that the shareholders, the managers and the workers may respectively play out their cognitive and physical roles as if they were team members while they are actually pursuing their own individualistic payoffs, if and only if they all believe that the value outcome of associational cognition is to be distributed according to the Shapley value. Thus, the social norm implicit in the Shapley value may be considered as an essential factor for embedding corporations as a cooperative venture. The actual content of the Shapley value depends on the type and depth of the respective cognitive assets of the different corporate stakeholders, as well as the way by which they are combined, however. He accordingly identifies possible five modes of organizational architecture and associated governance structures for the modern business corporation. With increasing complexity of the cognitive and physical environments of the corporation, the traditional assumption of shareholder primacy may not be taken for granted any more as the only one model of universal validity.

Katharina Pistor's chapter 9, 'On the Plasticity of the Corporate Form', takes a complementary look at the theory of the corporation from the theoretical perspective of the relation between law and economics. She argues that the core generic feature of the corporation is its existence as an entity separate from the asset claims of its members, with most of its other features being additions which reflect particular national traditions or temporal influences. The 'plasticity' of the corporate form implies that it can be adapted to a range of contexts without losing its essential organizational attributes. Pistor's analysis, similarly to that of Aoki, suggests that the orthodoxy of a single, optimal structure for the corporate form, regardless of context, has been misplaced.

The following two papers address the link between theory, practice and policy in the field of corporate governance. In Chapter 10, 'An End to Consensus? The Selective Impact of Corporate Law Reform on Financial Development', Simon Deakin, Prabirjit Sarkar and Ajit Singh draw on new empirical evidence to assess some core claims of the legal origin hypothesis, which associates the common law approach to corporate governance with superior economic outcomes. They track the global diffusion of the common law model of independent boards and legal support for hostile takeover bids over the course of the 1990s and 2000s, and demonstrate through time-series econometric analysis that its impact on financial development has not been uniform, being dependent on context, and also far from beneficial in all cases.

The final contribution to this volume, 'Government Banks and Growth: Theory and Evidence', by Svetlana Andrianova, Panicos Demetriades and Anja Shortland, presents an empirical analysis of the developmental properties of government-owned banks. Arguing from a modern view of 'developmental perspective' that government ownership may be efficient in contexts shaped by information asymmetries and weak institutions, they produce cross-country evidence to show that government ownership was associated with higher long-run growth rates in the years prior to the onset of the global financial crisis. Both these papers call into question central tenets of the legal origin hypothesis and place in doubt the wisdom of its implementation through the policies of international financial institutions during the 1990s and 2000s.

References

Aoki, M. (2001) *Toward a Comparative Institutional Analysis* (Cambridge MA: MIT Press).
Aoki, M. (2010) *Corporations in Evolving Diversity: Cognition, Governance and Institutions* (Oxford: Oxford University Press).
Gintis, H. (2009) *The Bounds of Reason: Game Theory and the Unification of the Behavioral Sciences* (Princeton, NJ: Princeton University Press).
Greif, A. (2006) *Institutions and the Path to the Modern Economy: Lessons from Medieval Trade* (New York and Cambridge, UK: Cambridge University Press).

Hansmann, H., and Kraakman, R. (2001) 'The End of History for Corporate Law', *The Georgia Law Journal,* vol. 89, pp. 439–468.

Hume, D. (1975) *Enquiries Concerning Human Understanding and Concerning the Principles of Morals* (Oxford: Clarendon Press; first published 1977).

Lewis, D. (1969) *Conventions: A Philosophical Study* (Cambridge, MA: Harvard University Press).

Rawls, J. (1972) *A Theory of Justice* (Cambridge, MA: Belknap Press of Harvard University Press).

Schelling, T. (1960) *The Strategy of Conflict* (Cambridge, MA: Harvard University Press).

Skyrms, B. (2010) *Signals: Evolution, Learning, and Information* (New York: Oxford University Press).

Part I
Theory and Empirical Reality

1
Theory and Reality in Economics: Insights from Three Allegories*

Michihiro Kandori
University of Tokyo, Japan

1.1 Introduction

A well-developed body of economic theory, which has evolved over more than 150 years, is now confronted with a rich and detailed set of data (either from field or experimental studies). There have been challenges from behavioral economists pointing out that the reality deviates systematically from the predictions of traditional economic theory. Those deviations are called *anomalies* and they have been attracting considerable attention from researchers.

A number of important questions have emerged from the debate between the neoclassical and behavioral economists. However, it is difficult to address these questions if they are posed in general and abstract terms. It is certainly more helpful to examine such questions in the context of particular economic problems, such as the provision of public goods, decision-making under uncertainty and so on. Unfortunately, even in specific economic contexts, we are often unable to obtain clear and decisive insights since *we have yet to understand why the reality deviates from the proposed theories in economics*. Without any detailed knowledge about the causes of anomalies, it is difficult to assess the relationship between theory and reality.

In an attempt to approach this problem, I will first move away temporarily from economics and consider three simple cases taken from (high school) natural sciences textbooks where the reason why reality deviates from theory (or theories) is *fully understood*. The three cases I consider are: Case 1, a falling leaf, Case 2, the motions of planets, and Case 3, which I will explain later in this paper. Following this I present three allegories; What if the relationship between theory and reality in economics is similar to that shown in Case 1, Case 2, or Case 3?

The merit of this thought experiment is that we have *full knowledge* about the actual causes of anomalies in Cases 1–3. These cases will provide us therefore with clearer insights into a number of issues including, but not limited to the following:

First of all, those allegories can help to *articulate* the views held by groups with different philosophies: the neoclassical researchers and the behavioral researchers.

Second, those allegories assist us to answer the following two methodological questions. The first question addresses the competing attitudes about how empirical or experimental studies should be organized:

- Should we use data/experiments to *test* a theory (the 'Top-down' attitude), or,
- should we use data/experiments to discover a regularity? In other words, should we *induce* a theory from data/experiments? (the 'Bottom-up' attitude)

The second of our questions concerns the extent to which a theory is of use:

- Should we discard a theory if it fails to: (i) fit the data; (ii) make accurate predictions; or (iii) provide useful recommendations?

Thirdly, the three allegories can be helpful in explaining the following puzzles and peculiarities about economics:

- Economics differs from any other discipline in that a substantial part of its research is devoted to highly sophisticated empirical techniques (econometrics). By contrast, we do not encounter disciplines such as 'physicometrics' or 'chemometrics.' Despite this devotion to sophisticated empirical techniques, the general public believes (or seems to believe) that economics provides very few (non-trivial) laws that are strongly confirmed by data. (The mathematician Stanislaw Ulam once teasingly challenged the economist Paul Samuelson as follows: 'Name me one proposition [in economics] which is both true and non-trivial.')
- Why does it take so long to receive referees' reports in economics? The process takes much longer in this area than it does in natural sciences and mathematics.
- Non-cooperative game theory took some 20 years to be accepted as a useful method in economics. Why did it take so long?

In the following sections, I will attempt to address all of these questions.

1.2   The first allegory: a falling leaf

According to the Newtonian law of motion, a leaf should fall at a constant acceleration, irrespective of its weight and shape. However, in reality, a falling leaf will oscillate and its speed is affected by both its weight and its shape. Suppose the traditional economic theory (neoclassical theory) is similar to the

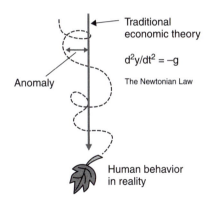

Figure 1.1 The first allegory

Newtonian law of motion and the human behavior in reality resembles the following trajectory of a falling leaf (Figure 1.1).[1]

Of course, there is no guarantee that this is a good allegory. However, let us focus on it for the moment and assess the relationship between neoclassical theory, behavioral theory and the reality according to this allegory.

The contributions of behavioral economics are: (i) to point out that reality deviates from the traditional theory in a systematic manner (that is, to highlight an anomaly); (ii) to offer models to describe the anomaly; and (iii) to show that taking the anomaly into account is useful in a variety of applications. This is certainly a substantial achievement. Compared with the situation in which people believe blindly that the leaf falls directly down according to Newtonian law and pay little attention to the actual trajectories of falling leaves, we certainly have a better understanding of reality.

However, there is some degree of weakness in behavioral economics. Whenever presenting a model to capture an anomaly, it has been a common practice in behavioral economics to choose one that is *tractable and parsimonious*. What is a tractable and parsimonious model to describe the oscillating trajectory of the falling leaf? A sine curve could be a good candidate. If the position of the leaf in Figure 1.1 is represented in x−y coordinate, the Newtonian Law asserts $x = $ constant (no horizontal movement) and $d^2y/dt^2 = -g$ (a constant acceleration downwards). The assumption of no horizontal movement ($x = $ constant) can be replaced with a tractable and parsimonious functional form of oscillation $x = a\sin(bt)$, and from the empirical data one can estimate parameters a and b to best fit the data (Figure 1.2).

This might appear to be a gross oversimplification of the work of behavioral economics; however, the value of this allegory is that it also articulates the views of the neoclassical researchers. (I will present a second allegory which allots more

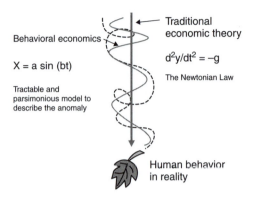

Behavioral economics

X = a sin (bt)

Tractable and
parsimonious model to
describe the anomaly

Traditional
economic theory

$d^2y/dt^2 = -g$

The Newtonian Law

Human behavior
in reality

Figure 1.2   A tractable and parsimonious model

credit to behavioral economics; see also Kahneman and Tversky's opinion cited below, which shares some similarities with this allegory).

In this allegory, behavioral economics provided a definitive contribution in drawing people's attention to reality. However, what it offers is a simple functional form to trace the data that are not able to capture fully the actual mechanisms that are operating beyond the anomalous behavior. To understand the falling leaf, it is not sufficient simply to fit a sine curve to the data. It is also important to have a fuller and deeper theoretical understanding of the various forces driving the motion of the leaf. The leaf is subject to air drag, whose magnitude and directions are affected by the shape, angle and current speed of the leaf. In addition, there might be several fine effects of the air turbulence created at the tail.

What are those 'true driving forces of anomalies' (which correspond to air drag and the effects of turbulence in the allegory) in economics? The pioneers of behavioral economics, Tversky and Kahneman, noted that the relationship between theory and reality, in the context of choice under uncertainty, is similar to this allegory (at least to some extent) and offered the following explanation:

> Despite its greater generality, [the improved version of prospect theory proposed in 1992] is unlikely to be accurate in detail. ... The present theory can be generalized ... but it is questionable whether the gain in descriptive validity ... would justify ... the cost of increased complexity. (Tversky and Kahneman 1992: 317)

Here, they stated clearly that their aim is to find a tractable and parsimonious functional form to *roughly trace* the data. What did they consider to be the true driving forces of human choice behavior?

> Theories of choice are at best approximate and incomplete. One reason for this pessimistic assessment is that choice is a constructive and contingent process. [P]eople use a variety of heuristic procedures... The heuristics of choice

do not readily lend themselves to formal analysis… (Tversky and Kahneman 1992: 317)

According to Tversky and Kahneman, the true driving force of human choice behavior is some *cognitive process* in the human brain. They take, however, a 'pessimistic' position that such cognitive mechanisms are so complex that they are unlikely to be captured by simple mathematical models. Note that the same is also true in the allegory of the falling leaf we have presented above. The effects of air drag and turbulence are so complex that they cannot possibly be captured by a simple functional form that is comparable to the Newtonian law of motion. At this point we should ask: should we simply be satisfied and stop at the stage of fitting a tractable functional form to data, so as to understand the reality?

It is also important to recognize that in the falling leaf allegory there is *no need to abandon the traditional theory, even after acknowledging the existence of anomalies*. In this instance the Newtonian law of motion does capture one of the forces driving the data. The law is worth teaching to students who are interested in falling leaves, together with the reasons why it does not offer a complete explanation of the data. It is also worth mentioning that the sine curve model is useful for some practical purposes. It does not make much sense, however, to replace the Newtonian law with the sine curve model.

1.3 The second allegory: the motions of planets

In the previous allegory, the traditional (neoclassical) theory is supposed to capture one of the principal driving forces of reality, and therefore that allegory may be biased in favor of the traditional theory. In my opinion, the first allegory describes the best-case scenario for the neoclassical theory. To obtain more critical perspectives, however, let us turn to the second allegory, the motions of planets.

Suppose that neoclassical economic theory corresponds to the *geocentric* model, which assumes that Mars orbits around the Earth (Figure 1.3a). This theory provides largely accurate predictions of the motions of planets, but close scrutiny reveals that Mars occasionally changes direction (a systematic deviation from the theory, an anomaly called *retrograde motion*. See Figure 1.3b). To address this anomaly, the geocentric model was modified to assume that Mars has a smaller orbit whose center moves along the original orbit presumed in the geocentric model (Figure 1.3c). Despite this modification, the geocentric model confronted a number of additional challenges from observed data (anomalies) and led to further modifications. All those modifications failed, however, and were eventually replaced with the simple and accurate sun-centered (or *heliocentric*) model. According to this second model, the retrograde motion anomaly of Mars can be explained very simply by a phenomenon that occurs when the

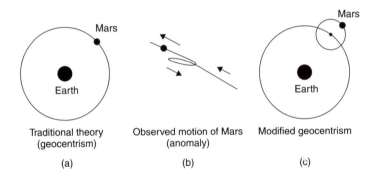

Figure 1.3   The motions of planets

Earth, which completes its orbit around the Sun in a shorter time than Mars, overtakes it.

In this particular allegory, the *anomaly shows that the traditional theory is fundamentally wrong* and that the old theory needs to be replaced by a new, more satisfactory theory. This allegory articulates the view of some of the behavioral economists who argue that neoclassical theory should be abandoned and replaced with behavioral models. This allegory, however, also reveals that there is a twist in the transition from old theory to new theory: any attempt to explain the anomaly by a minimum modification of the old theory (Figure 1.3(c)) is doomed to fail. Behavioral economists aim to discover new principles (which correspond to heliocentricism in this allegory), and the anomalies we observe may well be suggesting that this is the correct approach. The extent to which this endeavor has been successful to date, however, is subject to controversy. Do the behavioral models correspond to heliocentricism, or do they resemble the modified geocentrism in Figure 1.3(c), which failed but paved the way for the development of a more satisfactory model?

1.4   Lessons from the first and second allegories

The preceding two allegories are useful in assessing the competing attitudes toward how empirical or experimental studies should be organized. That is:

- Should we use data/experiments to *test* a theory (the 'Top-down' attitude)?, or,
- should we use data/experiments to discover a regularity? In other words, should we *induce* a theory from data/experiments? (the 'Bottom-up' attitude).

The presented allegories show clearly that the right answer is, 'it depends on the circumstances.'

If the relationship between theory and reality is similar to our second allegory about planets, then clearly the bottom-up induction drawn from empirical regularity offers an effective way of arriving at a satisfactory theory. However, if the situation is closer to the first allegory about a falling leaf, the bottom-up method is not so effective. It is apparent that no matter how much data are collected about falling leaves, it is very unlikely that a satisfactory theory can be formed by pure induction. It is necessary to resort to some level of theorizing to organize and interpret the data, and conducting controled experiments to test the proposed theory is clearly more effective. For example, one can abstract away from the eye-catching oscillating movements to confine attention to the decelerating effect of air drag. A simple theoretical conjecture might be that the air resistance is proportional to the squared speed of the falling object. Once this hypothesis is established, we can observe how well it matches the data (while not a perfect fit, the data may show some degree of truth), and we may also conduct an experiment by controling the shape of the falling object to best test this hypothesis (for example, by dropping balls rather than leaves).

Behavioral economists, who emphasize that clear empirical regularities of human behavior are firmly established in psychology, appear to have a view closer to the second allegory about planets. They are keen on introducing psychologically-established empirical regularities in economic analysis, but they are often indifferent (or even hostile) to attempts to *explain why* human behavior exhibits such regularities. Note, however, that even among psychologists, some researchers take the opposite view. Among this group is Toshio Yamagishi, an experimental psychologist, who has criticized the practice of traditional psychological research that confines itself to collecting a large amount of experimental data in the hope of finding empirical regularities without much theorization. Toshio Yamagishi has suggested that this line of research is similar to 'butterfly hunting in a never-ending summer vacation' (Yamagishi 2002). Yamagishi apparently finds that human behavior is more like the trajectory of falling leaf than the motions of a planet.

Which allegory is to be trusted? *Ex ante, there is no way of telling which is right.* In some cases, the first allegory is suitable, but there are certainly other cases where the second can be more appropriate. Only after all the dust has settled through the free competition of competing scientific research, would it become clear which allegory is valid. Of course, a researcher can conduct studies based on his/her own subjective belief about which allegory is more valid, but he/she should not be so dogmatic as to blindly dismiss the other way of seeing the relationship between theory and reality.

1.5   The third allegory: the falling leaf revisited

To gain further insights, let us now examine the third allegory, which is a variant of the first allegory about a falling leaf. Consider a hypothetical case in which it is *impossible to conduct fully controled experiments* about falling leaves. The rise of experimental economics and the recent developments in natural experiments may give an impression that controled experiments have finally become available in economics. However, if economic behavior is driven ultimately by some cognitive mechanisms in the human brain, then it appears that the means of control (of human cognitive mechanisms) at our disposal in economics may be rather limited. To represent this idea, let us consider the following hypothetical situation where human behavior is driven by a falling leaf in a tube embedded in the brain (Figure 1.4), and it is physiologically impossible to apply many potentially useful controls to the falling leaf in the brain. If we make the tube a vacuum, for example, the person dies, and there is no way of replacing the leaf in the brain with a ball.

This rather odd allegory is useful in articulating the views held by the majority of economists in defense of traditional economic theory.

In this allegory, there is no way to conduct a perfectly controled experiment to verify the pure effects of the traditional theory (the Newtonian law/neoclassical theory). With the limited control, the Newtonian law (or the neoclassical theory) is bound to be refuted empirically, its predictions fail in many cases, and its

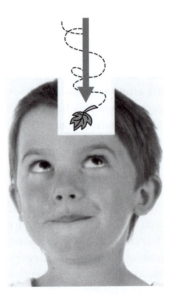

Figure 1.4   The third allegory

policy recommendations do not always solve the problems at hand. Neverthe-less, the traditional theory does capture an important driving force of human behavior in this allegory, and it can be appreciated as a model that *provides useful insights* despite all of its limitations. (This is my own interpretation of – and elab-oration on – Ariel Rubinstein's view, expressed in his 2006 presidential address for the Econometric Society). In this allegory, the Newtonian law/neoclassical theory is probably one of the most useful tractable mathematical models to gain insights into reality.

Of course, one serious problem of this allegory is that it is impossible to verify whether or not the traditional theory is actually accurate in the sense that it *does* capture one of the true driving forces of the falling leaf. If the scope of controled experiments is severely limited, how can one confirm that the leaf would fall at a constant acceleration in an ideal condition (that is, in a vacuum)? The long tradition of natural sciences teaches us that it is dangerous to believe in any theory, no matter how plausible it may appear, unless it is firmly verified by data. 'The test of all knowledge is experiment. Experiment is the sole judge of scientific "truth"', as Richard Feynman remarked in *The Feynman Lectures on Physics* (1964). In the next section I will elaborate further on this issue. In doing so, I will also offer some explanations for the puzzles (some peculiar aspects of economics) presented in the introduction.

1.6 Insights from the third allegory and the puzzles about economics

The main features of the third allegory can be summarized as follows:

1. The reality (the motions of the falling leaf) is rather chaotic and it is not easy to recognize clear empirical regularities.
2. Nonetheless, there is a simple law of motion (the Newtonian law) concealed under the chaotic data. However, due to limited available controls, it is difficult to create a situation where this law is actually observed in its pure form.
3. The traditional economic theory *indeed* captures such simple law operating beyond the rather chaotic data.

Those features listed above are presented in decreasing order of my own con-fidence about their validity. In my view, Feature 1 clearly captures a very important aspect of the subject matter of economics. In contrast, there is no guarantee that Feature 2 is largely true in economic data, and there is admittedly a possibility that the reality is exceedingly complicated that it 'does not readily lend itself to formal analysis' (recall the remarks by Tversky and Kahneman in section 1.2). Nonetheless, relying on the possibility of discovering a simple law and trying to find one is an acceptable attitude in scientific research. The third feature is definitely controversial as some natural scientists (recall Feynman's quote in the previous section) and the general public may disagree harshly with this assertion. In what follows, I will elaborate on those features of the third allegory to gain further insights.

1.6.1   The interocular trauma (IOT) test versus sophisticated statistical methods

In light of the third allegory, let us examine the first puzzle presented in the introduction: Why is there no counterpart of econometrics in physics or chemistry such as 'physicometics' or 'chemometrics'? Economics devotes a larger share of its resources to empirical technique, yet the general public appears to believe that physics and chemistry are far more reliable than economics can ever be.

What is happening? In physics and chemistry, researchers usually use only simple statistical methods (and sometimes *no* statistical testing) to confirm a theory by data. Their *modus operandi* is a hypothesis testing technique known as *the interocular trauma (IOT) test*: If the data fits the hypothesis so unambiguously that it 'hits you between the eyes', then it's significant.[2] Another important prerequisite for the confirmation of a theory in physics and chemistry is the *reproducibility* of experimental results. It means that the same theory should be able to pass the IOT test repeatedly in experiments conducted by different researchers in different locations.

Such verification procedure, based on the IOT test and reproducibility, is certainly the most effective way to convince us that a theory is accurate. Note that this is possible only when either (i) the raw data itself exhibits a high degree of regularity to pass the IOT test (e.g., the motions of planet), or (ii) controlled experiments are sufficiently effective in creating an ideal environment where the predicted phenomenon can be unambiguously observed (e.g., dropping a leaf in a vacuum). Unfortunately, the third mentioned allegory asserts that neither is likely in many economic problems. What should economists do in such a situation?

One possible attitude is to deduce that economists cannot come to any scientific conclusions. *However, sticking to this dictum and dismissing every attempt to explain economic data as equally unscientific is similar to throwing out the baby with the bath water.* This can be illustrated by the situation in which one tries to understand the motions of falling leaves under the constraint that one cannot release leaves in a vacuum. This constraint places severe limits on one's ability to confirm the Newtonian law of motion. Even worse, the constraint might hinder the conjecture that the Newtonian law of motion might be true. Despite being non-decisive, however, there are apparently both some 'good' and some 'bad' explanations of falling leaves, and the bad ones can be *really bad*. Hence attempting to discover good ones is far more productive than dismissing all explanations as being equally bad or unreliable. *Finding good explanations while only able to exercise very limited control over the data is exactly what economics is doing – or is forced to do.* To assist this goal, econometrics provides some systematic statistical techniques.

This view of economics, in light of the third allegory, leads to the following crucial question; what is a 'good explanation' in a situation where raw data do not show obvious regularity and where there are only limited means of control to observe a clear-cut regularity?

1.6.2   The definition of a good explanation?

So there stands the economist, eagerly watching falling leaves and trying to understand what drives the motions, under the constraint that he/she cannot apply much control to various factors which may affect the motions of leaves (inability to release leaves in a vacuum, for example). It is intuitively apparent that there are both good and bad explanations, and the goal of the economist is to identify good ones. The central problem here is that it is difficult to arrive at a clear definition of what constitutes a good explanation. At the moment, I do not personally have a good operational definition.

This is the fundamental dilemma in economics, which is, in my opinion, at the heart of a number of methodological questions. Let me summarize my argument:

1. In contrast to physics and chemistry, the raw data of economics do not usually exhibit a high degree of regularity.
2. Economic behavior is driven ultimately by cognitive mechanisms of which at present we have only a poor level of understanding. We also have only limited control over the cognitive mechanisms to discover clear regularity.
3. As a result, it is impossible to pin down 'the truth' with the same degree of accuracy as in the 'hard sciences' (such as physics and chemistry).
4. Economists disagree with the hardline position that nothing scientific can be said in such a situation. Trying to find good explanations is far more productive than dismissing all explanations as equally bad or unscientific.
5. The fundamental dilemma in economics is that it is rather hard to articulate the definition of 'good explanations.'

How is this problem of defining a good explanation addressed *in practice*? Rather than clearly articulating the definition of a good explanation or appointing a clever dictator who tells us what is good, economics seems to use the free competition approach. Researchers propose various explanations, and an explanation is regarded as a good one (at least temporarily) if it can win support from a majority of researchers. Of course, this is subject to a number of problems (for example, a majority can be, and actually has been, misguided, sometimes for a very long time; I will address this issue below), but this seems to be the practical criterion used in economics.

This view offers a systematic set of explanations for the puzzles I presented in the introduction. First, consider the extensive amount of time to receive a referee's report in economics. In physics and chemistry, the ultimate judgment of a good paper is the IOT test and reproducibility which are relatively easily verified by individual researchers.[3] Hence referees in the natural sciences are more concerned with the *type I errors* (rejecting good papers) than *type II errors* (accepting bad ones). Even if a bad paper is accepted, later researchers can find it relatively easy to confirm its quality. In economics, where the criterion of a good paper is more subtle, the refereeing process plays a more important role and referees seem to be more concerned with type II errors of accepting bad papers.

Secondly, when researchers are bound to use the free competition approach in the absence of an unambiguous definition of a good research paper, it may take a considerable length of time for a good idea to be accepted. For instance, the concept of the Nash equilibrium was established in 1950, but only after the mid-1970s did it become widely accepted as a fundamental concept in mainstream economics. This happens much less often in the natural sciences, where a good idea can be clearly detected by the IOT test and reproducibility, either because the raw data itself have a high degree of regularity or because fine data control methods are available.

1.7   The room for the IOT test and reproducibility in economics

As is suggested by the third of our allegories, the majority of economic problems are likely to have limited means of control over human cognitive mechanisms, and it is difficult to create an ideal environment where theoretical predictions can be observed unambiguously (such as releasing a leaf in a vacuum). Consequently, highly sophisticated statistical techniques have been developed and much attention has been focused on anomalies. However, is there actually no economic problem where: (i) theory provides a non-trivial prediction; (ii) data fit the prediction well in an intuitive sense (i.e., the theory passes the IOT test); and (iii) field and/or experimental data *repeatedly* confirm the theoretical prediction (reproducibility)? In what follows I argue that there are several good examples which satisfy (i)–(iii). Those good examples may have been overlooked (or undervalued) because economists are sometimes overly preoccupied with sophisticated statistical methods (this is the case for neoclassical researchers) or are too focused on finding anomalies (the case for behavioral researchers).

The first example is the mixed strategy equilibrium in a simple two-player card game invented by Barry O'Neil (1987). Each player has four cards, Joker, 1, 2, and 3, and draws one of them simultaneously with the other player. Player 1 wins if: (i) both choose Jokers; or (ii) both choose number cards (1,2, or 3) *and* the numbers were different. Otherwise, player 2 wins. As can be observed, the rules of the game are rather complicated and it is not obvious whether the rules favor player 1 or 2. Even less clear are the winning probabilities of players 1 and 2, and the frequencies with which the four cards are played. However, game theory provides very specific predictions. One can calculate the mixed strategy equilibrium and discover that the winning probability of player 1 is .4, and that each player assigns probability .4 to Joker and .2 to each number card. O'Neil (1987) found that those predictions fit his experimental data surprisingly well.

The first time that I observed this result, my thought was that Barry O'Neil was extremely fortunate to obtain such a good fit of data. I anticipated that there would be a large degree of variation in data when his experiment was repeated, and I was almost certain that data cannot always match the theory so favorably. In short, I was skeptical about the *reproducibility* of O'Neal's result. Hence I decided to verify it by conducting the same experiment in my classes over the past nine years. The results are summarized in the following tables.

Winning rate of player 1		
Equilibrium	**0.4**	Number of pairs
O'Neill (1987)	0.408	25
'02	0.397	9
'04	0.414	29
'06 a	0.39	30
'06 b	0.402	95
'09	0.409	102

	Frequencies of strategies							
	Player 1				Player 2			
	J	1	2	3	J	1	2	3
Equilibrium	**0.4**	0.2	0.2	0.2	**0.4**	0.2	0.2	0.2
O'Neill	**0.36**	0.22	0.22	0.20	**0.43**	0.23	0.18	0.17
'02	**0.32**	0.23	0.22	0.24	**0.41**	0.23	0.18	0.19
'06 a	**0.39**	0.21	0.20	0.21	**0.42**	0.21	0.17	0.19
'06 b	**0.32**	0.23	0.22	0.23	**0.37**	0.21	0.20	0.21
'09	**0.39**	0.21	0.20	0.20	**0.42**	0.20	0.19	0.19

The results are in the form of aggregate numbers (across all pairs, each of which played the game 105 times) and there was no monetary compensation to the subjects in my experiments. Furthermore, the subjects played the game before being exposed to the knowledge of mixed strategy equilibrium. As observed, the results closely resemble the prediction values (in an intuitive sense), and O'Neil's findings have very strong reproducibility. Thus, the presented game is an excellent example where: (i) economic theory provides non-trivial predictions; (ii) the theoretical predictions pass the IOT test; and (ii) the experimental results are reproducible.

The second example is a multi-unit auction game. In this game, four identical objects (for example, brand new PCs) are sold in a sealed bid auction. There are N bidders whose goal is to buy at most one unit of the object. The bidders simultaneously submit bids and the top four bidders obtain the objects and pay their own bid price. If each bidder's willingness to pay is identically and independently distributed according to the uniform distribution over [0,1], one can determine the symmetric Bayesian Nash equilibrium bidding function as follows.

$$b^*(V_i) = \frac{\dfrac{1}{N-3}V_i - 3\dfrac{1}{N-2}V_i^2 + 3\dfrac{1}{N-1}V_i^3 - \dfrac{1}{N}V_i^4}{\dfrac{1}{N-4} - 3\dfrac{1}{N-3}V_i + 3\dfrac{1}{N-2}V_i^2 - \dfrac{1}{N-1}V_i^3} \tag{1}$$

Here, V_i denotes the bidder's willingness to pay, and N is the number of bidders. This is obviously a highly non-trivial prediction of human behavior. Does the prediction fit the empirical data? To address this question, I conducted a series of experiments in my economics classes over a period of three years. The results are summarized in Figures 1.5–1.7.

The figures show all bidder's data and the curves represent the equilibrium bidding function. Again, no payment was made to the subjects. Admittedly, the prediction does not fit the observed data perfectly, but intuitively the theoretical prediction did a good job of describing the subjects' behavior. In my opinion, this is another example where the theory survives the IOT test and the experimental results are largely reproducible.

Why have such examples been largely undervalued or overlooked? The answer could include the possibility that economists are excessively preoccupied with sophisticated statistical methods and also are too directed towards finding anomalies.

When applying rigorous statistical tests to the experimental data of O'Neil's game, one can detect some systematic deviations of data from the equilibrium predictions. Despite the fact that aggregate data closely follow the theory predictions, individual data exhibit more variations than is predicted by the equilibrium. In addition, the theory predicts that strategies should be statistically independent over time, but actual data exhibit some serial correlation.

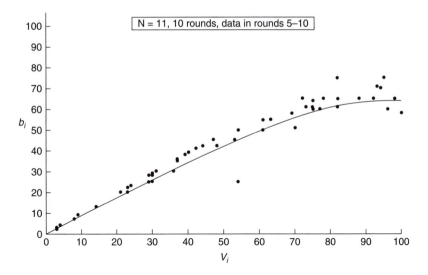

Figure 1.5   Observed strategies in multi-unit auction experiment in 2004

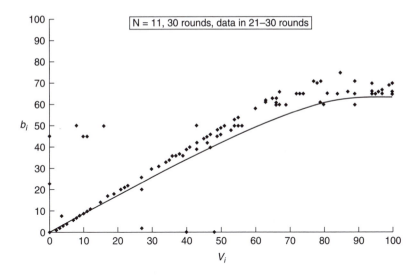

Figure 1.6   Observed strategies in multi-unit auction experiment in 2006

Hence, it has often been reported that the observed data do not fit the theory in O'Neil's game. Likewise, one can also detect that the data points are somewhat biased upwards in the multi-unit auction game. In fact, that was one of the focuses in the work by Cox, Smith and Walker (1984) who were the first to conduct experiments on this game. Accordingly, the multiple-unit auction game has

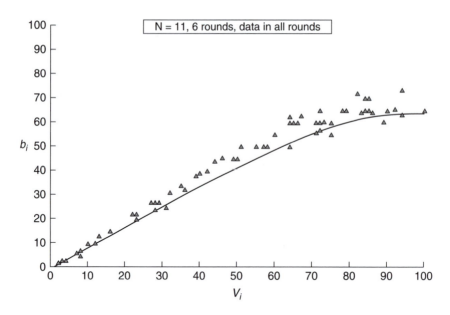

Figure 1.7   Observed strategies in multi-unit auction experiment in 2009

been regarded as just one of many instances where data systematically deviate from theory.

In my opinion, however, the most revealing features of those examples are: (i) the reasonably good fitness of data to the non-trivial predictions; and (ii) the fact that the experimental results are reproducible. Those features are much more noteworthy than the fine deviations from the theory. Note that the crucial judgment here is rather subjective. Typically, one is unimpressed if a theoretical prediction fits the data well when the prediction is trivial. In contrast, if a prediction is highly non-trivial, then a relatively good fitness of data and the reproducibility of such good fitness are worth noting. For that reason, in addition to the use of rigorous and sophisticated statistical technique, it is desirable for us to be more open minded to such (sound) subjective judgment, in the spirit of the IOT test, and also pay more attention to the reproducibility of experimental results.

Economic experiments are usually accompanied by anomalies, since it is difficult to control human cognitive mechanisms in order to directly observe the individual driving forces of economic behaviors. Therefore, researchers might just regard that theories as sources of useful insights and might be skeptical about the possibility that theories are clearly confirmed by experimental data. I subscribed to this view prior to the discovering of the aforementioned experimental results. Those findings, however, indicate that we might be overly pessimistic. There is value in using the IOT test and reproducibility in economics to uncover more examples where theory offers a good explanation of reality.

1.8 Summary and conclusion

I have attempted to assess the relationship between theory and reality in economics using three different allegories. The first allegory implies that the relationship between neoclassical theory and reality is perhaps similar to the relationship between the Newtonian law and the motions of a falling leaf. If this allegory is valid, then the neoclassical theory need not be abandoned due to the existence of anomalies in experimental data, since the neoclassical theory does indeed capture one of the main driving forces of falling leaves and thus continues to be an important building block of a more comprehensive model. In addition, the 'top-down' method of using experimental data to test a theory is useful in empirical or experimental studies. Since it is unlikely that one can come up with a satisfactory theory of falling leaves simply by accumulating millions of data of falling leaves, proposing a conjecture based on theoretical models would be a far more effective manner of detecting some of the laws that were in operation behind the data.

The second allegory, on the other hand, asserts that the relationship between neoclassical theory and reality is possibly similar to the relationship between geocentricism and the motions of planets. In this case, anomalies (such as the retrograde motion of Mars) indicate that the neoclassical theory is fundamentally wrong. It should be abandoned and replaced with a more satisfactory theory accounting for those anomalies (heliocentrism). This allegory also suggests that the 'bottom-up' method of identifying empirical regularities from carefully measured data is preferable in empirical/experimental studies. This allegory articulates the views held by some researchers in behavioral economics.

Which allegory should one believe? In my opinion, the right answer is 'It depends.' The point of constructing these allegories based on well-understood natural phenomena is to demonstrate that there is no reason to blindly deny one in favor of the other. One can conduct research according to his/her subjective probability of which allegory is more appropriate, but it is desirable to realize that the less preferred allegory in one case might be suitable in another situation.

The third allegory is a variant of the first one and considers a hypothetical situation where only limited controls can be applied to the assessment of falling leaves. This case reveals a concrete situation where a theory (the Newtonian law) provides good insights, even when theoretical predictions repeatedly fail and policy recommendations based on such theory are not always effective.

However, in the third allegory it is impossible to verify that the Newtonian law is *true* in an ideally controled environment. This allegory depicts an important aspect of economic research. In natural sciences, either raw data exhibit a high degree of regularity or it is possible to apply fine controls to data to create a situation where a theoretical prediction can be visualized unambiguously. Neither seems to be true in a majority of economic problems. The limitations of effective controls come from the fact that human behavior is produced by cognitive mechanisms of which we have only a poor understanding and that one can only apply indirect controls to those mechanisms in the field and in the lab.

Hence, the situation of economics is similar to explaining the motions of leaves under extremely limited controls. In such a case, it may be impossible to clearly single out *the truth*. However, attempting to discover good explanations is far more productive than dismissing all efforts of explanation for being equally unscientific or unreliable. Economics is struggling toward finding good explanations by trial and error and the free competition of research ideas. This view offers some systematic explanations for a number of puzzling phenomena which are observed only in economics (such as why it takes such a long time to receive a referee's report).

Finally, I presented two experimental examples to suggest that one should not be too pessimistic about the limitations of control. There are in fact some cases in which we can observe the implications of traditional theory rather clearly.

Notes

* This is partly based on my essay for the 75th anniversary of the Japanese Economic Association (Kandori 2010, in Japanese). A part of this paper was also presented at the Conference on Rationality and Irrationality, Stockholm School of Economics, 2011. I would like to thank Ken Binmore, Ariel Rubinstein, Stergio Skaperdas, Karl Warneryd and the conference participants for their helpful comments. I also thank Neil Nguyen for excellent editorial assistance.

1. Friedman (1953) also examined an allegory based on falling objects.

2. H. M. Markovitz, S. L. Savage, J. Danziger, *Flaw of Averages* (Hoboken, NJ: Wiley, 2009) attributes this to statistician Joe Berkson. In contrast, D. Friedman and S. Sunder associate the term with Leonard J. Savage (*Experimental Methods* [Cambridge: Cambridge University Press, 1994], p.92).

3. What about mathematics, which is not an empirical science and therefore cannot use the IOT and reproducibility? Isn't it similar to mathematical economics? Mathematicians seem to judge the value of research in the realm of pure theory and pay little attention to the scope of application in reality (even though good mathematical theory often turns out to be useful in real-life applications). Hence they do not face the dilemma of the economist in the third allegory, about the relationship between theory *and reality*.

References

Cox, J., V. Smith and J. Walker (1984) 'Theory and Behavior of Multiple Unit Discriminative Auctions', *The Journal of Finance*, vol. 39, no. 4, pp. 983–1010.

Friedman, M. (1953) 'The Methodology of Positive Economics', in *Essays in Positive Economics* (Chicago: University of Chicago Press).

Kandori, M (2010) 'What Has Economic Theory Taught Us, and Where is it Going?', chapter 6 in Japanese Economic Association (ed.), *Nihon Keizai Gakkai 75 Nenshi (The 75 Years of the Japanese Economic Association: Retrospect and Prospect)* (Tokyo: Yuhikaku) (in Japanese).

O'Neill, B. (1987) 'Nonmetric Test of the Minimax Theory of Two-Person Zerosum Games', *Proceedings of the National Academy of Sciences, U.S.A.*, vol. 84, pp. 2106–2109.

Rubinstein, A. (2006) 'Dilemmas of an Economic Theorist', *Econometrica*, vol. 74, no. 4, pp. 865–883.

Tversky, A. and D. Kahneman (1992) 'Advances in Prospect Theory: Cumulative Representation of Uncertainty', *Journal of Risk and Uncertainty*, vol. 5, pp. 297–323.

Yamagishi, T. (2002) 'New Directions of Research on Social Dilemmas', in H. Imai and A. Okada (eds), *Game Riron no Shin-Tenkai (Recent Developments in Game Theory)* (Tokyo: Keiso-Shobo) (in Japanese).

Part II
Complex Economic Dynamics: Agent-based and Analytical Models

2
The Dynamics of Pure Market Exchange

Herbert Gintis
Santa Fe Institute, USA and Central European University, Hungary

> The problem of a rational economic order is determined precisely by the fact that the knowledge of the circumstances of which we must make use never exists in concentrated or integrated form, but solely as the dispersed bits of incomplete and frequently contradictory knowledge which all the separate individuals possess. (F.A. Hayek 1945: 519)

2.1 Introduction

Adam Smith (2000 [1759]) envisioned a decentralized economy that sustains an efficient allocation of resources through the 'invisible hand' of market competition. Smith's vision was formalized by Léon Walras (1954 [1874]), and a proof of existence of equilibrium for a simplified version of the Walrasian economy was provided by Wald (1951 [1936]). Soon after, Debreu (1952), Arrow and Debreu (1954), Gale (1955), Nikaido (1956), McKenzie (1959), Negishi (1960), and others contributed to a rather complete proof of the existence of equilibrium in Walrasian economies. Such economies are particularly attractive because they capture the basic structural characteristics of market economies, and because a Walrasian equilibrium is Pareto-efficient (Arrow 1951; Debreu 1951, 1954; Hurwicz 1960).

The question of stability of the Walrasian economy was a central research focus in the years immediately following the existence proofs (Arrow and Hurwicz, 1958, 1959, 1960; Arrow, Block and Hurwicz, 1959; Nikaido 1959; McKenzie, 1960; Nikaido and Uzawa 1960; Uzawa 1960). The models investigated assumed that out of equilibrium, there is a system of *public prices* shared by all agents, the time rate of change of prices being a function of excess demand. The public price system was implemented by a single agent (the 'auctioneer') acting outside the economy to update prices in the current period on the basis of the current pattern of excess demand, using a process of 'tâtonnement', as was first suggested by Walras (1954 [1874]) himself.

The quest for a general stability theorem was derailed by Herbert Scarf's simple examples of unstable Walrasian equilibria (Scarf, 1960). There were attempts soon after to continue the analysis of tâtonnement by adding trading out of equilibrium (Uzawa 1959, 1961, 1962; Negishi 1961; Hahn 1962; and Hahn and Negishi 1962), but with only limited success.

General equilibrium theorists in the early 1970s harbored some expectation that plausible restrictions on utility functions might entail stability, because gross substitutability was known to imply global stability (Arrow et al., 1959) and gross substitutability was known to hold for Cobb–Douglas and many other utility functions (Fisher, 1999). However, gross substitutability is not a property of constant elasticity of substitution (CES) and more general utility functions. Moreover, Sonnenschein (1973), Mantel (1974, 1976), and Debreu (1974) showed that any continuous function, homogeneous degree zero in prices, and satisfying Walras' Law, is the excess demand function for some Walrasian economy.

However, Hahn and Negishi (1962) showed that if out-of-equilibrium trade is permitted and the so-called *Hahn condition* obtains, then the Walrasian equilibrium is stable under tâtonnement. The Hahn condition says that markets are sufficiently informationally complete that if there is aggregate excess demand then no individual experiences excess supply, and if there is aggregate excess supply, then no individual experiences excess demand. Fisher (1983) significantly broadened this model and proved stability assuming a expectational condition ('no favorable surprise') that should logically hold in any Walrasian equilibrium, plus a weakened Hahn condition, according to which lower-price sellers realize their plans before higher-price sellers do.

Nevertheless, surveying the state of the art some quarter-century after Arrow and Debreu's seminal existence theorems, Fisher (1983) concluded that little progress had been made toward a cogent model of Walrasian market dynamics. More recent studies have shown that the tâtonnement dynamic is stable only under extremely stringent conditions (Kirman, 1992). Indeed, chaos in price movements is the generic case for the tâtonnement adjustment processes (Saari, 1985; Bala and Majumdar, 1992). Saari (1995) and others have shown that the information needed by a price adjustment mechanism that can ensure stability include virtually complete knowledge of all cross-elasticities of demand in addition to excess demand quantities.

It is now more than another quarter-century since Fisher's seminal contributions, but it remains the case that, despite the centrality of the general equilibrium model to economic theory, we know nothing systematic about Walrasian market dynamics in realistic settings. We show that when the market system is modeled as a Markov process rather than a system of first-order differential equations, a powerful analytical dynamic emerges.

2.2 A Markov process primer

We will model the Walrasian economy as a Markov process, starting for illustrative purposes with a very elementary and purely didactic example. Our goal is to show that even a very simple finite Markov process may have too many states to permit an analytical solution, yet the global properties of the model are easily understood.

Consider an economy with k goods, each of which could serve equally well as a money good for the economy. Suppose there are n agents in the economy, and in each period, each agent is willing to accept exactly one good as money. Suppose further that in each period, one agent switches from his own preferred money to that of another randomly encountered agent. We can describe the state of the economy as a k-vector $(w_1 \ldots w_k)$, where w_i is the number of agents who accept good i as money. The total number of states in the economy is thus the number of different ways to distribute n indistinguishable balls (the n agents) into k distinguishable boxes (the k goods), which is $C(n+k-1, k-1)$, where $C(n,k) = n!/(n-k)!k!$ is the number of ways to choose k objects from a set of n objects. To verify this formula, write a particular state in the form

$$s = x \ldots x A x \ldots x A x \ldots x A x \ldots x$$

where the number of x's before the first A is the number of agents choosing good 1 as money, the number of x's between the $(i-1)^{\text{th}}$ A and the ith A is the number of agents choosing good i as money, and the number of x's after the final A is the number agents choosing good k as money. The total number of x's is equal to n, and the total number of A's is $k-1$, so the length of s is $n+k-1$. Every placement of the $k-1$ A's represents particular state of the system, so there are $C(n+k-1, k-1)$ states of the system.

For instance, if $n=100$ and $k=10$, then the number of states S in the system is $S = C(109,9) = 4,263,421,511,271$. Suppose in each period two agents are randomly chosen and the first agent switches to using the second agent's money good as his own money good (the two money goods may in fact be the same). This gives a determinate probability p_{ij} of shifting from one state i of the system to any other state j. The matrix $P = \{p_{ij}\}$ is called a *transition probability matrix*, and the whole stochastic system is called a *Markov process*. The Markov process is finite because it has a finite number of states.

What is the long-run behavior of this Markov process? Note first that if we start in state i at time $t=0$, the probability $p_{ij}^{(2)}$ of being in state j in period $t=2$ is simply

$$p_{ij}^{(2)} = \sum_{k=1}^{S} p_{ik} p_{kj} = (P^2)_{ij}. \tag{1}$$

This is true because to be in state j at $t = 2$ the system must have been in some state k at $t = 1$ with probability p_{ik}, and the probability of moving from k to j is just p_{kj}. This means that the two-period transition probability matrix for the Markov process is just P^2, the matrix product of P with itself. By similar reasoning, the probability of moving from state i to state j in exactly r periods, is P^r. Therefore, the time path followed by the system starting in state $s^0 = i$ at time $t = 0$ is the sequence $s^0, s^1, \ldots$, where

$$P[s^t = j | s^0 = i] = (P^t)_{ij} = p_{ij}^{(t)}.$$

The matrix P in our example has $S^2 \approx 1.818 \times 10^{15}$ entries. The notion of calculation P^t for even small t is quite infeasible. There are ways to reduce the calculations by many orders of magnitude (Gintis, 2009, Ch. 13), but even these are completely impractical with so large a Markov process.

Nevertheless, we can easily understand the dynamics of this Markov process. We first observe as that if the Markov process is ever in the state

$$s_*^r = (0_1, \ldots, 0_{r-1}, n_r, 0_{r+1} \ldots 0_k),$$

where all n agents choose good r money, then s_*^r will be the state of the system in all future periods. We call such a state *absorbing*. There are clearly only k absorbing states for this Markov process. We next observe that from any non-absorbing state s, there is a strictly positive probability that the system moves to an absorbing state before returning to state s. For instance, suppose $w_i = 1$ in state s. Then there is a positive probability that w_i increases by 1 in each of the next $n - 1$ periods, so the system is absorbed into state s_*^i without ever returning to state s. Now let $p_s > 0$ be the probability that Markov process never returns to state s. The probability that the system returns to state s at least q times is thus at most $(1 - p_s)^q$. Since this expression goes to zero as $q \to \infty$, it follows that state s *appears only a finite number of times with probability one*. We call s a *transient* state.

Because state s in the previous argument was an arbitrary non-absorbing state, it follows that *all non-absorbing states are transient*. It is also clear that with probability one there will be some period t such that no transient state reappears after period t. This means that with probability one the system is absorbed into one of the k absorbing states, from which it never emerges. Inevitably in this system one good emerges as the money good for the economy.

We can in fact often calculate the probability that a system starting out with w_r agents choosing good r as money, is absorbed by state s_*^r. Let us think of the Markov process as that of k gamblers, each of whom starts out with an integral number of k coins, there being n coins in total. The gamblers represent the goods and their coins are the agents who choose that good for money. We have shown that in the long run, one of the gamblers will have all of the coins, with probability one. Suppose the game is fair in the sense that in any period a gambler with a positive number of coins has an equal chance to increase or decrease his wealth by one coin. Then the expected wealth of a gambler in period $t + 1$ is just his wealth in period t. Similarly, the expected wealth $E[w^{t'}|w^t]$ in period $t' > t$ of a gambler whose wealth in period t is w^t is $E[w^{t'}|w^t] = w^t$. This means that if a gambler starts out with wealth $w > 0$ and he wins all the coins with probability q_w, then $w = q_w n$, so the probability of being the winner is just $q_w = w/n$.

We now can say that this Markov process, despite its enormous size, can be easily described as follows. Suppose the process starts with $w_r = w$. Then in a finite number of time periods, the process will be absorbed into one of the states $s_*^1, \ldots, s_*^k$, and the probability of being absorbed into state s_*^r is w/n. As it turns out, this description of a finite Markov process is completely general, except for a few technical points. In general, however, the process will not be absorbed into a single state, but rather into what is called an *irreducible Markov subprocess*, making transitions among a number of states, called *communicating recurrent states*. If the process is aperiodic, the fraction of time it is in each of these recurrent states state forms a probability distribution called the *stationary distribution* of the 'absorbing' Markov subprocess. If the process is periodic, it can be conveniently subdivided into a number of aperiodic subprocesses, each with a stationary distribution.

2.3   From differential equations to Markov processes

A plausible model of market dynamics should reflect two fundamental aspects of market competition. First, trades must be bilateral with separate budget equations for each transaction (Starr, 1972). The second is that in a decentralized market economy out of equilibrium, *there is no price vector for the economy at all*. The assumption that there is a system of prices that are common knowledge to all participants (we call these *public prices*) is plausible in equilibrium, because all agents can observe these prices in the marketplace. However, out of equilibrium there is no vector of prices determined by market exchange. Rather, assuming Bayesian rational agents, every agent has a subjective prior concerning prices, based on personal experience, that the agent uses to formulate and execute trading plans.

Consider, for instance, the wage rate for a particular labor service. In equilibrium, this price may be common knowledge, but out of equilibrium, every supplier of this service must have an estimate of the probability of selling his service as a function of his offer price. The supplier, if Bayesian rational, will have a subjective prior representing the shape of the demand function for the service. This prior will determine whether the supplier accepts a particular wage offer, or rejects the offer and continues searching for a better offer. The information needed to form this prior includes the distribution of subjective priors of demanders for the labor service, while the subjective prior of each demander will depend in a similar manner on the distribution of subjective priors of suppliers of the service. Thus in this case information is not simply asymmetrically distributed, but rather is effectively indeterminate, since the supply schedule depends on suppliers' assessment of demand conditions, and the demand schedule depends on demanders' assessment of supply schedules. The conditions under which each agent's choice is a best response to the others', even assuming common knowledge of rationality and common knowledge of the Markov process (which in this case is the game in which the players are engaged), are quite stringent and normally not present (Aumann and Brandenburger, 1995).

In analyzing market disequilibrium, we must thus assume that each agent's subjective prior includes a vector of *private* prices that is modified adaptively through the exchange experience. The admissible forms of experience in a decentralized market economy are those that result from observing the behavior of trading partners. This experience is the sole basis for a trader's updating his private price vector, and equilibrium can be achieved only if plausible models of inference and updating lead private prices to converge to equilibrium prices (Howitt and Clower, 2000).

In the interest of simplicity in dealing with a daunting problem that has defied solution for more than a century, we will assume that there are no institutions other than markets where individuals congregate to exchange their wares, there are no forms of wealth other than agents' production goods, all transactions take place in the current period, so there is no intertemporal planning, and there is no arbitrage beyond that which can be executed by an agent engaged in a series of personal trades using no information save that acquired through personal trading experience.

If we can show stability under these conditions (which we can) we then know that trader information concerning macro aspects of the economy plays no essential role in achieving market equilibrium, and indeed may well have a destabilizing effect (Gintis, 2007).

It follows logically that in so simple a market system with rational actors but no public institutions, *expectations are purely adaptive*. The 'rational expectations' notion that agents know the global structure of the economy and use macroeconomic information to form accurate expectations is not plausible in the decentralized context. This conclusion may, of course, require revision in a model with an institutional structure that creates public information, such as a credible government or national bank.

An appropriate candidate for modeling the Walrasian system in disequilibrium is a Markov process. The states of the process are vectors whose components are the states of individual agents. The state of each agent includes his holding of each good, an array of parameters representing his search strategies for buying and selling, parameters representing his linkage to others in a network of traders, and finally his vector of private prices, which the agent uses to evaluate trading offers.

If state s_i has a positive probability of making a transition to state s_j in a finite number of periods (i.e., $p_{ij}^{(t)} > 0$ for some positive integer t), we say s_i *communicates* with s_j. If all states in a Markov process communicate with each other, we say the process is *irreducible*. We cannot assume a Markov model of a Walrasian system is irreducible because, as in our elementary example above, where a good inevitably emerges as money, the states of the system with one good as money will not communicate with the states where a different good is money.

The Markov model of a Walrasian economy is finite if we assume there are a finite number of agents, a finite number of goods, a minimum discernible quantity of each good, and a finite inventory capacity for each good. A strictly positive probability of remaining in the same state for an agent then ensures that the Markov process is finite if aperiodic. Assuming for the moment that the Markov process is irreducible, being both and aperiodic implies the Markov process is *ergodic* (Feller, 1950), which means has a stationary distribution expressing the long-run probability of being in each state of the system, irrespective of its initial state.

We may not care about individual states of the process, but rather about certain aggregate properties of the system, including the mean and standard deviation of prices, and the aggregate pattern of excess demand. As we shall see, the ergodic theorem ensures that under appropriate conditions these aggregates have determinate long-term stationary distributions.

The Ergodic Theorem: Consider an n-state aperiodic and irreducible Markov process with transition matrix P, so the t-period transition probabilities are given by $P^{(t)} = P^t$. Then there is probability distribution $u = (u_1, \ldots, u_n)$ over the states of the Markov process with strictly positive entries that has the following properties for $j = 1, \ldots, n$:

$$u_j = \lim_{t \to \infty} p_{ij}^{(t)} \quad \text{for } i = 1, \ldots, n \tag{2}$$

$$u_j = \sum_{i=1}^{n} u_i p_{ij} \tag{3}$$

We call u the *stationary distribution* of the Markov process.

Equation (3) says that with probability one, u_j is the long-run frequency of state s_j in a realization $\{s^t\} = \{s^0, s^1, \ldots\}$ of the Markov process. Also, this frequency is strictly positive and independent from the starting state $s^0 = s_i$. By a well-known property of convergent sequences, (3) implies that u_j is also with probability one the limit of the average frequency of s_j from period t onwards, for any t. This is in accord with the general notion that in an ergodic dynamical system, the equilibrium state of the system can be estimated as an historical average over a sufficiently long time period (Hofbauer and Sigmund, 1998).

Equation (3) is the *renewal equation* governing stationary distribution u. It asserts that in the long run, the probability of being in state s_j is the sum over i of the probability that it was in some state s_i in the previous period, multiplied by the probability of a one-period transition from state s_i to state s_j, independent from the initial state of the realization $\{s^t\} = \{s^0, s^1, \ldots\}$.

A Markov process thus has only a one-period 'memory.' However, we can consider a finite sequence of states $\{s^{t-l}, s^{t-l+1}, \ldots, s^t\}$ of the Markov process of fixed length l as a single state, the process remains Markov and has as an l-period 'memory.' Because any physically realized memory system, including the human brain, has finite capacity, the finiteness assumption imposes no constraint on modeling systems that are subject to physical law.

To see this, suppose a Markov process has transition matrix $P = \{p_{ij}\}$ and consider two-period states of the form ij. We define the transition probability of going from ij to kl as

$$p_{ij,kl} = \begin{cases} p_{j,l} & j = k \\ 0 & j \neq k, \end{cases} \tag{4}$$

This equation says that ij represents 'state s_i in the previous period and state s_j in the current period.' It is easy to check that with this definition the matrix $\{p_{ij,kl}\}$ is a probability transition matrix, and if $\{u_1, \ldots, u_n\}$ is the stationary distribution associated with P, then

$$u_{ij} = u_i p_{i,j} \tag{5}$$

defines the stationary distribution $\{u_{ij}\}$ for $\{p_{ij,kl}\}$. Indeed, we have

$$\lim_{t \to \infty} p_{ij,kl}^{(t)} = \lim_{t \to \infty} p_{j,k}^{(t-1)} p_{k,l} = u_k p_{k,l} = u_{kl}$$

for any pair-state kl, independent from ij. We also have, for any ij,

$$u_{ij} = u_i p_{i,j} = \sum_k u_k p_{k,i} p_{i,j} = \sum_k u_{ki} p_{i,j} = \sum_{kl} u_{kl} p_{kl,ij}. \tag{6}$$

It is straightforward to show that pairs of states of P correspond to single states of $\{p_{ij,kl}\}$. These two equations imply the ergodic theorem for $\{p_{ij,kl}\}$ because equation 5 implies $\{u_{ij}\}$ is a probability distribution with strictly positive entries, and we have the defining equations of a stationary distribution; for any pair-state ij,

$$u_{kl} = \lim_{t \to \infty} p_{ij,kl}^{(t)} \tag{7}$$

$$u_{ij} = \sum_{kl} u_{kl} p_{kl,ij}. \tag{8}$$

An argument by induction extends this analysis to any finite number of sequential states of P.

An important question is the nature of collections of states of a finite Markov process. For instance, we may be interested in total excess demand for a good without caring how this breaks down among individual agents. From the case of two states j and k it will be clear how to generalize to any finite number. Let us make being in either state j or in state k into a new macro-state m. If P is the transition matrix for the Markov process, the probability of moving from state i to state m is just $P_{im} = P_{ij} + P_{ik}$. If the process is ergodic with stationary distribution u, then the frequency of m in the stationary distribution is just $u_m = u_j + u_k$. Then we have

$$u_m = \lim_{t \to \infty} P_{im}^n \tag{9}$$

$$u_m = \sum_i u_i p_{im} \tag{10}$$

However, the probability of a transition from m to a state i is given by

$$P_{mi} = u_j p_{ji} + u_k p_{ki}. \tag{11}$$

Now suppose states j and k are *interchangeable* in the sense that $p_{ji} = p_{ki}$ for all states i. Then (7) implies

$$u_i = \sum_r u_r p_{ri}, \tag{12}$$

where r ranges over all states except j and k, plus the macro-state m. In other words, if we replace states j and k by the single macro-state m, the resulting Markov process has one fewer state, but remains ergodic with the same stationary distribution, except that $u_m = u_j + u_k$. A simple argument by induction shows that any number of interchangeable states can be aggregated into a single macro-state in this manner.

More generally, we may be able to partition the states of M into cells $m_1, \ldots, m_l$ such that, for any $r = 1, \ldots, l$ and any states i and j of M, i and j are interchangeable with respect to each m_k. When this is possible, then $m_1, \ldots, m_l$ are the states of a derived Markov process, which will be ergodic if M is ergodic.

For instance, in a particular market model represented by an ergodic Markov process, we might be able to use a symmetry argument to conclude that all states with the same aggregate demand for a particular good are interchangeable. If so, we can aggregate all states with the same total excess demand for this good into a single macro-state, and the resulting system will be an ergodic Markov process with a stationary distribution. In general, this Markov process will have many fewer states, but still far too many to permit an analytical derivation of the stationary distribution.

2.4   The structure of finite aperiodic Markov processes

If a Markov process is finite and aperiodic but is not irreducible, its states can be partitioned into subsets $S^{tr}, S_1, \ldots S_k$, where every state $s \in S^{tr}$ is *transient*, meaning that for any realization $\{s^t\}$ of the Markov process, with probability one there is a time t such that $s \neq s^{t+t'}$ for all $t' = 1, 2, \ldots$; i.e., s does not reappear in $\{s^t\}$ after time t. It follows that also with probability 1 there is a time t such that no member of S^{tr} appears after time t. A non-transient state is called *recurrent*, for it reappears infinitely often with probability one in a realization of the Markov process.

If s_i is recurrent and communicates with s_j, then s_j is itself recurrent and communicates with s_i. For if j does not communicate with s_i, then every time s_i appears, there is a strictly positive probability, say $q > 0$ that it will never reappear. The probability that s_i appears k times is thus at most $(1 - q)^k$, so s_i reappears an infinite number of times with probability zero, and hence is not recurrent. If s_j communicates with s_i, then s_j must be recurrent, as can be proved using a similar argument.

It follows that communication of states is an equivalence relation over the recurrent states of the Markov process. We define $S_1, \ldots S_k$ to be the equivalence classes of the recurrent states of the Markov process with respect to this equivalence relation. It is clear that the restriction of Markov process to any one of the S_r, $r = 1, \ldots, k$ is an ergodic Markov process with a stationary distribution. Moreover, if $s_i \in S^{tr}$, there is a probability distribution q^i over $\{1, \ldots, k\}$ such that q_r^i is the probability, starting in s_i, the Markov process will eventually enter S_r, from which it will, of course, never leave. Thus for an arbitrary finite, aperiodic Markov process with transition matrix $P = \{p_{ij}\}$, we have the following.

Extended Ergodic Theorem: Let M be a finite aperiodic Markov process. There exists a unique partition $\{S^{tr}, S_1, \ldots, S_k\}$ of the states S of M, a probability distribution u^r over S_r for $r = 1, \ldots, k$, such that $u_i^r > 0$ for all $i \in S_r$, and for each $i \in S^{tr}$, there is a probability distribution q^i over $\{1, \ldots, k\}$ such that for all $i, j = 1, \ldots, n$ and all $r = 1, \ldots k$, we have

$$u_{ij} = \lim_{t \to \infty} P_{ij}^{(t)}; \tag{13}$$

$$u_j^r = u_{ij} \quad \text{if } i, j \in S_r; \tag{14}$$

$$u_j^r = \sum_{i \in S_r} u_i^r p_{ij} \quad \text{for } j \in S_r; \tag{15}$$

$$u_{ij} = q_r^i u_j^r \quad \text{if } s_i \in S^{tr} \quad \text{and} \quad s_j \in S_r. \tag{16}$$

$$u_{ij} = 0 \quad \text{if } s_j \in S^{tr}. \tag{17}$$

$$\sum_j u_{ij} = 1 \quad \text{for all } i = 1, \dots, n. \tag{18}$$

For a Markov process with few states, there are well-known methods for solving for the stationary distribution (Gintis, 2009: Ch. 13). However, for systems with a large number of states, these methods are impractical. Rather, we here create a computer model of the Markov process, and ascertain empirically the dynamical properties of the irreducible Markov subprocesses. We are in fact only interested in measuring certain aggregate properties of the subprocess rather than their stationary distributions. These properties are the long-run average price and quantity structure of the economy, as well as the short-run volatility of prices and quantities and the efficiency of the process's search and trade algorithms. It is clear from the quasi-ergodic theorem that the long-term behavior of an any realization of aperiodic Markov process is governed by the stationary distribution of one or another of the stationary distributions of the irreducible subprocesses $S_1, \dots, S_k$. Generating a sufficient number of the sample paths $\{s^t\}$, each observed from the point at which the process has entered some S_r, will reveal the long-run behavior of the dynamical system.

Suppose an aperiodic Markov process M with transient states S^{tr} and ergodic subprocesses $S_1, \dots, S_k$ enters a subprocess S_r after t_0 periods with high probability, and suppose the historical average over states from t_0 to t_1 is a close approximation to the stationary distribution of S_r. Consider the Markov process M^+ consisting of reinitializing M every t_1 periods. Then M^+ is ergodic, and a sufficiently large sample of historical averages starting t_0 periods after reinitialization and continuing until the next initialization will reveal the stationary distribution of M^+. This is the methodology we will used in estimating the aggregate properties of a Markov model of a market economy.

2.5 Scarfian instability revisited

To assess the effect of passing from differential equation to Markov process models, this section revisits Herbert Scarf's seminal example of Walrasian instability. Scarf's is a three-good economy in which each agent produces one good and consumes some of this good plus some of one other good, in fixed proportions. Labeling the goods X, Y, and Z, following Scarf, we assume X-producers consume X and Y, Y-producers consume Y and Z, and Z-producers consume Z and X, where the conditions of production are identical for all three goods. The utility functions for the three agents are assumed to be

$$u_X(x,y,z) = \min\{x,y\}, \tag{19}$$

$$u_Y(x,y,z) = \min\{y,z\}, \tag{20}$$

$$u_Z(x,y,z) = \min\{z,x\}. \tag{21}$$

It is straightforward to show that utility maximization, where p_x, p_y, and p_z are the prices of the three goods and x^d, y^d, and z^d are the final demands for the three goods, gives

$$x_X^d = y_X^d = \frac{p_x}{p_x+p_y} \tag{22}$$

$$y_Y^d = z_Y^d = \frac{p_y}{p_y+p_z} \tag{23}$$

$$z_Z^d = x_Z^d = \frac{p_z}{p_z+p_x} \tag{24}$$

These equations allows us to calculate total excess demand for each good as a function of the prices of the three goods. It is easy to check that the market-clearing prices, normalizing $p_z^* = 1$, are given by $p_x^* = p_y^* = 1$. The excess demand functions for the economy are then given by

$$E_x = x_X^d + x_Z^d - 1 = \frac{-p_y}{p_x+p_y} + \frac{p_z}{p_z+p_x} \tag{25}$$

$$E_y = y_X^d + y_Y^d - 1 = \frac{-p_z}{p_y+p_z} + \frac{p_x}{p_x+p_y} \tag{26}$$

$$E_z = z_Y^d + z_Z^d - 1 = \frac{-p_x}{p_z+p_x} + \frac{p_y}{p_y+p_z}. \tag{27}$$

The tâtonnement price adjustment process is given by

$$\dot{p}_i = E_i(p_x,p_y,p_z), \quad \text{where } i=x,y,z. \tag{28}$$

It is easy to show that the expression $p_x p_y p_z$ is constant on paths of the dynamical system, which implies that the equilibrium is neutrally stable, the system moving in closed paths about the equilibrium at every non-equilibrium point.

Before moving to the non-tâtonnement version of the Scarf economy, we will implement Scarf's differential equation solution as a Markov process in which time t becomes discrete, $t = 1,2,\ldots$, and the differential equations (28) are replaced by difference equations

$$p_x^{t+1} = p_x^t + E_x^t/\Delta \tag{29}$$

$$p_y^{t+1} = p_y^t + E_y^t/\Delta, \tag{30}$$

$$p_z^{t+1} = p_z^t + E_z^t/\Delta, \tag{31}$$

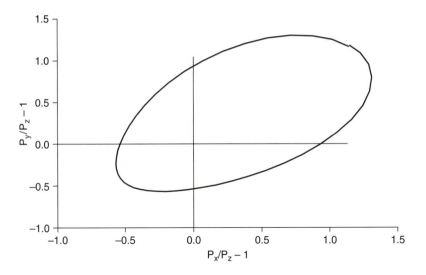

Figure 2.1 Neutral stability of three-good Scarf Economy, modeled as a Markov process with public prices and tâtonnement price adjustment

where prices are restricted to a bounded interval of rational numbers, and Δ is an integer chosen so that period-to-period price changes are small. Note that Δ affects the speed of adjustment of the system, but not the path of adjustment, provided it is not so small as to lead the system to violate the price bounds.

This system is a deterministic Markov process in which the current state is the vector of current prices. Suppose we start with disequilibrium prices $p_x = p_x^* + \delta_x$, $p_y = p_y^* + \delta_y$, $p_z = p_z^* = 1$, and in each period prices are updated according to the tâtonnement equations (29). The resulting path of deviations of prices p_x and p_y from equilibrium, with $p_z = 1$ as numeraire, after 5,200 periods with $\Delta = 100$, $\delta_x = 3$, and $\delta_y = -2$ is shown in Figure 2.1, and perfectly replicates the analytical results of Scarf (1960).

2.6   The Scarf economy without tâtonnement

For the Markov process version of the Scarf economy without tâtonnement, we maintain the above assumptions, except now we assume 1,000 traders of each of the three types, each trader endowed at time $t = 0$ with a set of private prices randomly drawn from a uniform distribution. We allow 50,000 generations and 10 periods per generation. At the start of each period, each agent's inventory is re-initialized to one unit of his production good and zero units of the other goods. Each agent in turn is then designated a trade initiator and is paired with a randomly chosen responder, who can either accept or reject the proposed trade. Each agent is thus an initiator exactly once and responder on average once per period. After a successful trade, agents consume whatever is feasible from their updated inventory.

In the reproduction stage, which occurs every ten periods, 5 per cent of agents are randomly chosen either to copy a more successful agent or to be copied by a less successful agent, where success is measured by total undiscounted utility of consumption over the previous ten periods. Such an agent is chosen randomly and assigned a randomly chosen partner with the same production and consumption parameters. The less successful of the pair then copies the private prices of the more successful. In addition, after the reproduction stage, each price of each agent is mutated with 1 per cent probability, the new price either increasing or decreasing by 10 per cent.

The trade procedure is as follows. The initiator offers a certain quantity of one good in exchange for a certain quantity of a second good. If the responder has some of the second good, and if the value of what get gets exceeds the value of what he gives up, according to his private prices, then he agrees to trade. If he has less of the second good than the initiator wants, the trade is scaled down proportionally. Traders are thus rational maximizers, where their subjective priors are their vectors of private prices, and each is ignorant of the other's subjective prior.

Which good he offers to trade for which other good is determined as follows. Let us call an agent's production good his P-good, the additional good he consumes his C-good, and the good which he neither produces nor consumes the T-good. Note that agents must be willing to acquire their T-good despite the fact that it does not enter their utility function. This is because X-producers want Y, but Y-producers do not want X. Only Z-producers want X. Since a similar situation holds with Y-producers and Z-producers, consumption ultimately depends on at least one type of producer accepting the T-good in trade, and then using the T-good to purchase their C-good.

If the initiator has his T-good in inventory, he offers to trade this for his C-good. If this offer is rejected, he offers to trade his T-good for his P-good, which will be a net gain in the value of his inventory provided his subjective terms of trade are favorable. If the initiator does not have his T-good but has his P-good, he offers this in trade for his C-good. If this is rejected, he offers to trade half his P-good for his T-good. If the trade initiator had neither his T-good nor his P-good, he offers his C-good in trade for his P-good, and if this fails he offers to trade for his T-good. In all cases, when a trade is carried out, the term are dictated by the initiator and the amount is the maximum compatible with the inventories of the initiator and responder.

Figure 2.2 shows that within a relatively few periods, the randomly initialized private prices move to *quasi-public* prices, in which the standard error of prices for the same good across individuals is relatively small. Quasi-public prices are

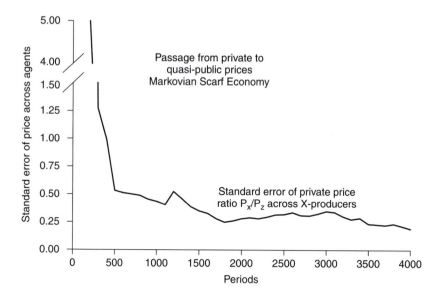

Figure 2.2 The Markov process version of the Scarf economy initialized with random prices quickly transitions to quasi-public prices (private prices with low standard error across traders)

the closest the Markov process comes to approximating the public prices of standard Walrasian general equilibrium theory.

The Markov dynamic in this case is a stationary distribution depicted in Figure 2.3. It is clear that by the time quasi-public prices have become established, the Markov process has attained its stationary distribution, which is a cycle around the equilibrium. This is the only behavior of the stationary distribution observed, independent of the initial state of the system, so it is the stationary distribution version of a limit cycle. In all observed cases, the stationary distribution has approximately the same period and amplitude.

In sum, we have developed a dynamic mathematical model of Scarfian exchange in the form of a Markov process. The transition probabilities of the Markov process are specified implicitly by the algorithms for agent pairing, trading, updating and reproduction. Except for the trade algorithm, for which alternative algorithms are plausible, all modeling choices are uniquely determined by the standard conception of the Walrasian general equilibrium model.

The equilibrium of the Markov process is a stationary distribution that can be analytically specified in principle, but in practice is orders of magnitude too large to calculate, even with the fastest and most powerful conceivable computational aids. Thus, as in the natural sciences, we are obliged to investigate the stationary distribution by running the process on a computer with a variety

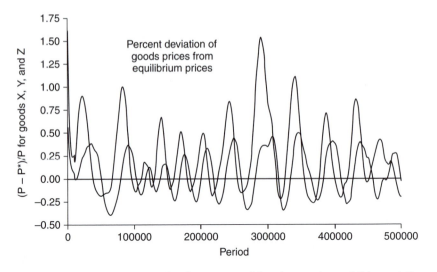

Figure 2.3 The Markov process Scarf economy with private prices exhibits a stationary distribution akin to a limit cycle. The average excursion from equilibrium and the approximate period of the stationary distribution are independent from initial conditions

of choices of numerical parameters. Such calculations are subject to statistical error, but our results are so robust that we are virtually certain to have captured the characteristics of system equilibrium almost perfectly. The most caution conclusion we can offer is that we have proven, for the first time, that there exist Scarfian economies that without tâtonnement that exhibit cycles around the equilibrium price vector, with private prices and a completely decentralized dynamical system of price adjustment. The long-run average price of each good in this model is approximately the market-clearing price.

2.7   A multi-good market economy with simple production

Despite its considerable historical value, the Scarf economy's extreme assumptions are uncharacteristic of a normal market economy, and as we shall see, it is the extreme assumptions that account for the Scarfian economy's lack of stability. The remainder of this paper will deal with a canonical case of a pure market economy with only one institution – the marketplace, but with highly heterogeneous agents. We assume each agent produces one good, in fixed amount, using only personal labor, but consumes a variety of goods produced by others. Agents are endowed with subjective priors concerning the value of all goods, which we call their *private prices*. They have no information about the economy other than that gathered from private experience in trade, including periodically discovering the private price vector of another agent they have encountered and copying it, with some possible mutation, if that agent appears to be more successful than himself. The only serious design decision is that of the trade algorithm which, while much more straightforward than in the case of the Scarf economy, is still in principle somewhat underspecified by the logic of Walrasian exchange. Happily, the details of the trade protocol do not affect the dynamical movement to Walrasian equilibrium as far as we can ascertain.

We assume there are n sectors. Sector $k = 1, \ldots, n$ produces good k in 'styles' $s = 1, \ldots, m$ (we use 'styles' to enrich the heterogeneity of goods in the model without seriously increasing the computational resources needed to estimate the stationary distribution of the resulting Markov process). Each agent consumes a subset of non-production goods, but only a single style of any good. In effect, then, there are nm distinct goods g_s^k, but only n production processes and correspondingly n equilibrium prices, since goods g_s^k and g_t^k with styles s and t respectively, have the same production costs and hence the same price in equilibrium. We write the set of goods as $G = \{g_s^k | k = 1, \ldots, n, s = 1, \ldots m\}$. We also write $g = g^k$ when $g = g_s^k$ for some style s.

A producer of good g_s^k, termed a g_s^k-agent, produces with no inputs other than personal labor an amount q_k of good g_s^k which depreciates to zero at the end of a trading period. In a non-monetary economy, only the production good is carried in inventory, but when individuals are permitted to acquire non-consumption goods, as in later sections of the paper, a trade inventory includes all goods that are not the agent's consumption goods.

The Markov process is initialized by creating N agents, each of whom is randomly assigned a production good g_s^k. Thus, in an economy with goods in m styles, there are Nnm traders. Each of these traders is assigned a private price vector by choosing each price from a uniform distribution on $(0, 1)$, then normalizing so that the price of the nth good is unity. Each g_s^k-agent is then randomly assigned a set $H \subseteq G$, $g_s^k \notin H$ of consumption at most one style of a given good.

The utility function of each agent is the product of powers of CES utility functions of the following form. Suppose an agent consumes r goods. We partition the r goods into k segments (k is chosen randomly from $1 \ldots r/2$) of randomly chosen sizes $m_1, \ldots, m_k$, $m_j > 1$ for all j, and $\sum_j m_j = n$. We randomly assign goods to the various segments, and for each segment, we generate a CES consumption with random weights and an elasticity randomly drawn from the uniform distribution on an interval $[\epsilon_*, \epsilon^*]$. Total utility is the product of the k CES utility functions to random powers f_j such that $\sum_j f_j = 1$. In effect, no two agent have the same utility function.

For example, consider a segment using goods $x_1, \ldots, x_m$ with prices $p_1, \ldots, p_m$ and (constant) elasticity of substitution s, and suppose the power of this segment in the overall utility function is f. It is straightforward to show that the agent spends a fraction f of his income M on goods in this segment, whatever prices he faces. The utility function associated with this segment is then

$$
u(x_1, \ldots, x_n) = \left(\sum_{l=1}^{m} \alpha_l x_l^{\gamma} \right)^{1/\gamma},
\tag{32}
$$

where $\gamma = (s-1)/s$, and $\alpha_1, \ldots, \alpha_m > 0$ satisfy $\sum_l \alpha_l = 1$. The income constraint is $\sum_{l=1}^{m} p_l x_l = f_i M$. Solving the resulting first-order conditions for utility maximization, and assuming $\gamma \neq 0$ (i.e., the utility function segment is not Cobb-Douglas), this gives

$$
x_i = \frac{Mf_i}{\sum_{l=1}^{m} p_l \phi_{il}^{1/(1-\gamma)}},
\tag{33}
$$

where

$$
\phi_{il} = \frac{p_i \alpha_l}{p_l \alpha_i} \quad \text{for } i, l = 1, \ldots, m.
$$

When $\gamma = 0$ (which occurs with almost zero probability), we have a Cobb-Douglas utility function with exponents α_l, so the solution becomes

$$
x_i = \frac{Mf_i \alpha_i}{p_i}.
\tag{34}
$$

By creating such a complex array of utility functions, we ensure that our results are not the result of assuming an excessively narrow set of consumer characteristics. However, the high degree of randomness involved in creating a large number of agents ensures all goods will have approximately the same aggregate demand characteristics. If we add to this that all goods have the same supply characteristics, we can conclude that the market-clearing Walrasian equilibrium will occur when all prices are equal. This in fact turns out to be the case. If we assume heterogeneous production conditions, then we cannot calculate equilibrium prices, but we can still judge that the dynamical system is asymptotically stable by the long-run standard error of the absolute value of excess demand, which will be very small in equilibrium.

For each good $g_s^k \in G$ there is a *market* $m[k, s]$ of traders who sell good g_s^k. In each period, the traders in the economy are randomly ordered and are permitted one by one to engage in active trading. When the g_t^h-agent A is the current active trader, for each good g_t^h for which A has positive demand (i.e, $x_h^{A*} > 0$), A is assigned a random member B $\in m[h, t]$ who consumes g_s^k. A then offers B the maximum quantity y_k of g_s^k, subject to the constraints $y_k \leq i_k^A$, where i_k^A represents A's current inventory of good g_s^k, and $y_k \leq p_h^A x_h^A / p_k^A$, where x_h^A is A's current demand for g_t^h. This means that if A's offer is accepted, A will receive in value at least as much as he gives up, according to A's private prices. A then offers to exchange y_k for an amount $y_h = p_k^A y_k / p_h^A$ of good g_t^h; that is, he offers B an equivalent value of good g_t^h, the valuation being at A's prices. B accepts this offer provided the exchange is weakly profitable at B's private prices; that is, provided $p_k^B y_k \geq p_h^B y_h$. However, B adjusts the amount of each good traded downward if necessary, while preserving their ratio, to ensure that what he receives does not exceed his demand, and what he gives is compatible with his inventory of g_t^h. If A fails to trade with this agent, he still might secure a trade giving him g_s^k, because A $\in m[k,s]$ may also be on the receiving-end of trade offers from g_t^h-agents at some point during the period. If a g_s^k-agent exhausts his supply of g_s^k, he leaves the market for the remainder of the period.

The assumption that each trading encounter is between agents each of whom produces a good that the other consumes could be replaced by the assumption is that each g_s^k-producer A can locate the producers of his consumption goods, but that finding such a producer who also consumes g_s^k will require a separate search. We simply collapse these two stages, noting that when a second search is required and its outcome costly or subject to failure, the relative inefficiency of the non-monetary economy, by comparison with the monetary economies described below, is magnified. Note, however, that while A's partner is a consumer of g_s^k, he may have fulfilled his demand for g_s^k for this period by the time A makes his offer, in which case no trade will take place.

The trade algorithm involves only one substantive design choice, that of allowing A to make a single 'take-it-or-leave-it' relative price offer, while obliging A to accept quantity terms that are set by B, when it is feasible to do so. Such alternatives as allowing B to make the take-it-or-leave-it offer, and choosing the mean of the two offers provided that each is acceptable to the other, or using a Nash bargaining solution, do not alter the market dynamics.

After each trading period, agents consume their inventories provided they have a positive amount of each good that they consume, and agents replenish the amount of their production good in inventory. Moreover, each trader updates his private price vector on the basis of his trading experience over the period, raising the price of a consumption or production good by 0.05 per cent if his inventory is empty (that is, if he failed to purchase any of the consumption good or sell all of his production good), and lowering price by 0.05 per cent otherwise (that is, if he succeeded in obtaining his consumption good or sold all his production inventory). We allow this adjustment strategy to evolve endogenously according to an imitation processes.

After a number of trading periods, the population of traders is updated using the following process. For each market $m[k,s]$ and for each g_s^k-trader A, let f^A be the accumulated utility of agent A since the last updating period (or since the most recent initialization of the Markov process if this is the first updating period). Let f_* and f^* be the minimum and maximum, respectively, over f^A for all g_s^k-agents A. For each g_s^k-agent A, let $p^A = (f^A - f_*)/(f^* - f_*)$, so p^A is a probability for each A. If r agents are to be updated, we repeat the following process by r times. First, choose an agent for reproducing as follows. Identify a random agent in $m[k, s]$ and choose this agent for reproduction with probability p^A. If A is not chosen, repeat the process until one agent is eventually chosen. Note that a relatively successful trader is more likely to be chosen to reproduce than an unsuccessful trader. Next, choose an agent B to copy A's private prices as follows. Identify a random agent B in $m[k, s]$ and choose this agent with probability $1 - p^B$. If B is not chosen, this process is repeated until B is chosen. Clearly, a less successful trader is likely to be chosen this criterion. Repeat until an agent B is chosen. Finally, endow B with A's private price vector, except for each such price, with a small probability μ = randomly increase or decrease its value by a small percentage ϵ. The resulting updating process is a discrete approximation of a monotonic dynamic in evolutionary game theory, and in differential equation systems, all monotonic dynamics have the same dynamical properties (Taylor and Jonker, 1978; Samuelson and Zhang, 1992). Other monotonic approximations, including the simplest, which is repeatedly to choose a pair of agents in $m[k, s]$ and let the lower-scoring agent copy the higher-scoring agent, produce similar dynamical results.

Using utility as the imitation criterion is quite noisy, because utility functions are heterogeneous and individuals who prefer goods with low prices do better than agents who prefer high-priced goods independent of the trading prowess. Using alternative criteria, such as the frequency and/or volume trading success, with results similar to those reported herein.

The result of the dynamic specified by the above conditions is the change over time in the distribution of private prices. The general result is that the system of private prices, which at the outset are randomly generated, in rather short time evolves to a set of *quasi-public* prices with very low inter-agent variance. Over the long term, these quasi-public prices move toward their equilibrium, market-clearing levels.

2.8   Estimating the stationary distribution

I will illustrate this dynamic assuming $n = 9$, $m = 6$, and $N = 300$, so there are 54 distinct goods which we write as $g_1^1, \ldots, g_6^9$, and 16,200 traders in the economy. There are then nine distinct prices $p_1^A, \ldots, p_9^A$ for each agent A. We treat g^9 as the numeraire good for each trader, so $p_9^A = 1$ for all traders A. A g^k-agent produces one unit of good k per period. We assume that there are equal numbers of producers of each good from the outset, although we allow migration from less profitable to more profitable sectors, so in the long run profit rates are close to equal in all sectors. The complexity of the utility functions do not allow us to calculate equilibrium properties of the system perfectly, but we will assume that market-clearing prices are approximately equal to unit costs, given that unit costs are fixed, agents can migrate from less to more profitable sectors, and utility functions do not favor one good or style over another, on average. Population updating occurs every ten periods, and the number of encounters per sector is 10 per cent of the number of agents in the sector. The mutation rate is $\mu = 0.01$ and the error correction is $\epsilon = 0.01$.

The results of a typical run of this model are illustrated in Figures 2.4 to 2.6. Figure 2.4 shows the passage from private to quasi-public prices over the first 20,000 trading periods of a typical run. The mean standard error of prices is computed as follows. For each good g we measure the standard deviation of the price of g across all g-agents, where for each agent, the price of the numeraire good g_9 is unity. Figure 2.4 shows the average of the standard errors for all goods. The passage from private to quasi-public prices is quite dramatic, the standard error of prices across individuals falling by an order of magnitude within 300 periods, and falling another order of magnitude over the next 8,500 periods. The final value of this standard error is 0.029, as compared with its initial value of 6.7.

Figure 2.5 shows the movement of the average standard error of the absolute value of excess demand over 50,000 periods for nine goods in six styles each. Using this measure, after 1,500 periods excess demand has decreased by two orders of magnitude, and it decreases another order of magnitude by the end of the run.

It is not surprising, given the behavior of excess demand for this model, that prices would approach their Walrasian equilibrium values. This process

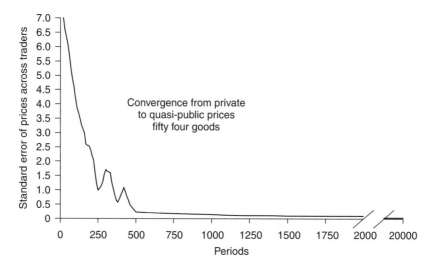

Figure 2.4 Convergence of private prices to quasi-public prices in a typical run with nine goods in 6 sytles each (fifty-four goods)

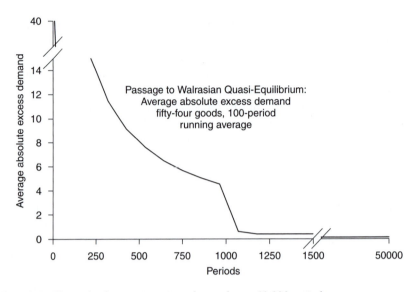

Figure 2.5   The path of aggregate excess demand over 50,000 periods

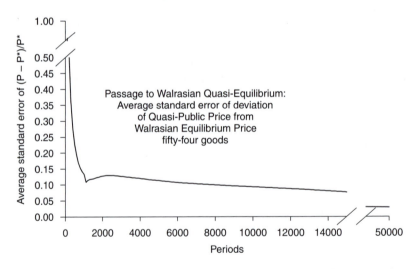

Figure 2.6   The passage from private to quasi-public prices in the Markovian Scarf economy. The long-run standard error of prices across traders is rather high, due to the fact that the system does not tend to Walrasian equilibrium

is illustrated in Figure 2.6. After 50,000 periods, the standard error of the deviation of prices from (our calculated) equilibrium values are about 3 per cent of its starting value.

The distinction between low-variance private prices and true public prices is significant, even when the standard error of prices across agents is extremely small, because stochastic events such as technical changes propagate very slowly when prices are highly correlated private prices, but very rapidly when all agents react in parallel to price movement. In effect, with private prices, a large part of the reaction to a shock is a temporary reduction in the correlation among prices, a reaction that is impossible with public prices, as the latter are always perfectly correlated.

There is nothing special about the parameters used in the above example. Of course, adding more goods or styles increases the length of time until quasi-public prices become established, as well as the length of time until market quasi-equilibrium is attained. Increasing the number of agents increases the length of both of these time intervals.

2.9   The emergence of money

There is no role for money in the Walrasian general equilibrium model because all adjustments of ownership are carried out simultaneously when the equilibrium prices are finally set. When there is actual exchange among individual agents in an economy, two major conditions give rise to the demand for money, by which we mean a good that is accepted in exchange not for consumption or production, but rather for resale at a later date against other intrinsically desired goods. The first is the failure of the 'double coincidence of wants' (Jevons, 1875), explored in recent years in this and other journals by Starr (1972) and Kiyotaki and Wright (1989, 1991, 1993). The second condition is the existence of transactions costs in exchange, the money good is likely to be that which has the lowest transactions cost (Foley, 1970; Hahn, 1971, 1973; Kurz, 1974b, 1974a; Ostroy, 1973; Ostroy and Starr, 1974; Starrett, 1974). We show that these conditions interact in giving rise to a monetary economy. When one traded good has very low transactions costs relative to other goods, this good may come to be widely accepted in trade even by agents who do not consume or produce it. Moreover, when an article that is neither produced nor consumed can be traded with very low transactions costs, this good, so-called *fiat* money. will emerge as a universal medium of exchange.

We now permit traders to buy and sell at will any good that they neither consumer nor produce. We call such a good a *money good*, and if there is a high frequency of trade in one or more money goods, we say the market economy is a *money economy*. We assume that traders accept all styles of a money good indifferently. We first investigate the emergence of money from market exchange by assuming zero inventory costs, so the sole value of money is to facilitate trade between agents, even though the direct exchange of consumption and production goods between a pair of agents might fail because one of the parties is not currently interested in buying the other's production good. The trade algorithm in case agents accept a good that they do not consume is as follows. At the beginning of each period, each agent calculates how much of each consumption good he wants to acquire during that period, as follows. The agent calculates the market value of his inventory of production and money goods he holds in inventory, valued at his private prices. This total is the agent's income constraint. The agent then chooses an amount of each consumption good to purchase by maximizing utility subject to this income constraint. The trade algorithm is similar to the case of the pure market, except that either party to a trade may choose to offer and/or accept a money good in the place of his production good.

We evaluate the performance of this economy using the same parameters as in our previous model, including zero inventory costs. Figure 2.7 shows that the use of money increases monotonically over the first 2,000 periods, spread almost equally among the remaining goods. From period 2,000 to period 4,000, one good becomes a virtually universal currency, driving the use of the others to low levels. It is purely random which good becomes the universal medium of exchange, but one does invariable emerge as such after several thousand periods. If we add inventory costs with g^1 being lower cost than the others, g^1 invariably emerges as the medium of exchange after 1,000 periods, and the other goods are not used as money at all. I did not include graphs of the passage to quasi-public prices or other aspects of market dynamics because they differ little from the baseline economy described above.

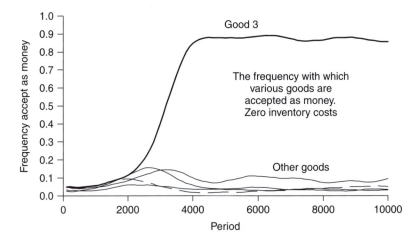

Figure 2.7 The emergence of money in a market economy. The parameters of the model are the same as in the baseline case treated previously. inventory costs are assume absent

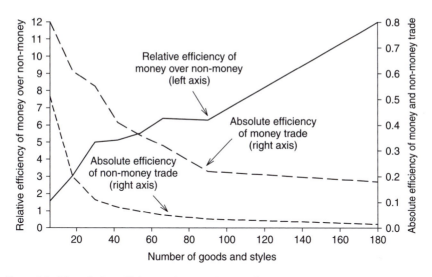

Figure 2.8 The relative efficiency of money in a market economy

As in traditional monetary theory (Menger, 1892; Wicksell, 1911; Kiyotaki and Wright, 1989, 1991) money emerges from goods trade both because it is a low transactions cost good and it solves the problem of the 'double coincidence of wants' that is required for market exchange (Jevons, 1875). The relative efficiency of money over direct goods trade increases with the number of goods, as illustrated in Figure 2.8. While with six goods and one style the relative efficiency of money is only 150 per cent, for nine goods and twenty styles (180 goods), the relative efficiency is 1,200 per cent.

2.10 The resilience of the decentralized market economy

We now show that the above Markov model is extremely resilient in the face of aggregate shocks when the number of producers per good is sufficiently large, but becomes unstable when this number falls below a certain (relatively high) threshold. We illustrate this in the context of a *fiat* money economy. We take the non-monetary economy described above, with nine goods in six styles each, and add a single new good that is neither produced nor consumed, and has zero inventory storage costs. When such a good is available, it quickly becomes a universal medium of exchange for the economy, accepted by almost 100 per cent of market traders. The nature of market dynamics in a *fiat* money economy is not noticeably different from the economies described above.

In this *fiat* money economy with 300 producers per good, every 1,000 periods, we impose an aggregate shock on the economy consisting of a reduction in the *fiat* money holdings of each trader to 20 per cent of its normal level, as shown in

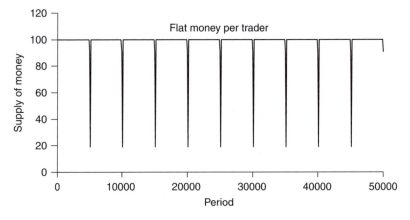

Figure 2.9 To test the resilience of the Markov economy, we impose a periodic shock, sustained for 100 periods, that reduces the money supply to 20% of its normal level

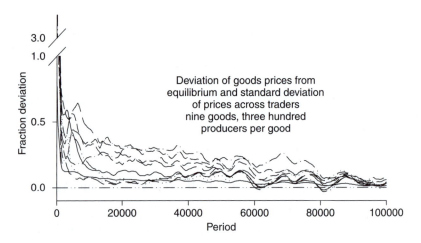

Figure 2.10 Walrasian equilibrium is reilient to aggregate shocks. With 300 producers per good, we impose an aggregate shock on the Markov process consisting of halving the money supply every 1000 periods, and restoring the money supply after 100 periods have elapsed with the smaller money supply. There is virtually no effect on the passage to a quasi-Walrasian equilibrium

Figure 2.9. The reduced holding are maintained for 100 periods, after which the money holdings of each trader is multiplied by two, restoring the money stock for the economy to its initial level. Figure 2.10 shows the effect of the period shock on average prices and on the standard error of prices across traders; there

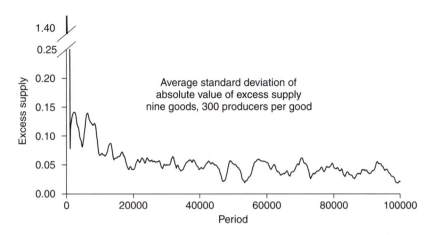

Figure 2.11 Excess demand is resilient in the face of large macro-level shocks. The parameters are as in the previous figure. Note that there is virtually no effect on aggregate excess demand in any sector of the economy

is no noticeable effect. Figure 2.11 shows that the quantity side of the economy is also virtually unaffected by the system of aggregate shocks.

2.11   Conclusion

The search for stability of market exchange using differential equations with public prices, while producing some brilliant mathematical analyses, was doubly defective. First, no plausible dynamic price and quantity adjustment mechanism was found. Second, such a dynamic, even were it found, would be of doubtful value because out of equilibrium public prices cannot exist in a decentralized market economy. By modeling market exchange as a Markov process, we have shown that under plausible conditions we get convergence to a quasi-equilibrium. However, under the extreme conditions of the Scarf economy (only three goods, three traders, and fixed coefficients utility functions) we get a stationary distribution akin to a limit cycle in continuous models. With a plain-vanilla Walrasian economy with individual production, we find global stability under a wide range of parameters. Yet we do not have the analytical machinery to ascertain when Scarf instability will hold, when global stability holds, or whether there are other possible dynamic characteristics of a Markovian market system.

On the positive side, we have proved that certain Markov models of market dynamics are globally stable over a wide range of parameters. This is an existence theorem possibly as informative as the existence proofs for general equilibrium. Computational proofs, however, are not as powerful as purely analytical proofs.

Those unused to working with complex dynamical systems may object that a computational proof is no proof at all. In fact, a computational proof may not be a mathematical proof, but it is a scientific proof: it is evidential rather than tautological, and depends on induction rather than deduction. The natural sciences, in which complex systems abound, routinely use mathematical to models that admit no closed-form analytical solutions, ascertain their properties through approximation and simulation, and justify these models by virtue of how they conform empirical reality. This appears to be the current state of affairs with respect to Markov processes and general equilibrium theory.

References

Arrow, Kenneth and Leonid Hurwicz (1958) 'On the Stability of the Competitive Equilibrium, I', *Econometrica*, vol. 26, pp. 522–552.

Arrow, Kenneth and Leonid Hurwicz (1959) 'Competitive Stability Under Weak Gross Substitutability: Nonlinear Price Adjustment and Adaptive Expectations', Technical Report, Office of Naval Research Contract Nonr-255, Department of Economics, Stanford University, Technical Report No. 78.

Arrow, Kenneth and Leonid Hurwicz (1960) 'Some Remarks on the Equilibria of Economics Systems', *Econometrica*, vol. 28, pp. 640–646.

Arrow, Kenneth, H.D. Block and Leonid Hurwicz (1959) 'On the Stability of the Competitive Equilibrium, II', *Econometrica*, vol. 27, pp. 82–109.

Arrow, Kenneth J. 'An Extension of the Basic Theorems of Classical Welfare Economics', in J. Neyman (ed.), *Proceedings of the Second Berkeley Symposium on Mathematical Statistics and Probability* (Berkeley: University of California Press, 1951), pp. 507–532.

Arrow, Kenneth J. and Gérard Debreu (1954) 'Existence of an Equilibrium for a Competitive Economy', *Econometrica*, vol. 22, no. 3, pp. 265–290.

Aumann, Robert J. and Adam Brandenburger (1995) 'Epistemic Conditions for Nash Equilibrium', *Econometrica*, vol. 65, no. 5, pp. 1161–1180.

Bala, V. and M. Majumdar (1992) 'Chaotic Tâtonnement', *Economic Theory*, vol. 2, pp. 437–445.

Debreu, Gérard (1951) 'The Coefficient of Resource Utilization', *Econometrica*, vol. 19, 273–292.

Debreu, Gérard (1952) 'A Social Equilibrium Existence Theorem', *Proceedings of the National Academy of Sciences*, vol. 38, pp. 886–893.

Debreu, Gérard (1954) 'Valuation Equilibrium and Pareto Optimum', *Proceedings of the National Academy of Sciences*, vol. 40, pp. 588–592.

Debreu, Gérard (1974) 'Excess Demand Function', *Journal of Mathematical Economics*, vol. 1, pp. 15–23.

Feller, William (1950) *An Introduction to Probability Theory and Its Applications*, vol. 1 (New York: John Wiley & Sons).

Fisher, Franklin M. (1983) *Disequilibrium Foundations of Equilibrium Economics* (Cambridge: Cambridge University Press).

Fisher, Franklin M. (1999) *Microeconomics: Essays in Theory and Applications*, ed. Maarten Pieter Schinkl (Cambridge, UK: Cambridge University Press).

Foley, Duncan (1970) 'Economic Equilibria with Costly Marketing', *Journal of Economic Theory*, vol. 2, pp. 276–291.

Gale, David (1955) 'The Law of Supply and Demand', *Math. Scand.*, vol. 30, pp. 155–169.

Gintis, Herbert (2007) 'The Dynamics of General Equilibrium', *Economic Journal*, vol. 117, pp. 1289–1309.

Gintis, Herbert (2009) *Game Theory Evolving*, second edition (Princeton, NJ: Princeton University Press).

Hahn, Frank (1962) 'A Stable Adjustment Process for a Competitive Economy', *Review of Economic Studies*, vol. 29, pp. 62–65.

Hahn, Frank (1971) 'Equilibrium with Transactions Costs', *Econometrica*, vol. 39, pp. 417–439.

Hahn, Frank (1973) 'On Transactions Costs, Inessential Sequence Economies and Money', *Review of Economic Studies*, vol. 40, pp. 449–461.

Hahn, Frank and Takashi Negishi (1962) 'A Theorem on Non- tâtonnement Stability', *Econometrica*, vol. 30, pp. 463–469.

Hayek, F.A. (1945) 'The Use of Knowledge in Society', *American Economic Review*, vol. 35, no. 4, pp. 519–530.

Hofbauer, Josef and Karl Sigmund (1998) *Evolutionary Games and Population Dynamics* (Cambridge: Cambridge University Press).

Howitt, Peter and Robert Clower (2000) 'The Emergence of Economic Organization', *Journal of Economic Behavior and Organization*, vol. 41, pp. 55–84.

Hurwicz, Leonid (1960) 'Optimality and Informational Efficiency in Resource Allocation Processes', in *Mathematical Methods in Social Sciences* (Stanford, CA: Stanford University Press), pp. 27–46.

Jevons, William Stanley (1975) *Money and the Mechanism of Exchange* (London: D. Appleton Co.).

Kirman, Alan P. (1992) 'Whom or What does the Representative Individual Represent?', *Journal of Economic Perspectives*, vol. 6, pp. 117-136.

Kiyotaki, Nobuhiro and Randall Wright (1989) 'On Money as a Medium of Exchange', *Journal of Political Economy*, vol. 94, no. 4, 927–954.

Kiyotaki, Nobuhiro and Randall Wright (1991) 'A Contribution to a Pure Theory of Money', *Journal of Economic Theory*, vol. 53, no. 2, 215–235.

Kiyotaki, Nobuhiro and Randall Wright (1993) 'A Search-Theoretic Approach to Monetary Economics', *American Economic Review*, vol. 83, no. 1, pp. 63–77.

Kurz, Mordecai (1974a) 'Equilibrium in a Finite Sequence of Markets with Transactions Costs', *Econometrica*, vol. 42, pp. 1–20.

Kurz, Mordecai (1974b) 'Equilibrium with Transactions Cost and Money in a Single Market', *Journal of Economic Theory*, vol. 7 pp. 418–452.

Mantel, Rolf (1974) 'On the Characterization of Aggregate Excess Demand', *Journal of Economic Theory*, vol. 7, pp. 348–353.

Mantel, Rolf (1976) 'Homothetic Preferences and Community Excess Demand Functions', *Journal of Economic Theory*, vol. 12, pp. 197–201.

McKenzie, L.W. (1959) 'On the Existence of a General Equilibrium for a Competitive Market', *Econometrica*, vol. 28, pp. 54–71.

McKenzie, L.W. (1960) 'Stability of Equilibrium and Value of Positive Excess Demand', *Econometrica* 28 (1960): 606–617.

Menger, Karl (1982) 'On the Origin of Money', *Economic Journal*, vol. 2, pp. 239–255.

Morishima, Michio (1960) 'A Reconsideration of the Walras–Cassel–Leontief Model of General Equilibrium', in *Mathematical Methods in Social Sciences* (Stanford, CA: Stanford University Press), pp. 63–76.

Negishi, Takashi (1960) 'Welfare Economics and the Existence of an Equilibrium for a Competitive Economy', *Metroeconomica*, vol. 12, pp. 92–97.

Negishi, Takashi (1961) 'On the Formation of Prices', *International Economic Review*, vol. 2, pp. 122–126.

Nikaido, Hukukaine (1956) 'On the Classical Multilateral Exchange Problem', *MetroEconomica*, vol. 8, 135–145.

Nikaido, Hukukaine (1959) 'Stability of Equilibrium by the Brown–von Neumann Differential Equation', *MetroEconomica* 27 (1959): 645–671.

Nikaido, Hukukaine and Hirofumi Uzawa (1960) 'Stability and Nonnegativity in a Walrasian Tâtonnement Process', *International Economic Review*, vol. 1, pp. 50–59.

Ostroy, Joseph (1973) 'The Informational Efficiency of Monetary Exchange', *American Economic Review*, vol. 63, 597–610.

Ostroy, Joseph and Ross Starr (1974) 'Money and the Decentralization of Exchange', *Econometrica*, vol. 42, pp. 1093–1113.

Saari, Donald G. (1985) 'Iterative Price Mechanisms', *Econometrica*, vol. 53, pp. 1117–1131.

Saari, Donald G. (1995) 'Mathematical Complexity of Simple Economics', *Notices of the American Mathematical Society*, vol. 42, no. 2, pp. 222–230.

Samuelson, Larry and Jianbo Zhang (1992) 'Evolutionary Stability in Asymmetric Games', *Journal of Economic Theory*, vol. 57, no. 2 pp. 363–391.

Scarf, Herbert (1960) 'Some Examples of Global Instability of Competitive Equilibrium', *International Economic Review*, vol. 1, pp. 157–172.

Smith, Adam (2000 [1759]) *The Theory of Moral Sentiments* (New York: Prometheus).

Sonnenschein, Hugo (1973) 'Do Walras' Identity and Continuity Characterizethe Class of Community Excess Demand Functions?', *Journal of Ecomonic Theory*, vol. 6, pp. 345–354.

Starr, Ross (1972) 'The Structure of Exchange in Barter and Monetary Economies', *Quarterly Journal of Economics*, vol. 86, no. 2, pp. 290–302.

Starrett, David (1974) 'Inefficiency and the Demand for "Money" in a Sequence Economy', *Review of Economic Studies*, vol. 40, pp. 437–448.

Taylor, Peter and Leo Jonker (1978) 'Evolutionarily Stable Strategies and Game Dynamics', *Mathematical Biosciences*, vol. 40, pp. 145–156.

Uzawa, Hirofumi (1959) 'Edgeworth's Barter Process and Walras' Tâtonnement Process', Technical Report, Office of Naval Research Contract NR-047-004, Department of Economics, Stanford University. Technical Report No. 83.

Uzawa, Hirofumi (1961) 'The Stability of Dynamic Processes', *Econometrica*, vol. 29, no. 4, 617–631.

Uzawa, Hirofumi (1962) 'On the Stability of Edgeworth's Barter Process', *International Economic Review*, vol. 3, no. 2, pp. 218–231.

Wald, Abraham (1951 [1936]) 'On Some Systems of Equations of Mathematical Economics', *Econometrica*, vol. 19, no. 4, pp. 368–403.

Walras, Leon (1954 [1874]) *Elements of Pure Economics* (London: George Allen and Unwin).

Wicksell, Knut (1967 [1911]) *Lectures in Political Economy, Vol. 2. Money* (New York: Kelley).

3

Toward an Analytical Solution for Agent-Based Models: An Application to a Credit Network Economy*

Corrado Di Guilmi
University of Technology, Australia

Mauro Gallegati
Università Politecnica delle Marche, Italy

Simone Landini
IRES Piemonte, Italy

Joseph E. Stiglitz
Columbia University, USA

3.1 Introduction

The mainstream approach, as it is formalized in the DSGE (dynamic stochastic general equilibrium) models, is based on the process of intertemporal maximization of utility in the market-clearing context of the standard competitive equilibrium theory. It is built upon the representative agent (RA) framework, which rules out direct interactions among agents by assumption. Its fundamental hypotheses trivially lead to conclusions that there can be no inefficiencies and any pathology in general.[1]

In short, the RA framework of the DSGE models adopts the most extreme form of conceptual reductionism in which macroeconomics and the financial network are reduced to the behavior of an individual agent.[2] The deep understanding of the interplay between the micro and macro levels is ruled out, as well as any 'pathological' problems, such as coordination failure. The RA in economics is tantamount to stating that 'macroeconomics equals microeconomics.'

We believe that a change of focus is necessary: an appropriate micro-foundation should consider the interaction at the agent-based level. This is feasible if the economy is represented by a framework with heterogeneous agents. The development of sound micro-founded models should also involve the links among agents in a networked economy. This approach can provide better insights on how a crisis emerges from the microeconomic interaction and how it propagates in the economic system.

The literature provided, up to now, two different tools for dealing with interaction and heterogeneity: game theory and computational economics (CE). In the game theory framework, each agent takes into account the behavior of every other, which is supposed to be known. But a complete network populated by rational and fully informed agents would require infinite computational ability, which is beyond any plausible assumption. On the other hand, there has been a strong development of CE models, populated by interacting and boundedly rational agents. In these models, macro outcomes are very sensitive to different configurations of the parameters. Furthermore, the relationship between results and initial conditions is undefined, not to mention the issue of the trade-off between tractability and realism.

The idea of this paper is neither to ignore interactions between agents, nor to get hopelessly mired in complicated details by trying to model those interactions in their completeness, but rather to strike for some middle ground in which the consequences of interconnectedness can be at least crudely assessed. To achieve this, we start with a 'minimal' model of the economy as a credit network, in which firms interact directly with banks. Rather than simulating these interactions, we represent them by means of probabilities, and derive equations describing the evolution of the network and how its structure changes with time. The equations we derive provide some qualitative insights into the systemic fragility of the credit network.

The results of the present paper are based on the solution algorithms proposed by Di Guilmi et al. (2011) and are here presented without the full detail of the derivation. The complete demonstrations are available upon request. The remainder of the paper is structured as follows: section 3.2 presents the general hypotheses of the model, introducing firms and banks; section 3.3 illustrates the solution of the model dynamics; section 3.4 interprets the results and proposes some policy implications; section 3.5 offers some final remarks.

3.2   The model

This section introduces the main hypotheses about the structure of the model, concerning the firms, the banks and their match on the credit market.

3.2.1   The firms sector

The productive sector is modeled along the lines of Delli Gatti et al. (2010). Each firm sets the optimal quantity of output on the basis of its financial condition, according to the following rule

$$Q_{f,t} = \alpha A_{f,t}^{\beta},$$

(1)

where $\alpha > 0$ and $\beta \in (0,1)$ are constant parameters and A is the net worth of firm f. As shown in Greenwald and Stiglitz (1993), equation (1) comes from a profit maximization problem, when bankruptcy is costly and the probability of default is inversely related to the net worth. For the sake of simplicity, all firms are assumed to have the same linear production function, defined as

$$Q_{f,t} = (1/\varpi)N_{f,t}, \tag{2}$$

where Q is the physical output, N is the quantity of labor and $\varpi > 0$ is the inverse of labor productivity, assumed to be a constant parameter. From (1) and (2) it follows that $N_{f,t} = \varpi\alpha A_{f,t}^{\beta}$. The wage bill W is

$$W_{f,t} = wN_{f,t}, \tag{3}$$

where the nominal wage w is constant and uniform across firms.

Firms do not know in advance the quantity of goods that will be demanded and this can produce uncertainty about the final price. For this reason, following Greenwald and Stiglitz (1993), we model the selling price for each firm u_f as a stochastic variable coming from a uniform distribution, defined in the interval $[u_{min}, u_{max}]$.

Because of imperfect information there is a hierarchy in the sources of firms financing, from internal to external finance. The firms that can finance their whole wage bill with internal resources are defined as *self-financing* (SF), while the others are *non-self-financing* (NSF). The latter ones resort to the credit market as, by assumption, they are completely rationed on the equity market. The demand for credit for a NSF firm is given by

$$D_{f,t} = W_{f,t} - A_{f,t}, \tag{4}$$

while $D_{f,t} = 0$ for SF firms. Firms' profits $\pi_{f,t}$ are defined as

$$\pi_{f,t} = u_{f,t}Q_{f,t} - W_{f,t} - r_{f,t}D_{f,t}, \tag{5}$$

where r is the rate of interest. The net worth of firms is the sum of past profits:

$$A_{f,t+1} = A_{f,t} + \pi_{f,t} \tag{6}$$

If $A < 0$ the firm goes bankrupt and it is replaced by a new one, such that the total number of firms is constant in time.

3.2.2 The banking sector

A bank can lend to different firms and sets unilaterally the interest rate for each of them. In particular, the bank b asks to the firm f an interest rate which is inversely related to the financial soundness of borrower and lender, according to the formula

$$r_{b,t}^{f} = a\left[A_{b,t}^{-a} + \left(\frac{D_{f,t}}{A_{f,t}}\right)^{a}\right] = a\left[A_{b,t}^{-a} + v_{f,t}^{a}\right] \tag{7}$$

where $a > 0$, $A_{b,t}$ is the bank's net worth and $v_{f,t}$ is the firm leverage ratio.

The dependence on $A_{b,t}$ represents the fact that, for a bank, the lower its equity, the higher is its probability of default. Consequently, the owners of the bank's capital will demand a premium for risk which is inversely proportional to its internal financial resources. As a consequence, a higher net worth means a lower premium paid by the bank to investors and allows the bank to charge a lower interest rate to customers (Gambacorta, 2008). The second factor in the interest rate formula, $(v_{f,t})^a$, quantifies the higher risk premium requested by the bank to highly-leveraged firms.

This formula analytically devices the mechanism described by Stiglitz and Greenwald, (2003, p. 145): 'The high rate of bankruptcy is a cause of the high interest rate as much as a consequence of it.' This is because the demise of one or more firms generates bad debt for the lender and, thus, brings about a deterioration in its financial conditions (a lower $A_{b,t}$). As a consequence, the bank will raise the interest rates, worsening the positions of its customers and, possibly, leading to the bankruptcy of some of them. The new bad debt has further negative impact on the financial soundness of the lender in a downward spiral.

The profits of the bank b are given by

$$\pi_{b,t} = \sum_{f}(1 + r^f_{b,t})D^f_{b,t},\tag{8}$$

where $D^f_{b,t}$ is the credit supplied by the bank b to the firm f. The bank's net worth is computed as

$$A_{b,t+1} = A_{b,t} + \pi_{b,t} - BD_{b,t}\tag{9}$$

where BD is the bad debt, which is the debt that cannot be paid back due to the bankruptcy of borrowers. If $A_{b,t} < 0$, the bank goes bankrupt, and it is replaced by a new one. Thus, also the number of banks is constant.

3.2.3   Partner selection and network evolution

A NSF firm signs a one-period credit contract with one bank. In order to capture the fact that firms have limited information about the credit market, at each point in time a NSF firm can demand for credit only to a subset of banks. If we indicate with B the total number of banks in the economy, the number of banks that are 'visible' to a firm is given by mB, where $m \in (0, 1]$ is a parameter constant across firms and in time. The subset of banks for each firm is randomly selected at each period. Hence every firm possibly surveys a different pool of banks every period.

The firm sorts the banks in its randomly selected pool according to the proposed interest rates and then sends a signal to the bank which offers the lowest interest rate, demanding for credit.

Credit rationing can arise as the banks must comply with a regulatory framework. In particular, the monetary authority determines an adequacy ratio along the lines of the Basel II accord. Consequently, the total lending of the bank b, denoted by $L_{b,t}$, must be lower than $\overline{\Theta} A_{b,t}$ where $\overline{\Theta} \geq 1$ is a constant parameter. Let us define

$$\overline{L}_{b,t} = A_{b,t} \overline{\Theta} \tag{10}$$

as the limit for lending that the bank b can supply.

In order to select how many and which requests for credit will be satisfied, the bank adopts a prudential criterion. It first sorts the potential customers in ascending order of leverage ratios v. Then it considers the demand for credit starting from the firm with the lowest v and accepts their demand as long as condition (10) is satisfied.

When a firm is refused credit from a bank, it sends a signal to the bank which follows in its list, that is a bank who offers a higher interest rate. If all the banks in the firm's pool decline to supply credit, the firm must reduce its production in order to meet its financial constraint. It can pay salaries only with its internal resources, and, accordingly, the quantity produced by a fully credit rationed firm is equal to $q_{f,t} = A_{f,t}/(w\varpi)$.

The structure of the network is represented by a series of islands, or cliques: each island is composed by the lending bank and its borrowing firms. The composition and the number of cliques vary from a period to another. The composition changes as a NSF firms can become SF (therefore not connected to any bank) or change its lender. The number of cliques is variable as a bank can have no customers at a given time (and so not be included in the network) and been chosen by one or more firms in the following period (forming a clique).

3.3 Solution of the model

This section introduces and applies the analytical techniques for the solution of the model. We have already partitioned the population of firms into two groups: SF and NSF. The evolution of the density for the number of agents belonging to a particular cluster can be modeled by means of the master equation (ME). The ME is a differential equation which describes the variation of the probability of observing a certain number of agents in a given group; it can be solved under asymptotic conditions. In this treatment, the final outcome of the solution is a system of equations which describes the evolution of the network and the degree distribution. To this aim we first need to quantify the number of NSF firms, as they compose the network, and then use this result to study the evolution of the network. We set up two master equations:

- the first one (NSF-ME) to describe the evolution of the number of NSF firms; the solution of this ME will be plugged in
- the second one (K-ME) which models the dynamics of the degree and, through further passages, makes possible the identification of the degree distribution.

One of the novelties is in that the first ME is *nested* into the second to model the dependence between the two.

In the first subsection the NSF-ME is introduced and solved. It is worth noticing that the transition rates for this ME are endogenous and dependent upon the financial conditions of firms. The second subsection presents the K-ME and its solution.

3.3.1   Stochastic evolution of firms

The evolution of two different groups of firms is modeled along the lines of Di Guilmi et al. (2010), who study an analogous problem using a ME to model the dynamics of the densities of different groups of firms. The ME is a function of the transition probabilities for the agents to move between the two groups. In this model, each firm has a different transition probability, which is dependent on its financial condition (the equity A) and on the price shock u. In order to make the problem analytically tractable we need to quantify an average probability for each of the two transitions. Therefore, we identify two *representative* firms, one SF and one NSF by taking the average net worth, indicated respectively by A_0 for SF and A_1 for NSF firms. This reduction in the degrees of freedom of the problem is defined as *mean-field approximation* in statistical mechanics. From these two values we can compute the targeted productions, the costs and the financial needs for the two average firms by using equations (1)–(4).

3.3.1.1   The transition rates and the NSF-ME

The probability for a NSF firm f to become SF depends on the capacity of the firm of having at time $t-1$ a profit large enough to pay the salary bill at time t. This condition can be expressed as

$$A_{f,t-1} + \pi_{f,t-1} \geq W_{f,t},$$

which, using equation (5), becomes

$$A_{f,t-1} + u_{f,t-1}Q_{f,t-1} - W_{f,t-1} - r_{f,t-1}D_{f,t-1} \geq W_{f,t}. \tag{11}$$

The only exogenous variable in (11) is the price u_f and thus it is convenient to specify the probability of switching as a function of it. In particular, since the distribution of u is known, it is possible to quantify the minimum price threshold above which the NSF firm can obtain a profit sufficient to become

SF. We denote this threshold with $\bar{u}$. Rearranging equation (11) and using the subscript 1 for the mean-field variables of the representative NSF firm, we can write

$$u_{1,t-1} \geq \frac{W_{1,t} + W_{1,t-1} + r_1 D_{1,t-1} - A_{1,t-1}}{Q_{1,t-1}} = \bar{u}_t. \tag{12}$$

Using the uniform probability function of u, we can write the probability of becoming SF ι as

$$\iota_t = 1 - F(\bar{u}_t) = 1 - \frac{\bar{u}_t - u_{min}}{u_{max} - u_{min}}. \tag{13}$$

In the same fashion, we can specify the condition for the mean-field SF firm to become NSF as

$$A_{0,t-1} + u_{0,t-1} Q_{0,t-1} - W_{0,t-1} < W_{0,t}, \tag{14}$$

which can be written as follows

$$u_{0,t-1} < \frac{W_{0,t} + W_{0,t-1} - A_{0,t-1}}{Q_{0,t-1}} = \underline{u}_t, \tag{15}$$

where $\underline{u}$ is the upper threshold of the price shock. Denoting with ζ the probability of becoming NSF and making use of the known uniform probability function of u, we can write

$$\zeta_t = F(\underline{u}_t) = \frac{\underline{u}_t - u_{min}}{u_{max} - u_{min}}. \tag{16}$$

In order to obtain the transition rates, the transition probabilities need to be conditioned on the probability of being NSF or SF. In particular, the probability to find a firm belonging to one particular group is higher the larger is the size of that group. This fact can be modelled by means of the two following environmental externality functions

$$\psi_{1,t} = \psi_1 \left(\frac{N_{1,t} - \vartheta}{N} \right) = \frac{b_1 + b(N_{1,t} - \vartheta)}{N},$$

$$\psi_{0,t} = \psi_0 \left(\frac{N_{1,t}}{N} \right) = \frac{b_0 + b[N - (N_{1,t} - \vartheta)]}{N}, \tag{17}$$

where $b > 0$, $b_1 > -bN_1$, $b_0 > -b(N - N_1)$, $\vartheta = \{0, 1\}$ is the observed variation in N_1 and ψ_1 and ψ_0 are constants. Accordingly the transition rates β and δ are given by the following homogeneous functions

$$N\beta_t = \left(\frac{N_{1,t} - \vartheta}{N} \right) = N\zeta_t \left[\frac{b_1 + b(N_{1,t} - \vartheta)}{N} \right] \left[\frac{N - (N_{1,t} - \vartheta)}{N} \right],$$

$$N\delta_t = \left(\frac{N_{1,t} + \vartheta}{N} \right) = N\iota_t \left\{ \frac{b_0 + b[N - (N_{1,t} + \vartheta)]}{N} \right\} \left(\frac{N_{1,t} + \vartheta}{N} \right). \tag{18}$$

The NSF-ME is a differential equation which quantifies the variation in the probability to observe a given number of NSF firms $N_{1,t}$. It is given by the probability of observing $N_{1,t} + 1$ or $N_{1,t} - 1$ and having a transition of one firm, respectively, out from or in the NSF condition, less the probability of already having a number $N_{1,t}$ of NSF firms and observing any transition. Consequently, we have

$$\frac{dP_t(N_{1,t})}{dt} = \underbrace{[\beta_t(N_{1,t} - 1)P_t(N_{1,t} - 1) + \delta_t(N_{1,t} + 1)P_t(N_{1,t} + 1)]}_{\text{in flow probabilities}}$$

$$\underbrace{- [(\beta_t(N_{1,t}) + \delta_t(N_{1,t}))P_t(N_{1,t})].}_{\text{out flow probabilities}} \tag{19}$$

3.3.1.2   ME solution and dynamics of the proportions of firms

The solution algorithm involves three main steps:

1. split the state variable N_1 in two components:
   – the *drift* (ϕ), which is the expected value of $n_1 = N_1/N$;
   – the *spread* (ϵ), which quantifies the aggregate fluctuations around the drift.

Accordingly, the state variable is re-formulated in the following way (Aoki, 1996):

$$N_{1,t} = N\phi_t + \sqrt{N}\epsilon_t; \tag{20}$$

2. expand in Taylor's series the modified master equation;
3. equate the terms with the same order of power for N.

This process yields an ordinary differential equation, known as macroscopic equation, which describes the dynamics of the trend, and a stochastic partial differential equation, known as Fokker–Planck equation, which describes the dynamics of the density R of the fluctuations (see Aoki, 1996; van Kampen, 1992). Hence, the final solution is given by the mean-field system of coupled equations

$$\begin{cases} \dot{\phi} - \Delta_t(\phi) = \beta_t(\phi) - \delta_t(\phi) = \rho_t\phi - \rho_t\phi^2 \\ \partial_t R_t(\epsilon) = -\partial_\phi \Delta_t(\phi)\partial_\epsilon(\epsilon R_t(\epsilon)) + \frac{1}{2}\sum_t(\phi)\partial_\epsilon^2 R_t(\epsilon) \end{cases} \tag{21}$$

where $\rho_t = b(\zeta_t - \iota_t)$ and $\sum_t(\phi) = \beta_t(\phi) + \delta_t(\phi)$.

The first of the (21) is a logistic equation with two equilibrium points: $\phi^* = \{0, 1\}$. The system approaches the two boundaries without hitting them. Indeed, the quadratic term $-\rho_t\phi^2$ acts as a break with increasing intensity as ϕ_t approaches one of the equilibrium points. Both equations depend on the transition rates and, therefore, on the average financial conditions of the firms.

Following van Kampen (1992), we substitute the formulation of the transition rates (18) into (21) and integrate the resulting expression. The final solution, with the trend dynamics ϕ and the distribution probability for the fluctuation component ϵ, can be written as

$$
\begin{cases}
\phi(t) = \left[1 + \left(\frac{1}{\phi_0} - 1\right)\exp(-\rho_t t)\right]^{-1}, \\
\epsilon(t) \xrightarrow{i.i.d} \mathcal{N}\left(\mu_{\epsilon,t}, \sigma_{\epsilon,1}^2, t\right) & \text{s.t.} \\
\qquad\qquad\qquad \mu_{\epsilon,t} = \langle\epsilon_0\rangle e^{\Delta_t'(\phi)} \\
\qquad\qquad\qquad \sigma_{\epsilon,1}^2 = \langle\epsilon_e^2\rangle(1 - e^{2\Delta_t'(\phi)t}),
\end{cases}
\tag{22}
$$

with $\phi_0 \in [0,1)$ and $\langle\epsilon_e^2\rangle = -\sum_t(\phi)/(2\Delta_t'(\phi))$.

By using the mean-field values of the average production of the firms in the two groups Q_1 and Q_0, it is possible to obtain the trend and the fluctuations of the aggregate output, as for equation (20). The total output can be expressed as

$$
\begin{aligned}
Q_t &= N_{1,t}Q_{1,t} + (N - N_{1,t})Q_{0,t} \\
&= N\{[\phi_t + N^{-1/2}\epsilon_t]Q_{1,t} + [1 - \phi_t - N^{-1/2}\epsilon_t]Q_{0,t}\} \\
&= N\{Q_{0,t} - [\phi_t + N^{-1/2}\epsilon_t][Q_{0,t} - Q_{1,t}]\}.
\end{aligned}
\tag{23}
$$

It is possible to show that $Q_1 < Q_0$, therefore the dynamics of trend and fluctuations of aggregate production are dependent upon ϕ and ϵ in system (22).

3.3.2 Stochastic evolution of the network: K-ME

In this section we develop the ME for the network degree. The NSF-ME is nested into the K-ME; to the best of our knowledge, this method has never been developed before. The problem is analysed by studying the evolution of the probability for two firms to be financed by the same bank. This (indirect) connection between two firms defines an (indirect) link in the network. The solution algorithm makes use of the concept of *giant component*, which is the node with the highest number of connection. In this model, it represents the bank which has the largest number of customers.[3]

As done for the NSF-ME, in the same fashion we split the state variable in the trend and fluctuations components. The volume of NSF firms N_l that are borrowers from a bank with degree K_l is assumed to be given by

$$
N_{l,t} = N_{1,t}[K_l\phi_{l,t} + \sqrt{K_l}\epsilon_{l,t}],
\tag{24}
$$

where ϕ_l is the expected value and ϵ_l is the fluctuations component. Equation (24) shows a direct correlation between N_1 and the expected number of borrowers for a bank. It can be rearranged and written in intensive form as

$$
n_{l,t} = \frac{N_{l,t}}{N_{1,t}} = K_l\phi_{l,t} + \sqrt{K_l}\epsilon_{l,t}.
\tag{25}
$$

3.3.2.1   The transition rates and the K-ME

The transition probabilities in this setting concern the creation or destruction of a link between two firms. We introduce the variable ω and set $\omega_{i,j} = 1$, if there is a link between the two firms i and j (they share the same bank), and $\omega_{i,j} = 0$ otherwise. Accordingly, the creation and destruction rates are equal to, respectively,

$$\mathbb{P}(\omega_{t+1,i,j} = 1|\omega_{t,i,j} = 0) = \zeta,$$
$$\mathbb{P}(\omega_{t+1,i,j} = 0|\omega_{t,i,j} = 1) = \iota. \tag{26}$$

Analogously to the NSF-ME case, two externality functions need to be defined in order to quantify the transition rates. These functions are assumed to be dependent on the size of the giant component. In particular, the market share of the largest bank (the giant component) is given by $\gamma_t = S_t/N_{1,t}$, where S_t is the number of its customers. Due to the interest rate formula in equation (7), the size of the giant component impacts on the morphology of the network by exerting a *gravitational* effect. The larger is a bank, the higher is its capacity to attract new borrowers by offering a lower interest rate. Thus, the greater is the giant component, the more it attracts firms and, consequently, the smaller are the chances of an inflow of firms into another component of the network. Accordingly, the externality function $\psi_{1,l,t}$ for the inflows into a generic component (bank) is assumed to be an inverse function of γ_t and $k_l = K_l^{-1}$. Symmetrically, the outflow externality function $\psi_{0,l,t}$ is a direct function of the two quantities. The externality functions can be specified as follows

$$\psi_{1,l,t} = \exp(p_1^2(1 - \gamma_t)(\phi_l^0/k_l)), \tag{27}$$
$$\psi_{0,l,t} = \exp(p_1^2\gamma_t(\phi_l^0/k_l)), \tag{28}$$

where p_1 is the firm-bank matching probability.[4] Consequently the formulations of the transition rates are the following

$$\beta_t(n_{l,t} - \vartheta\rho_{l,t}) = \lambda_{l,t}[1 - (n_{l,t} - \vartheta\rho_{l,t})],$$
$$\delta_t(n_{l,t} + \vartheta\rho_{l,t}) = \mu_{l,t}[n_{l,t} + \vartheta\rho_{l,t}], \tag{29}$$

where $\lambda_{l,t} = \zeta\psi_{1,l,t}$ and $\mu_{l,t} = \iota\psi_{0,l,t}$. The term $\pm\vartheta\rho_{l,t}$ introduces a correction to take into account that the number of firms in this case is variable, being represented by the NSF firms. In section 3.1, the total population of firms is constant and equal to N; for the network dynamics we need to consider only the firms who enter the credit market, whose number comes from the solution of the NSF-ME. In particular, we indicate with ϑ the observed variation in $n_{l,t}$ and $\rho_{l,t} = \rho(K_{l,t}, N_{1,t})$.

The K-ME describes the evolution of the probability distribution for the degree in each level. It can be expressed as

$$\frac{dP_t(n_{l,t})}{dt} = \underbrace{[\beta_t(n_{l,t}-1)P_t(n_{l,t}-1) + \delta_t(n_{l,t}+1)P_t(n_{l,t}+1)]}_{\text{inflow probability}}$$

$$\underbrace{- (\beta_t(n_{l,t}) + \delta_t(n_{l,t}))P_t(n_{l,t})}_{\text{outflow probability}}. \tag{30}$$

3.3.2.2   ME solution: dynamics of the degree and degree distribution

In order to solve (30), we adopt the same methodology used for the NSF-ME. Also in this case, the final solution is a system analogous to (22). Splitting the state variable as in (24) and following the steps of the solution algorithm defined in subsection 3.3.1.2, we obtain the following equation for the trend

$$\phi_{l,t} = (\phi_l^0 - \phi_l^*)\exp\{-\rho_{l,t}[\lambda_{l,t} + \mu_{l,t}]t\} + \phi_l^* \tag{31}$$

where

$$\phi_l^* = [1 + \mu_{l,t}/\lambda_{l,t}]^{-1} \tag{32}$$

is the steady-state value of the degree.

Finally, the Fokker–Planck equation provides a Gaussian law for the fluctuations about the expected l-th degree level with mean $\mu_{\epsilon_{l,t}} = \langle \epsilon_l^0 \rangle \exp(-\rho_{l,t}\Delta_t'(\phi_l)t)$ and variance $\sigma_{\epsilon_{l,t}}^2 = \langle \epsilon_l^{*2} \rangle [1 - \exp(2\rho_{l,t}\Delta_t'(\phi_l))t]$, where ϵ_l^2 is the stationary value of fluctuations in the l-th degree level and ϵ_l^0 is the initial condition.

The trend equation and the distribution of fluctuations can be used to compute the degree distribution and its evolution in time. If we define a vector of possible initial starting points ϕ_0 for the average degree, there will be a different trajectory for each starting point according to the dynamics described by equation (32). Consequently, at each point in time, the empirical distribution of the degree is obtained by the different values of ϕ generated by the different trajectories.

3.4   Results

The systems of equations that compose the solution illustrate the role that the levels of indebtedness and concentration play in shaping the dynamics of the network evolution. The description of the network by means of the ME makes possible an analytical representation of the concept of *too big to fail* (proxied by the giant component) and *too interconnected to fail* (the degree). The model is also able to endogenously generate a dynamics for the proportion of NSF and SF firms, and, consequently, of aggregate production. These dynamics affect the size and the evolution of the network.

3.4.1   Interpretation

The analytical solution of the model describes the effects of the interaction among agents in the system. Indeed, the dynamics of the degree is modeled as dependent on the interaction among firms through the banking system. In particular, the solution shows how the interaction can cause coordination failures; as a consequence, the system oscillates between different steady states. The transition from an equilibrium point to another can be originated by avalanches of bankruptcies of firms and banks when the level of concentration becomes critical.

In order to identify the effects of the level of concentration on the market structure, we need to study the effect of the size of the giant component on the equilibrium solution. We can substitute the definitions of λ and μ into (32) and take the derivative with respect to γ. It can be demonstrated that this derivative is always positive. As a consequence, both the value of the degree during the adjustment and its steady value positively depend on the size of the giant component. The variance of the fluctuations of the degree is directly proportional to its steady-state value and, therefore, to the giant component. Consequently, a market with a relatively high level of concentration (large giant component and large degree) will display a higher volatility, due to the expected larger fluctuations in the average degree. Therefore, the degree distribution will appear as platycurtik. Since in the model the degree distribution is a proxy of the size distribution of banks, this implies larger instability, due to the possibility of rapid and deep modifications in the market structure. This analytical result is confirmed by the numerical analysis of the model[5] as shown by Figure 3.1.

In respect of the aggregate output of the economy, the solution shows that instability in the credit market structure brings about higher volatility in output. An increase in the number of NSF firms has a negative effect on aggregate output, as shown by equation (23), and brings about an increase in the average degree, as for equation (24). Moreover, due to the solution equations, a larger N_1 causes a larger volatility in output due to equation (23); in the same way, the bigger is the average degree, the larger is the variance of its fluctuations. Accordingly, there is a positive correlation between variance of the degree and variance of output.

With regard to the dynamics of the network, the increasing concentration follows the growth of the economy: as firms and banks profit, interest rates decrease due to the accumulation of internal finance. Sounder banks are able to attract customers and grow faster. This virtuous cycle can lead to the emergence of a *big bank* which controls the biggest share of the credit market (represented by the giant component). This builds the set-up for the subsequent crisis, according to a pattern analogous to the one envisaged by Minsky (1982): during a boom credit becomes cheaper and firms are led to increase their production, as they

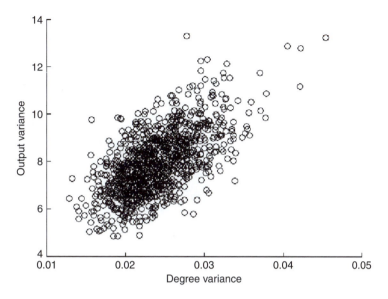

Figure 3.1 Variance of the degree and of the output. Monte Carlo simulation (correlation: 0.62)

accumulate profits. This growth increases the concentration in the credit market and makes firms and banks more vulnerable to negative shocks. Indeed, the presence of a big bank can have a destabilizing effect on the system through the variance of the distribution of the fluctuations of the degree. Every bank is potentially subject to large shocks, which consequently impact on the conditions of credit for firms through equation (7); as a consequence, borrowers can experience substantial variation in the cost of debt and, in the case of a significant negative shock, become insolvent, worsening the conditions of other banks and eventually spiraling down the whole system. The network economy displays an endogenous cyclical behavior, in which the tendency to concentration heightens the probability for the system to be hit by systemic financial distress (Figures 3.2 and 3.3).

3.4.2 Policy implications

Despite the fact that the representation of the credit market is simplified, the model captures the basic features of a credit network economy, such as the emergence of nodes with systemic relevance and the possibility of crises through propagation effects, when these nodes are in financial distress (De Masi et al., 2010).

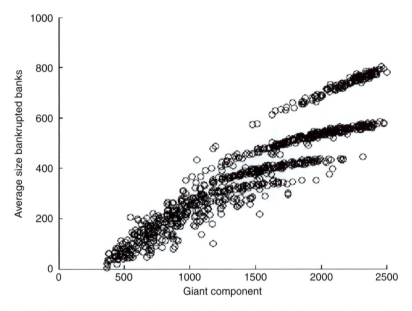

Figure 3.2   Giant component and average lending of bankrupted banks. Single simulation (correlation in Monte Carlo simulations: 0.71)

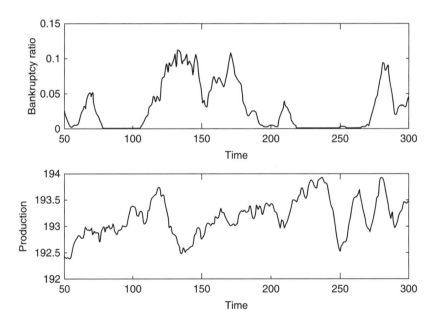

Figure 3.3   Banks' bankruptcy ratio and aggregate output

The model provides all the measures of systemic risk measures identified by the European Central Bank: (i) the degree of connectivity; (ii) the degree of concentration; and (iii) the size of exposures. Furthermore it analytically describes their dynamics and highlights the causal relationship among them. For these reasons, the framework can be helpful for a preliminary assessment of a stabilization policy.

The main policy tool embedded in the model is the adequacy ratio requirement $\overline{\Theta}$. By handling this parameter, the policymaker can influence the dynamics of the model and reduce the probability of a systemic collapse through different channels. The capital requirement directly influences the structure of the market in two ways. On the one hand, a reduction in $\overline{\Theta}$ defines a ceiling for the size of the giant component, diminishing the chances of the emergence of a big bank. As detailed in subsection 3.4.1, a smaller giant component reduces the variance of the distribution of fluctuations of the degree. The final effect is a smaller chance of large and sudden modifications in the market structure and a higher stability. On the other hand, the average degree (and thus the average size of banks) is directly proportional[6] to $\overline{\Theta}$. This effect is amplified by the fact that a smaller $\overline{\Theta}$ is also likely to increase the competition in the credit market, lowering the interest rate spread among banks. The ultimate outcome is therefore a higher dispersion in the market and no big banks. Hence, the model illustrates that the size limit is also a limit on the interconnectivity, linking the concepts of *too big to fail* and *too interconnected to fail*. The introduction of a capital requirement allows the policymaker to shape the network topology and the market structure.

The parameter $\overline{\Theta}$ indirectly affects the probability of bankruptcy for firms. In fact, with stricter lending limits for banks, a firm with high leverage ratio is likely to be credit rationed, due to the banks' selection process, and thus to reduce its production and financial needs, consequently lowering its chances of bankruptcy.

At the micro level, $\overline{\Theta}$ indirectly influences the transition rates. A lower lending limit will bring about, on average, smaller interest rates, through equation (7), as only the NSF firms with the lowest debt ratio will be financed. The threshold $\overline{u}$ in (12) will be lower, increasing the probability for a NSF firm to become SF. This chain of effects is particularly relevant as it allows the policymaker to influence the path of evolution of the system between different equilibriums. Indeed the economic policy, by influencing the transition rates, can impact on the dynamics described by the first of the (22). In this way, it can drive the proportion of NSF between the two limits 0 and 1 in order to set the economy on the preferred equilibrium path. The impact of the variations in $\overline{\Theta}$ in the numerical simulations are illustrated by Figure 3.4.

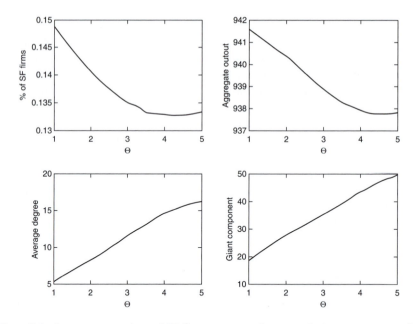

Figure 3.4 Average proportion of SF firms, output, degree and giant component for different values of q. Monte Carlo simulation

Summarizing, with reference to the three measures of systemic risk, the model shows that the capital requirement threshold influences: (i) the degree of connectivity, as it impacts on the average degree of network; (ii) the degree of concentration, as it directly determines the maximum size of banks and, indirectly, their average size; (iii) the level of exposures, by imposing a limit to lending. The solution of the model makes possible a quantitative and qualitative analysis of the impact of such a policy on the average degree, on the shape of the degree distribution and on the resilience of the credit market structure.

Through the stabilization of the credit market, policymakers can also influence the dynamics of production. An increase in the probability for NSF firms to become SF brings about a lower number of NSF firms in steady state and, consequently, a lower variance of the fluctuation component ϵ in equation (22). Equation (23) demonstrates that it causes a higher level and a smoother dynamics for aggregate output. Indeed, as the dynamics of output is dependent on the density of NSF firms, a lower variance of this density is accompanied by a smaller variance of output.

3.5   Concluding remarks

In this paper we propose a technique for the analytical solution for models with heterogeneous and interacting agents and apply it to a credit network model. In particular, we describe the dynamics of the behavior of the agents by means of two MEs, one nested into the other. Their asymptotic solutions yield the trend and fluctuations of the two state variables: the proportion of NSF firms and the network degree.

The solution identifies some emerging properties of a credit network. We find that rising economic output, and the consequent increase in the overall wealth of firms, turns out to be proportional to how much the loans in the system come to be concentrated among a few banks. In network terms, this concentration can be measured by the average degree for banks. There is a natural tendency for this quantity to rise as the economy expands and banks and firms profit. This rise in concentration is potentially destabilizing for the system: the failure of a single bank can bring trouble to a large number of firms, which pass it on to other banks, leading to further failures, in a downward spiral. Cascades of failures put financial pressure on all firms, raising the costs of borrowing and slowing down the economy.

The model is able to endogenously generate feedback between economic growth and rising interconnectedness which leads to cycles of booms and busts. The solution of the model highlights the causal links among micro-, meso- and macro-variables. In this perspective, the present work provides a starting point for the development of more refined models of the credit network in order to test possible stabilization policies.

Notes

* With the usual caveats we thank the participants to the Eastern Economic Association meeting 2011 in New York, the International Economic Association meeting in Beijing, the DGES in Paris, the CIES in Wien and the Econonophysics Colloquium 2011 for very helpful comments.

1. There are attempts of reconciling the empirical evidence with the mainstream model by introducing various imperfections. Unfortunately, small departures from the perfect information hypothesis have been shown to undermine most of the key propositions of the standard competitive model (Greenwald and Stiglitz, 1986).

2. In natural sciences, the notion of reductionism is much more limited since it amounts to represent the nature of macro-phenomena by analysing the constitutive elements, whose interaction allows for emergent phenomena, i.e. characteristics that are not present in the single element.

3. In the solution algorithm, without loss of generality, we consider it as an exogenous stochastic random variable.

4. This probability can be quantified as the product of the probability for a bank to be in a firm's pool, m, and the probability of being chosen by the firm. The latter should be different for each bank, as it is dependent on $\bar{\Theta}$ and A_b. Since the probability of matching needs to be defined at the mean-field level, we express it as a function only of $\bar{\Theta}$ and write it as: $1 - exp(-c\bar{\Theta})$, with $c > 0$. Accordingly, p_1 is given by

$$p_1(\bar{\Theta}) = m[1 - exp(-c\bar{\Theta})]. \tag{33}$$

As a consequence, the probability for two firms to be connected to the same bank is p_1^2.
5. Computer simulations of the model with full degree of heterogeneity for banks and firms have been performed in order to provide some insights on the dynamics generated by the behavioral rules of agents. It is worth stressing that, in our study, numerical simulations are used just as a test of the analytical outcomes.
6. See equation (29).

References

Aoki, M. (1996) *New Approaches to Macroeconomic Modeling* (Cambridge: Cambridge University Press).

De Masi, G., Y. Fujiwara, M. Gallegati, B. Greenwald and J.E. Stiglitz (2010) 'An Analysis of the Japanese Credit Network', *Evolutionary and Institutional Economics Review*, vol. 7, no. 2, pp. 209–232.

Delli Gatti, D., M. Gallegati, B. Greenwald, A. Russo and J.E. Stiglitz (2010) 'The Financial Accelerator in an Evolving Credit Network', *Journal of Economic Dynamics and Control*, vol. 34, no. 9, pp. 1627–1650.

Di Guilmi, C., M. Gallegati and S. Landini (2010) 'Financial Fragility, Mean-field Interaction and Macroeconomic Dynamics: A Stochastic Model', in N. Salvadori (ed.), *Institutional and Social Dynamics of Growth and Distribution* (Cheltenham: Edward Elgar), pp. 323–351.

Di Guilmi, C., Gallegati, M. and Landini, S. (2011) *Interactive Macroeconomics*. Available online at http://finance.uts.edu.au/staff/corradodg/Interactive% 20Macroeconomics.pdf.

Gambacorta, L. (2008) 'How Do Banks Set Interest Rates?', *European Economic Review*, vol. 52, no. 5, pp. 792–819.

Greenwald, B. and J.E. Stiglitz (1993) 'Financial Markets Imperfections and Business Cycles', *Quarterly Journal of Economics*, vol. 108, no. 1, pp. 77–114.

Greenwald, B.C. and J.E. Stiglitz (1986) 'Externalities in Economies with Imperfect Information and Incomplete Markets', *The Quarterly Journal of Economics*, vol. 101, no. 2, pp. 229–264.

Minsky, H.P. (1982) *Inflation, Recession and Economic Policy* (New York: M.E. Sharpe).

Stiglitz, J.E. and B. Greenwald, B. (2003) *Towards a New Paradigm in Monetary Economics*. (Cambridge: Cambridge University Press).

van Kampen, N.G. (1992) *Stochastic Processes in Physics and Chemistry* (Amsterdam: North-Holland).

4

The EURACE Macroeconomic Model and Simulator*

Silvano Cincotti
DOGE.I-CINEF, Università di Genova, Italy

Marco Raberto
DOGE.I-CINEF, Università di Genova, Italy

Andrea Teglio
Universitat Jaume I, Spain

4.1 Introduction

EURACE is a macroeconomic model and simulator which has been under development since 2006 when the project began within a EU-funded research grant under the sixth framework program. The aim of EURACE is to design and implement an agent-based macroeconomic simulation platform able to integrate different sectors and markets, in particular, goods markets, labor markets, financial markets and credit markets. The EURACE project proposes an innovative approach to macroeconomic modeling and economic policy design according to the new field of agent-based computational economics (Tesfatsion and Judd 2006; Raberto et al. 2006a,b, 2008a).

The simulator and the economic model have been constantly evolving since the start of the project in 2006 and the EURACE model is probably by far the largest and most complete agent-based model developed in the world nowdays. It represents a fully integrated macroeconomy consisting of three economic spheres: the real sphere (consumption goods, investment goods and labor market), the financial sphere (credit and financial markets) and the public sector (government(s), central bank and Eurostat).

In the following, we will outline the main features of the single-country EURACE model characterized by a single government and no spatial features.

4.2   General features

4.2.1   Closure

EURACE is one of the very rare fully-specified agent-based models of a complete economy. EURACE is dynamically complete, that is, it specifies all real and financial stocks and flows and will allow us to aggregate upward from the micro-specifications to the macroeconomic variables of interest.

4.2.2   Decision processes

In modeling agent decision processes, the model follows the usual and realistic assumptions of agent-based economics about bounded rationality, limited information gathering and storage capacities, and limited computational capabilities of the economic agents. These assumptions lead us to use simple heuristics to model the agents' behavior, derived from the management literature for firms, and from experimental and behavioral economics for consumers/investors. We also make use of experimental evidence from the psychological literature on decision-making. The rules used by the agents are simple but not necessarily fixed. Their parameters can be subject to learning, and thus adapted to a changing economic environment. Here we can make a distinction between adaptive agents and learning agents: the first use simple stimulus-response behavior to only adapt their response to their environment, while the last use a conscious effort to learn about the underlying structure of their environment.

4.2.3   Market protocols

The modeling of the market protocols is empirically inspired by real world markets. The consumption goods market is decentralized and characterized by one-to-one interactions between firms and consumes. This is a simple form to model localized markets with potential rationing on both sides. Households go shopping on a weekly basis.

In particular, market protocols capture important market frictions based on problems of search, matching and expectation formation in turbulent environments that are present in real world labor and goods markets. The labor market functions by way of a local 'search-and-match' protocol that likewise resembles a real world job search by unemployed workers. For the artificial financial market we model a real world market protocol: the clearing house. Government bonds are usually sold by auction. For the credit market we use a firm-bank network interaction mechanism. This reflects how real world firms appear to manage their credit lines as emerges from the empirical data that have been examined concerning firm–bank network interactions.

4.2.4   Use of a balance sheet approach as a modeling paradigm

In the EURACE model, a double-entry balance sheet with a detailed account of all monetary and real assets as well as monetary liabilities is defined for each agent. Monetary and real flows, given by agents' behaviors and interactions, such as market transactions, determine the period-by-period balance sheet dynamics. Stock-flow consistency checks have then been done at the aggregate level to verify that all monetary and real flows are accounted for, and that all changes to stock variables are consistent with these flows. This provides us with a solid and economically well-founded methodology to test the consistency of the model. See Teglio et al. 2010b for further details.

4.2.5   Timing of decisions

The choice of time scales for the agents' decision-making has been made in order to reflect the real time scales in economic activities. The agents' financial decisions are made on a shorter time scale (day) than the economic decision-making, for example, consumption and production, where the proper time horizon can be a week, a month, or a quarter.

4.2.6   Asynchronous interactions

In reality, most human decision-making and interaction is asynchronous, due to the autonomous decisions of the agents. We model this asynchronous decision-making by letting agents have different activation days. This means that on a single market different agents are active on different days. Thus, who interacts with whom changes from day to day. Some activities, however, are synchronized. This is in particular the case when they are institutionally initiated as, for instance, yearly tax payments or monthly wage payments. We use synchronous decision-making/interactions whenever it reflects the reality.

4.2.7   Scalable number of agents

One of the main goals of EURACE is to analyze how far qualitative properties of the phenomena arising in economies with interacting heterogeneous agents change as there is an increase in the number of involved agents. This is a research topic that has been to a large extent ignored in previous work in agent-based computational economics. Based on this goal, the implementation of the EURACE platform is designed to be scalable to a large number of agents.

4.2.8   Innovative software framework and parallelization

The EURACE model has been implemented in FLAME (Flexible Large-scale Agent-based Modelling Environment – www.flame.ac.uk). The FLAME framework is specifically designed to provide a formal and very flexible approach to agent-based modeling and enables the creation of agent-based models that can be run on high-performance computers. The framework is based on the logical communicating extended finite state machine theory (Xmachine) which gives the agents more power to enable the writing of complex models for large complex systems. The agents are modeled as communicating X-machines allowing them to communicate through messages being sent to each other as designed by the modeler. This information is automatically read by the FLAME framework and generates a simulation program which enables these models to be parallelized efficiently over different computers.

4.3   Producers

Consumption goods producers, henceforth firms, are the bulk of the production sector in the EURACE model. They employ labor and capital goods to produce consumption goods by means of a Cobb–Douglas technology. Quantity and price decisions are based on standard inventory planning and mark-up pricing rules. Firms ask loans to the banking system in order to finance their production plans and to fulfill their payments commitments, that is, taxes, dividends, interests, and loan repayments. If rationed in the credit market, firms issue new shares to raise the required money in the equity market. Production, investment and financing decisions are taken, processed and completed by firms once a month on their assigned activation day. Activations days are different and specific to each firm.

Table 4.1 presents the typical balance sheet of a firm f at a given business day. Liquidity M^f and inventories I^f are updated daily following firms' cash flows and sales, while physical capital K^f is updated once a month following capital accumulation due to investments and capital depreciation. Debt D^f is also computed once a month (at the same day of capital, that is, at the activation day) following the outcomes in the credit market, that is, borrowing of new loans and repayment of old loans. Equity E^f is also updated once a month at the activation day as residual according to the usual accounting rule:

$$E^f = M^f + p^C I^f + p^K K^f - \sum_{b \in \{banks\}} D_b^f \tag{1}$$

where p^C is the monthly consumption goods price index and p^K is the price of capital goods, both referred to the calendar month. A business month is defined by a set of n business days, henceforth simply days, and any activation day sets the start of a business month which is specific for any firm and does

Table 4.1   Balance sheet snapshot of firm f

Assets	Liabilities
M^f: liquidity deposited at a given bank	$D^f = \sum_{b \in \{banks\}} D_b^f$: total debt (sum of outstanding loans)
I^f: inventories	
K^f: physical capital	E^f: equity

not correspond to calendar months, which have an equal duration of n days but start at days 1, $n+1$, $2n+1$, etc...

4.3.1 The planning of production

Each firm keeps a stock of its unsold production as inventories I^f. Once every business month, during its activation day, the firm checks if its stock needs to be refilled. According to the approach of using standard managerial methods wherever applicable, a standard inventory rule for managing the stock holding is employed. Let us suppose that at activation day t, which sets the start of business month τ, firm f has an inventories stock I_t^f and expects a demand $\hat{Q}_\tau^f$ for the business month τ. It is worth noting that planned, desired or expected amounts of economic variables (such as production, capital and investments) will be denoted by the hat symbol to distinguish them from realized amounts that will depend on market and simulation outcomes. Standard results from inventory theory suggest that the firm should choose to produce a quantity $\hat{q}_\tau^f$ for month τ given by:

$$\hat{q}_\tau^f = \begin{cases} 0 & I_t^f \geq \hat{Q}_\tau^f \\ \hat{Q}_\tau^f - I_t^f & I_t^f < \hat{Q}_\tau^f, \end{cases} \tag{2}$$

Expected demand $\hat{Q}_\tau^f$ is estimated using a linear regression based on the sales of previous months. The realized production volume q_τ^f can deviate from the planned output $\hat{q}_\tau^f$ due to rationing on the production factor markets. Production times are not explicitly taken into account and the produced quantities are delivered on the same day when production takes place. The local stock level is therefore updated accordingly.

4.3.2 Production technology, demand of production factors and investment

The production technology is represented by a Cobb–Douglas type production function with complementarities between the quality of the investment good and the specific skills of employees for using that type of technology. See Dawid et al. 2008 and 2009 for details about this approach. Every worker v has a level of general skills $b^v \in \{1, ..., b_{\max}\}$ and a level of specific skills $\hat{b}_t^v$. The specific skills of worker v indicate how efficiently the corresponding technology is exploited by the individual worker. Building up those specific skills depends on collecting experience by using the technology in the production process. The shape of the evolution of productivity follows a concave curve, the so-called learning curve, when the organizational productivity is recorded after implementing a new production method or introducing a new good. Concavity in this context means that the productivity rises with the use of the production method or production of the new good, but this increase emerges at a decreasing rate. We transfer this pattern of organizational learning on the individual level and assume that the development of individual productivity follows a learning curve. The specific skills are updated once in each production cycle of one month. Furthermore, we assume that updating takes place at the end of the cycle. A crucial assumption is the positive relationship between the general skills b^v of a worker and his ability to utilize his experiences. Building up worker's technology-specific skills depends on a worker's level of general skills, that is, their education and the other general abilities which are not directly linked to the particular technology. Taking the relevance of the general skill level into account the specific skills of a worker v for technology j is assumed to evolve according to,

$$\bar{b}_\tau^v = \bar{b}_{\tau-1}^v + \chi(b^v)(A_{\tau-1}^f - b_{\tau-1}^v), \tag{3}$$

where we denote with $A_{\tau-1}^f$ the average quality of the capital stock of firm f where worker v is employed. The function χ is increasing in the general skill level of the worker. Note that this formulation captures the fact that in the absence of technology improvements marginal learning curve effects per time unit decrease as experience is accumulated and the specific skills of the worker approaches the current technological frontier.

Factor productivity is determined by the minimum of the average quality of physical capital and the average level of relevant specific skills of the workers. Capital K^f and labor N^f inputs are substitutable with a constant elasticity and we assume constant returns to scale. Accordingly, output for a consumption goods producer is given by

$$q_\tau^f = \min[B_\tau^f, A_\tau^f](N_\tau^f)^\alpha (K_\tau^f)^\beta, \tag{4}$$

where B_τ^f denotes the average specific skill level in firms and $\alpha + \beta = 1$.

Given the planned production quantity $\hat{q}_\tau^f$ set according to Eq. 2 and the available Cobb–Douglas technology set by Eq. 4, firms have to decide the desired amount of both capital $\hat{K}_\tau^f$ and labor $\hat{N}_\tau^f$ to fulfill their production plans. The choice is made according to the standard rule of cost minimization given a production goal. The solution is the labor and capital amounts at which the marginal rate of substitution between the two factors equates the ratio of their costs, that is,

$$\frac{\alpha \hat{K}_\tau^f}{\beta \hat{N}_\tau^f} = \frac{w_\tau^f}{c_{K,\tau}^f} \tag{5}$$

where w_τ^f is the average wage currently paid by the firm to its employees and $c_{K,\tau}^f$ is given by

$$c_{K,\tau}^f = \left(\bar{r}_\tau^f + \xi\right) p_\tau^K, \tag{6}$$

where $\bar{r}_\tau^f$ is the average cost of capital, ξ is the monthly depreciation rate, and p_τ^K is the present unit cost of capital. It is worth noting that $\bar{r}_\tau^f$ is computed as a weighted average of different loan rates paid by firm f for any loan, where the weights are given by the relative amount of the loan.

Taking into account the planned production quantity $\hat{q}_\tau^f$, Eq. 5 in conjunction with the production function defined by Eq. 4, where $\alpha + \beta = 1$, yields the desired demands for capital and labor:

$$\hat{K}_\tau^f = \left(\frac{\beta w_\tau^f}{\alpha c_{K,\tau}^f} \right)^\alpha \frac{\hat{q}_\tau^f}{\min \left[B_\tau^f, A_\tau^f \right]} \tag{7}$$

$$\hat{N}_\tau^f = \left(\frac{\alpha c_{K,\tau}^f}{\beta w_\tau^f} \right)^\beta \frac{\hat{q}_\tau^f}{\min \left[B_\tau^f, A_\tau^f \right]} \tag{8}$$

If $\hat{K}_\tau^f > (1 - \xi)K_{\tau-1}^f$, i.e., the desired capital amount is higher than the capital endowment of firm f at the end of the previous business month, considering also the expected capital depreciation, then the firm demands an investment $\hat{I}_\tau^f = \hat{K}_\tau^f - (1 - \xi)K_{\tau-1}^f$ in new physical capital to fill the gap. On the other hand, if the desired capital amount is lower than the available capital, considering depreciation, i.e., if $\hat{K}_\tau^f < (1 - \xi)K_{\tau-1}^f$, then all the amount of capital $(1 - \xi)K_{\tau-1}^f$ available at month τ should be used, because its cost is already paid. In this case, the desired amount of labor is recomputed considering the present capital endowment by using Eq. 5.

The monthly realized operating profit of a consumption goods producer is the difference in sales revenues during the previous period and production costs given by the wage bill, the interest bill and the cost of capital depreciation. Wages for the full month are paid to all workers on the day when the firm updates its labor force. Investment goods are paid on the day when they are delivered.

4.3.3 Pricing

Consumption good producers employ a standard mark-up pricing rule in setting prices. In particular, the new sale price p_τ^f at month τ is set considering a fixed mark-up μ on unit costs c_τ^f as follows:

$$p_\tau^f = (1 + \mu) c_\tau^f, \tag{9}$$

where units costs c_τ^f are calculated as a weighted average of the unit costs $\bar{c}_\tau^f$ related to realized production q_τ^f and the unit costs $c_{\tau-1}^f$ related to previous periods production which is still unsold and stocked in the inventories I_t^f, i.e.,

$$c_\tau^f = \frac{\bar{c}_\tau^f q_\tau^f + c_{\tau-1}^f I_t^f}{q_\tau^f + I_t^f}. \tag{10}$$

Present production unit costs $\bar{c}_\tau^f$ are given by the sum of labor costs $w_\tau N_\tau^f$, the interest bill B_τ^f and the cost of capital depreciation $\xi p_\tau^K K_{\tau-1}^f$, all divided by the present production amount q_τ^f, i.e.,

$$\bar{c}_\tau^f = \frac{w_\tau N_\tau^f + B_\tau^f + \xi p_\tau^K K_{\tau-1}^f}{q_\tau^f}. \tag{11}$$

4.3.3.1   Financing

We follow the pecking-order theory (Myers and Majluf 1984) which states that, because of information asymmetries present in both credit and equity markets, firms prefer to meet their financial payments first by using their internal liquidity, then by means of new debt, if liquidity is not sufficient, then by issuing new equity if rationed in the credit market. Each firm faces liquidity needs necessary to finance the production and investment plans as well as the scheduled financial payments. In particular, scheduled financial payments consist in the interest bill B_τ^f, that is, the interest payments on the amount of outstanding debt, the loans repayments Γ_τ^f, taxes T_τ^f and the dividends payout. The tax bill is a constant fraction of previous month gross earnings (or gross profits), while the dividends payout is a variable fraction of previous month net earnings (or net profits). In particular, each firm decides the planned per-share dividend $\hat{a}_\tau^f$. Consequently, the expected dividends payout is simply given by $e^f \hat{a}_\tau^f$ where e^f is the number of outstanding equity shares of firm f. It is worth noting that both taxes and dividends are set to zero in the case of negative gross earnings. Gross earning at sale month $\tau - 1$ are given by revenues $R_{\tau-1}^f$, earned during the month, minus labor costs and the interest bill $B_{\tau-1}^f$. Revenues are computed as $R_{\tau-1}^f = p_{\tau-1}^f q_{\tau-1}^f$ where $q_{\tau-1}^f$ is the quantity sold during the previous month and $p_{\tau-1}^f$ the sale price. Labor costs are given by $w_{\tau-1} N_{\tau-1}^f$ where $w_{\tau-1}$ is the money wage and $N_{\tau-1}^f$ the number of employees of firm f during month $\tau - 1$. The total foreseen liquidity needs L_τ^f of firm f at month τ are therefore given by summing all scheduled financial payments, the foreseen production and investment costs referred to the production planned for month τ. Costs include the foreseen labor costs, i.e., $w_\tau \hat{N}_\tau^f$, where $\hat{N}_\tau^f$ is the labor demand, and investments costs $p_\tau^k \hat{\iota}_\tau^f$. It is worth noting that effective costs may be lower than the foreseen ones, because $N_\tau^f \leq \hat{N}_\tau^f$ due to the possible rationing of firm f in the labor market and thus its inability to hire all the planned employees. On the contrary, given that we stipulate a job production for capital goods producers, effective investments $\hat{\iota}_\tau^f$ should be expected to be always equal to planned ones, unless the firm f is unable to collect the necessary liquidity needs L_τ^f. The foreseen liquidity needs are then given by:

$$L_\tau^f = B_\tau^f + T_\tau^f + \Gamma_\tau^f + e^f \hat{a}_\tau^f + w_\tau \hat{N}_\tau^f + p_\tau^K \hat{\iota}_\tau^f. \tag{12}$$

Finally, it is worth noting that the interest bill, taxes and loans repayments are determined out of the firm's control, while dividends, labor and investments costs can be scaled down in the case that the firm is unable to raise the necessary monetary resources in the credit market or in the stock market.

Following the pecking-order theory, any firm f meets its liquidity needs first by using its internal liquid resources P_τ^f, that is, the cash account deposited at a given bank; then, if $P_\tau^f < L_\tau^f$, the firm asks for a loan of amount $\lambda_\tau^f = L_\tau^f - P_\tau^f$ to the banking system in order to be able to cover entirely its foreseen payments. Credit linkages between firm f and any bank b are defined by a connectivity matrix which is randomly created whenever a firm enters the credit market in search of funding. In order to take into account search costs as well as incomplete information , each firm links with a limited number of banks, which are chosen in a random way.

Firms have to reveal to the linked banks information about their current equity and debt levels, along with the amount of the loan requested λ_τ^f. Using this information, each contacted bank b communicates the amount of money $\ell_\tau^{b,f}$ it is willing to lend to firm f, where $\ell_\tau^{b,f} \leq \lambda_\tau^f$. The amount $\ell_\tau^{b,f}$ is determined according to the decision rules outlined in the next section. Each contacted bank calculates also the interest rate $r_\tau^{b,f}$ associated to the loan offer and communicates it to the firm. Then the firm f agrees to get the loan from the bank applying the lowest interest rate. Banks receive demands by firms sequentially and deal with them on a 'first come, first served' basis. As explained with more detail in the following section, the firm can be credit-rationed. If a firm cannot obtain a sufficient amount of credit from the bank that is offering the best interest rate, the firm will ask for credit from the bank offering the second-best interest rate, and so on until the connected bank offering the highest interest rate is contacted. It is worth noting that, although the individual firm asks loans to the bank with the lowest lending rate, the total demand for loans does not depend directly on the interest rates of loans.

When firm f receives a loan from bank b, its cash account P_τ^f is increased by the corresponding amount $\ell_\tau^{b,f}$. If the firm is unable to collect the necessary credit amount, that is, if P_τ^f is still lower than L_τ^f, the firm still has the possibility to issue new equity shares and sell them on the stock market. If the new shares are not sold out, the firm enters a state called *financial crisis*. When a firm is in financial crisis, we mainly distinguish two cases: if the firm's available internal liquidity is still sufficient to meet its committed financial payments, that is, taxes, the debt instalment and interests on debt, then these financial payments are executed and the dividend payout and the production schedule are rearranged to take into account the reduced available liquidity; otherwise, if the firm is unable to pay its financial commitments, it goes into bankruptcy.

The model designs two types of bankruptcies, called insolvency and illiquidity bankruptcies. The first type is when firm's equity goes negative. The second type is when the firm is unable to pay its financial commitments but still has a positive equity. The significative difference between the two types of bankruptcies is the following: in the case of insolvency bankruptcy, firm's debt is restructured according to a new target level of debt that has to be a fraction of the firm's total assets. The part of debt exceeding the target is cancelled and the corresponding loan in the bank's assets is written-off. On the contrary, illiquidity bankruptcy does nto entail debt restructuring.

In both cases, when a firm goes into bankruptcy, it fires all its employees, stopping production for a period τ_B^f. During this period, the firm tries to rise new capital in the financial market in order to increase its liquidity.

4.3.4   Investment goods producers (IG firms)

There exists a single type of technology for investment goods. The investment good is offered with infinite supply by investment goods producers, which follow a job production process and therefore have no inventories. Energy and raw materials are the only factors of production and are assumed to be imported from abroad. The assumptions about job production and production factors imply that investment good producers have no financing needs. The price of energy and raw materials is exogenously given. The price of capital goods p^K is a mark-up on energy prices. The profits of investment good producer are distributed in equal shares among all households. Put differently, it is assumed that all households own equal shares of capital goods producers and that shares are not traded in the market. Therefore, the amount payed by consumption goods producers for investment goods is partially (the part related to mark-up) channeled back into the economy, while the part related to energy costs leaves the EURACE economy.

4.4   Households

Households are simultaneously taking the roles of workers, consumers and financial market traders. Households' total monthly income is made by both labor and capital income. Gross labor income is given by the monthly money wage w_τ, paid by the employer, or by an unemployment benefit received from the government. The unemployment benefit is set at a fixed percentage η of the last salary received. Households receive gross capital income from the equity shares and government bonds held in their financial portfolio. Capital income is given by dividends payed by firms on a monthly basis and by monthly government bond coupons. Households pay taxes on both labor and capital income. Labor and capital income taxes are fixed percentages, ξ^{Hw} and ξ^{H_K}, respectively, of the gross income. Households' financial wealth is given by their

Table 4.2 Household (H): balance sheet overview

Assets	Liabilities
M^h: liquidity deposited at a given *bank*	
n_g^h: government bonds holdings	(none)
n_f^h, n_b^h: equity shares holdings of firm f and bank b	

assets portfolio and by the liquidity deposited at a given bank. We stipulate that households have no liabilities. Table 4.2 presents the typical balance sheet of an household.

Once households receive their labor income or unemployment benefit, at the activation day of the firm where they are employed, they set the consumption budget for the entire duration of the month. Saving-consumption decision is modeled according to the theory of buffer-stock saving behavior (Carroll 2001, Deaton 1992), which states that households consumption depends on a precautionary saving motive, determined by a target level of wealth to income ratio. Consider household h receiving a gross money wage w_τ on a particular day. Consider the total net income of the household y_τ^h which includes the after-tax money wage as well as the net capital income earned during the previous month. Consider also the financial wealth W_τ^h of household h at month τ which includes its assets portfolio, valued at the most recent market prices, as well as liquidity. Following the buffer stock theory of consumption, the household sets the budget for consumption c_τ^h in the following month as:

$$c_\tau^h = \bar{y}^h + \varphi^H (W_\tau^h - x\bar{y}^h),$$

(13)

where $\bar{y}^h$ is the average total net income of household h in the last v months and x is the target wealth to income ratio. The rationale of the rule is that if, for instance, the present wealth to average income ratio is higher then the target one, i.e., $W_\tau^h/\bar{y}^h > x$, then the household spends more than his or her income in order reach the target value. The parameter ϕ^H sets the adjustment speed.

Households can either invest their savings in the asset market, by trading stocks or bonds, or put them in a saving account that pays a fixed, risk-free interest rate. The financial market operates on a daily basis and is characterized by a clearing house mechanism for price formation which is based on the matching of the demand and supply curves. Households' portfolio allocation is modeled according to a preference structure designed to take into account the psychological findings that emerged in the framework of behavioral finance and, in particular, of prospect theory (Kahneman and Tversky 1979; Tversky and Kahneman 1992). In particular, a key prospect theory insight, that is, myopic loss aversion, is considered. Myopic loss aversion depends on the limited foresight capabilities characterizing humans when they are forming their beliefs about financial returns (Benartz and Thaler 1995). Further details about the belief formation and the preference structure are provided in Raberto et al. 2008b and Teglio et al. 2009.

Once the monthly consumption budget c_τ^h has been determined, household h samples on a weekly basis the prices of different consumption goods producers and then decides which goods to buy. We assume that the decision is random and that follows a probability distribution given by a logit model. This approach is standard in the marketing literature where logit models are intended to represent the stochastic influence of factors not explicitly taken into account. Denote by F_h the set of consumption goods producers whose goods have been sampled by household h in the given week. Since in our set-up there are no quality differences between consumption goods, the choice probability $Prob_{h,f}$ of good $f \in F_h$ produced by the f-th consumption goods producer depends solely on relative prices as follows:

$$Prob_{h,f} = \frac{\exp(-\Lambda \log p^f)}{\sum_{f \in F_h} \exp(-\Lambda \log p^f)}, \tag{14}$$

where Λ parameterizes the intensity of market competition, that is, the bigger Λ is, the more price sensitive probabilities are and the more competitive the market is. Once the consumer has selected a particular consumption good producer f, he spends his entire weekly consumption budget, that is, $c_\tau^h/4$, for good f provided that the inventory is sufficiently large. In case the consumer cannot spend all his budget on the product selected first, he spends as much as possible, removes that product from the list F_h, updates the logit values and selects another product on which to spend the remaining consumption budget. If he is rationed again, he spends as much as possible on the second selected product and rolls over the remaining budget to the following week.

4.5   The banking sector

The primary purpose of the banking sector is to finance consumption goods producers by means of bank loans. Any bank meets the demand for a loan from a firm, provided that the risk–reward profile of the loan is considered acceptable by the bank. The reward is given by the interest rate which is charged and the risk is defined by the likelihood that the loan will default. Given the loan request amount λ^f by firm f, bank b calculates the probability π^f that the firm will not be able to repay its debts as:

$$\pi^f = 1 - \exp\left(-\frac{D^f + \lambda^f}{E^f}\right). \tag{15}$$

The default probability π^f correctly increases with the firm's leverage and is used as a risk weight in computing the risk-weighted loan portfolio of banks, henceforth W^b. D^f and E^f are firm's debt and equity, respectively. According to the computed credit worthiness of the firm, the bank informs it about the interest rate that would be applied to the requested loan:

$$r^{b,f} = r^{cb} + \gamma^b \pi^f, \tag{16}$$

where r^{cb} is the base interest rate set by the central bank and $\gamma^b \pi^f$ is the risk spread depending on the firm's credit risk π^f. The parameter γ^b sets the spread sensitivity to the creditworthiness of the firm. The central bank acts as the 'lender of last resort', providing liquidity to the banking sector at the base interest rate r^{cb}. It is worth noting that banks' lending rate does not depend on the expected demand for loans but only on the evaluation of firm's credit risk.

Banks can then lend money, provided that firms wish to take out new loans, and that their regulatory capital requirements are fulfilled. Let us note that granting new loans inflates the balance sheet of the banking system because it also generates new deposits. Indeed, when a loan is taken and spent, it creates a deposit in the bank account of the agent to whom the payment is made. In particular, firms pay wages to workers and pay new physical capital to investment firms, that are owned by households and redistribute net earnings to them.

The model regulatory capital requirements are inspired by the Basel II accords and state that the capital ratio of banks, given by the equity E^b divided by the risk-weighted assets W^b, has to be higher than a given threshold, defined as $\frac{1}{\alpha}$, where α is the key policy parameter used in this study. Hence, if firm f asks for a loan λ^f, bank b supplies a credit amount ℓ^{bf} determined as follows:

$$\ell^{bf} = \begin{cases} \lambda^f & \text{if } \alpha E^b \geq W^b + \pi^f \lambda^f, \\ \frac{\alpha E^b - W^b}{\pi^f} & \text{if } W^b < \alpha E^b < W^b + \pi^f \lambda^f, \\ 0 & \text{if } \alpha E^b \leq W^b. \end{cases} \tag{17}$$

The value of risk-weighted assets W^b is computed by the weighted sum of outstanding loans of bank b where the weights are given by the default probability (the default risk) of each loan defined in Eq. 15. Bank's liquidity, i.e., M^b as in Table 4.3, is an asset but its default risk shall be considered zero, therefore it does not enter into the computation of W^b.

Table 4.3 Bank's balance sheet

Assets	Liabilities
M^b: liquidity deposited at the *central bank*	S^b: standing facility (debt to the *central bank*)
Υ^b: bank's loan portfolio	D^b: total (households' and firms') deposits at the bank
	E^b: equity

The parameter α can be interpreted as the leverage level banks are allowed to have. Equation 17 states that bank b is available to satisfy entirely the loan demand λ^f if it does not push W^b above the Basel II threshold, set at α time the net worth (equity) of the bank, otherwise the bank can satisfy the loan demand only partially or even is not allowed to lend any money at all, and firm f is rationed in the credit market. Thus, it can be argued that banks are quantity takers and price setters in the loans market, with the policy constraint of a fixed capital adequacy ratio.

In order to better visualize the stock-flow accounts for banks, a typical balance sheet of a bank is reported in Table 4.3. For any bank b, the stocks of total deposits D^b and loans Υ^b are updated daily following the changes in their stock levels, that is, changes in the private sector (households and firms) deposits due to payments (i.e. flows of money among private sector agents) and changes in the loan portfolio due to the granting of new loans and old loan repayments. The stock of liquidity M^b of bank b is then updated accordingly, following the standard accounting rule $M^b = S^b + D^b + E^b - \Upsilon^b$. If M^b becomes negative, S^b, that is, the standing facility with the central bank, is increased to set $M^b = 0$. If M^b is positive and the bank has a debt with central bank, i.e. $S^b > 0$, S^b is partially or totally repaid for a maximum amount equal to M^b.

Finally, at the end of the trading day, both liquidity M^b and equity E^b are updated in order to take into account money flows which regard bank b, that is, interest revenues and expenses, taxes and dividends. The bank can choose whether or not to pay dividends to shareholders, and this choice is crucial for driving its equity dynamics. In particular, if a bank is subject to credit supply restriction due to a low net worth compared to the risk-weighted assets portfolio, then it stops paying dividends in order to raise its equity capital and to increase the chance to match in the future the unmet credit demand. Finally, loans are extinguished in a predetermined and fixed number of constant installments, n_ℓ.

4.6   The government

The government is responsible for the fiscal and welfare policies. It collects taxes on corporate profits, household labor and capital income, and sets the three corresponding tax rates. Taxes are collected on a monthly basis while tax rates are revised yearly downward or upward by a given percentage tick in order to pursue a zero budget deficit goal. Taxes constitute the revenues side of government budget.

Government expenses are given by unemployment benefits and interest rates on the outstanding government debt, all paid on a monthly basis. Unemployed benefits are set to a percentage of the last salary of the unemployed worker. The government debt is made by infinitely-lived government bonds that pay a fixed monthly coupon, determined by the nominal bond interest rate and the

Table 4.4 Government's balance sheet

Assets	Liabilities
M^g: liquidity deposited at the central bank	n^g: number of outstanding bonds (long-term debt)

bond face value. The nominal bond interest rate is anchored with a mark-up to the central bank base interest rate. Government bonds are owned by households and traded in the financial market. The government deficit is financed by issuing and selling in the market new infinitely-lived bonds. Government liquidity M^g is deposited at the central bank.

Table 4.4 presents the sketch of assets, i.e. liquidity, and liabilities, i.e., bonds of the government in EURACE.

4.7 The central bank

The central bank plays several important roles in the EURACE economy. It provides a standing facility to grant liquidity in infinite supply to commercial banks, when they are in short supply, and sets the base interest rate (or policy rate), which is the cost of liquidity provided to banks and the lowest reference value considered by banks when setting interest rates of loans to firms. Furthermore, the central bank may pursue an unconventional monetary policy, named quantity easing, which consists of buying government bonds directly in the market, easing the funding conditions for the budgetary authorities. Table 4.5 shows the typical balance sheet of a central bank.

The monetary policy of the Central Bank follows a Taylor rule (see Taylor 1993) for a discussion), and the short-term nominal interest rate is set as:

$$r_\tau^{cb} = \pi_\tau + a_\tau^\pi (\pi_\tau - \pi_\tau^*) + a_\tau^u (u_\tau^* - u_\tau) \tag{18}$$

where π_τ is the yearly inflation rate for month τ, π_τ^* is the desired rate of inflation, u_τ is the unemployment rate for month τ, and u_τ^* mimics the natural rate of unemployment, or the full-employment rate (that we exogenously set to 0 for simplicity).

This version of the Taylor rule departs from the standard one for its use of the unemployment rate instead of the output, and therefore for measuring an unemployment gap instead of the more classic output gap. It is plain that the two measures are strongly interconnected and the unemployment gap is certainly a satisfactory indicator of economic recession.

The rule for policymakers is to raise interest rates when inflation is above target or when unemployment is very low and therefore output is close its potential level. The central bank should lower rates when inflation therefore is below

Table 4.5   Central bank' balance sheet

Assets	Liabilities
n_g^{CB}: government bonds (QE)	Outstanding fiat money
M^{CB}: liquidity	M_g^{CB}: governments liquidity
L_b^{CB}: loans to banks (standing facility)	M_b^{CB}: banks reserves
Gold	E^{CB}: equity

the target level or when the unemployment rate is high and output is below potential. When inflation is on target and output is growing at its potential, rates are said to be neutral. This rule aims to stabilize the economy in the short term and to stabilize inflation over the long term.

If the policy rate set by the central bank is very low, that is, $r^{cb} < r^l$, quantitative easing will be activated by letting the central bank purchase government bonds in the financial market. The money creation channel through quantitative easing is intended to facilitate the funding of the government budget deficit in a situation of a depressed economy. The rational behind the triggering mechanism activating QE states that when the interest rate is already low, the central bank is no longer able to pursue an expansionary monetary policy by lowering rates, and it has to do it by purchasing bonds in the market.

4.8   Computational experiments

Computational experiments have been performed considering a simulation setting characterized by 2,000 households, 20 consumption goods producers, three banks, one investment goods producer, one government and one central bank. The objective of the computational experiments is to assess the macroeconomic implications of the different settings of capital adequacy ratios for banks, as determined by α. Values of α have been set in the range from 5 to 10, where $\alpha = 5$ corresponds to the case of the tightest capital requirement and $\alpha = 10$ to the most permissive case. The duration of each simulation is set to 240 months (20 years). For each setting of α, two different monetary policies have been considered. As described in section 7, the first policy follows the conventional Taylor rule, while the second one encompasses, beside the Taylor policy, the unconventional practice of quantitative easing, where the central bank buys government bonds in the secondary market, if interest rates are already too low and cannot be decreased further to keep the economy on track.

Each parameter's setting is then characterized by one of the six values of α considered and by a flag 'no' or 'yes' which denotes whether the quantitative easing (QE) monetary policy has been adopted. The total number of parameters settings then sums up to 12. In order to corroborate the significance of results, for each setting of parameters, eight different simulation runs have been considered, where each run is characterized by a given seed of the pseudo-random numbers generator. The same set of eight random seeds has been employed for the setting of all parameters.

Tables 4.6 and 4.7 report the simulation results for the main nominal and financial variables of the economy, respectively, obtained with the 12 parameters' settings considered. In particular, Table 4.6 presents the amount of total credit outstanding, which is an important counterpart of the monetary aggregates in the economy. We name as credit money the part of monetary aggregates whose counterpart is given by the total amount of credit outstanding. The dynamics of credit money then depends on the supply of credit by the banking system, which is constrained by its equity base, and depends also on the amount of loans demanded by firms to finance their activity. Thus, it is worth noting that the dynamics of credit money is fully endogenous in the EURACE model.

Different dynamic paths for credit money are given by the different values of α. It is worth remembering also that in a previous study on EURACE (Cincotti et al. 2010), different dynamic paths for the endogenous credit money were created by setting exogenously the dividends–earnings ratio of firms, which now, more properly, is endogenous. (See also Teglio et al. 2010a for further discussions about this new model feature.) The dynamics of fiat money depends on the central bank monetary policy. In particular, if the QE policy is active, the central

Table 4.6 Ensemble averages and standard errors (in brackets) of the total amount of credit outstanding, fiat money, price and wage levels referred to the whole 240 months of simulation length. The two different monetary policies have been considered as well as different values of α. Statistics are computed over 8 seeds of the random number generator

α	QE	Total credit outstanding	Fiat money from CB	Price index	Wage index
5.0	no	436394 (24425)	4919 (0)	0.70 (0.01)	2.06 (0.04)
	yes	386295 (29709)	6618 (196)	0.69 (0.02)	1.96 (0.05)
6.0	no	393740 (21671)	4919 (0)	0.74 (0.02)	1.95 (0.04)
	yes	462327 (29846)	6375 (65)	0.78 (0.02)	2.09 (0.05)
7.0	no	484467 (11216)	4919 (0)	0.77 (0.01)	2.16 (0.02)
	yes	508371 (20532)	5973 (73)	0.78 (0.01)	2.19 (0.04)
8.0	no	589120 (38233)	4919 (0)	0.81 (0.01)	2.17 (0.19)
	yes	588997 (12685)	5489 (105)	0.83 (0.01)	2.32 (0.04)
9.0	no	705142 (28790)	4919 (0)	0.91 (0.01)	2.56 (0.03)
	yes	641226 (20026)	5171 (76)	0.88 (0.01)	2.47 (0.04)
10.0	no	719864 (27612)	4919 (0)	0.95 (0.01)	2.60 (0.04)
	yes	737517 (15188)	5469 (85)	0.94 (0.01)	2.64 (0.04)

bank may buy government bonds directly on the market, thus increasing the overall amount of fiat money in the economy. In this case, the intervention of the central bank is helpful sustaining government bond prices and thus facilitating the financing of government debt. The average levels of price and wage are also reported in Table 4.6. A clear finding emerging from Table 4.6 is how the total amount of credit outstanding increases as the value of α increases, in particular for the lowest value of α. Actually, as α increases, banks are allowed to lend more money to producers in the economy, therefore this is not a surprising result. However, it is interesting to observe how the growth of total credit becomes flat as α approaches its highest values. This fact can be easily explained considering that the equity base of banks is subject to possible debt write-offs due to firms' insolvency bankruptcies, and these events are more likely as α increases, because firms, being less constrained in the credit market, become increasingly leveraged and therefore more financially fragile. Table 4.7 clearly shows how the average firm leverage and the occurrence of insolvency bankruptcies increases with α, while, on the other hand, the likelihood of bankruptcies due to illiquidity decreases for higher α, due to the easier credit conditions. The reduction of banks' equity due to insolvency bankruptcies can then counterbalance the increase of α.

Finally, Table 4.6 clearly shows that the amount of fiat money increases if the QE monetary policy is in place and that that the size of increase diminishes as

Table 4.7 Ensemble averages and standard errors (in brackets) of main financial varables referred to the whole 240 months of simulation length. The two different monetary policies have been considered as well as different values of α. Statistics are computed over 8 seeds of the random number generator

α	QE	Interest rate (%)	Firms' leverage	Illiquidity bankruptcies	Insolvency bankruptcies
5.0	no	3.09 (0.08)	0.78 (0.02)	178.6 (12.5)	0.0 (0.0)
	yes	3.12 (0.05)	0.77 (0.02)	172.6 (13.8)	0.0 (0.0)
6.0	no	3.73 (0.14)	0.93 (0.01)	121.9 (11.3)	0.0 (0.0)
	yes	3.72 (0.10)	0.98 (0.03)	122.8 (12.3)	0.0 (0.0)
7.0	no	4.96 (0.10)	1.18 (0.02)	88.9 (6.2)	0.3 (0.3)
	yes	4.96 (0.12)	1.24 (0.05)	112.9 (10.6)	0.4 (0.3)
8.0	no	5.87 (0.09)	1.53 (0.03)	77.9 (10.7)	0.6 (0.4)
	yes	5.86 (0.13)	1.45 (0.04)	69.8 (11.5)	0.1 (0.1)
9.0	no	6.52 (0.13)	1.90 (0.09)	55.6 (7.9)	0.3 (0.2)
	yes	6.28 (0.10)	1.62 (0.02)	64.0 (6.9)	0.0 (0.0)
10.0	no	6.89 (0.11)	2.14 (0.12)	49.6 (6.9)	1.1 (0.2)
	yes	6.81 (0.14)	2.17 (0.09)	58.6 (9.0)	1.3 (0.3)

α increases, that is, when the amount of credit money is higher. Furthermore, the fiat money component in the monetary aggregate is generally much smaller than that of credit money. Actually, credit money is generally beneficial for the economy and can be seen as a partial substitute of fiat money. This argument can explain why the increase of fiat money is lower for higher α and, considering the relative amounts of fiat money and credit money, why the QE policy does not give, except of course for the values of fiat money, statistically different results in Tables 4.6 and 4.7 and, in particular, for what concerns the outcomes of real variables, as reported in Table 4.8.

Table 4.8 presents the most important real variables in the EURACE artificial economy, that is, the average real GDP level and its components – consumption and investments – as well as the unemployment rate. A clear indication emerges for a better macroeconomic performance, that is, lower unemployment, and higher level of real GDP related to higher levels of credit money in the economy, i.e., higher values of α as shown in Table 4.6. It is worth noting, however, that the improvement in economic performance flattens at the highest α. This finding is consistent with the previous one observed for nominal values, and it is due again to the higher financial fragility that firms have at big α. Loose capital requirements foster economic activity and growth in an initial phase but in the long run they bring more insolvency bankruptcies, debt write-offs, a reduction in the equity base of banks, and possible credit rationing which is harmful to

Table 4.8 Ensemble averages and standard errors (in brackets) of main real variables referred to the whole 240 months of simulation length. The two different monetary policies have been considered as well as different values of α. Statistics are computed over 8 seeds of the random number generator

α	QE	Cons. goods production	Invest. goods production	Real GDP level	Unemployment rate (%)
5.0	no	13325 (676)	4661 (372)	17986 (1036)	19.51 (3.67)
	yes	12534 (892)	4191 (430)	16725 (1317)	23.15 (4.95)
6.0	no	11928 (574)	3526 (283)	15454 (843)	26.25 (3.10)
	yes	12558 (432)	4146 (320)	16704 (740)	23.52 (2.28)
7.0	no	13293 (215)	4026 (132)	17319 (322)	18.29 (1.25)
	yes	13365 (362)	4281 (245)	17646 (586)	18.12 (2.05)
8.0	no	13303 (1052)	4424 (504)	17726 (1523)	18.26 (5.54)
	yes	14257 (157)	4533 (136)	18791 (210)	13.40 (0.70)
9.0	no	14965 (182)	4879 (205)	19843 (385)	10.36 (0.87)
	yes	14686 (185)	4550 (178)	19237 (349)	11.59 (0.91)
10.0	no	14858 (175)	4831 (262)	19688 (430)	10.21 (0.82)
	yes	15076 (120)	5186 (219)	20262 (335)	9.40 (0.54)

Table 4.9 Ensemble averages and standard errors (in brackets) of main real variables referred to the first 60 months of simulation length. The two different monetary policies have been considered as well as different values of α. Statistics are computed over 8 seeds of the random number generator

α	QE	Cons. goods production	Investment goods production	Real GDP level	Unemployment rate (%)
5.0	no	7685 (70)	2866 (18)	10552 (81)	40.93 (0.67)
	yes	7661 (59)	2878 (20)	10539 (68)	41.13 (0.61)
6.0	no	8260 (44)	3224 (18)	11483 (59)	36.07 (0.30)
	yes	8150 (56)	3224 (17)	11375 (67)	36.94 (0.53)
7.0	no	9113 (87)	3794 (31)	12908 (118)	29.00 (0.82)
	yes	9005 (65)	3746 (29)	12751 (91)	30.04 (0.62)
8.0	no	9761 (67)	4216 (27)	13977 (91)	23.89 (0.60)
	yes	9579 (97)	4126 (47)	13704 (141)	25.32 (0.84)
9.0	no	10114 (87)	4366 (28)	14480 (112)	20.85 (0.72)
	yes	10211 (83)	4408 (14)	14619 (90)	20.07 (0.72)
10.0	no	10544 (65)	4514 (40)	15057 (81)	17.19 (0.64)
	yes	10403 (47)	4498 (38)	14900 (51)	18.38 (0.45)

the economy. This argument is confirmed by Table 4.9, where the averages of real variables are computed in the first five years of simulation. In this case, the improvement in economic conditions is present also at the highest values of α, because the insolvency problems of overly leveraged firms have not yet reached the peak.

Figures 4.1, 4.2 and 4.3 present a sample of simulation paths whose averages over different seeds have been shown in the previous tables. Only two values of α, that is, $\alpha = 5$ and $\alpha = 10$, and the conventional monetary policy based on the Taylor rule have been considered. In particular, Figure 1 shows the total production of consumption goods as well as the unemployment, while the path of real investments is plotted in the bottom part of Figure 4.3. The trajectories of the two GDP components show that the EURACE model is able to exhibit endogenous short-term fluctuations as well as endogenous long-run growth. The endogenous business cycles can be explained by the strong fluctuations in the investment in physical capital and disruptions in the supply chain as well as mass layoffs due to firms' bankruptcies. Furthermore, investment decisions as well as firms' bankruptcies depend strongly on interest rates, on the availability of internal liquidity and on bank credit. Therefore, there is a strict relation between real economic activity and its financing through the credit sector. Long-run economic growth is due to the growth of firms' physical capital resulting from the endogenous investment decisions. The increase in labor productivity due to the improvement of the skills of workers is the other reason

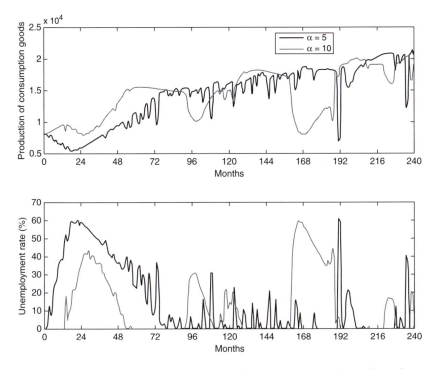

Figure 4.1 Simulation paths for production and unemployment. Two values of *a* are considered, i.e., *a* = 5 (black line) and *a* = 10 (grey line)

which explains long-run growth. Finally, the comparison of the trajectory at $\alpha = 5$ with the one at $\alpha = 10$ clearly shows how in the short run high values of α, that is, loose capital requirements for banks, boost the economy, while in the long run the higher financial fragility and insolvency bankruptcies may reverse the situation.

4.9   Concluding remarks

This paper presents a set of computational results realized by mean of the agent-based model and simulator EURACE. In particular, results show the real effects on the EURACE economy of the dynamics of monetary aggregates, that is, endogenous credit money supplied by commercial banks and fiat money created by the central bank by means of quantitative easing. The dynamics of credit money is endogenous. Different dynamic paths have been obtained by different settings of the regulatory capital requirements for banks. A quantity-easing monetary policy, activated in case of low interest rates and high unemployment, failed to provide a better macroeconomic performance.

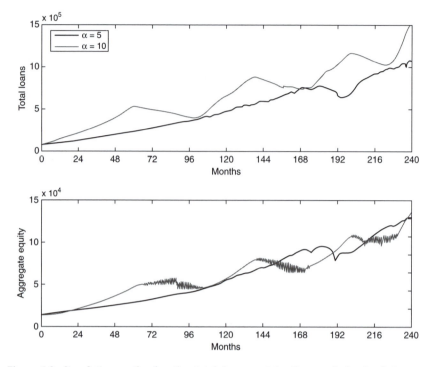

Figure 4.2 Simulation paths for the total loans outstanding and the banks' aggregate equity base. Two values of *a* are considered, i.e., *a* = 5 (black line) and *a* = 10 (grey line)

Results also show the emergence of endogenous business cycles which are mainly due to the interplay between real economic activity and its financing through the credit market. In particular, the amplitude of the business cycles strongly raises with bankruptcy of firms and, in fact, firms' leverage, defined as the debt–equity ratio, can be considered as a proxy of the likelihood of bankruptcy.

Finally, from a more general perspective, the results show the possibility of explaining the emergence of business cycles based on the complex internal functioning of the economy, and in particular based of the investment–finance linkage as in the Minsky perspective (Minsky 1986), without considering any ad-hoc exogenous shocks, as in the standard DSGE framework (De Grauwe 2010). The adopted agent-based framework has been able to address this complexity, and these results reinforce the validity of the EURACE model and simulator for future research in economics.

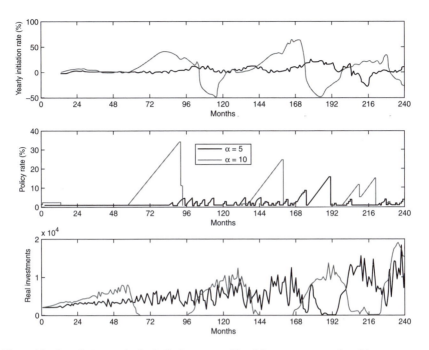

Figure 4.3 Simulation paths for inflation, central bank interest rates and real investments. Two values of *a* are considered, i.e., *a* = 5 (black line) and *a* = 10 (grey line)

Note

* This work has been partly supported by the University of Genoa and by the European Commission under EURACE project (EU IST FP6 STREP grant: 035086).

References

Benartzi, S. and R.H. Thaler (1995) 'Myopic Loss Aversion and the Equity Premium Puzzle', *The Quarterly Journal of Economics*, vol. 110, no. 1, pp. 73–92.

Carroll, C.D. (2001) 'A Theory of the Consumption Function, With and Without Liquidity Constraints', *Journal of Economic Perspectives*, vol. 15, no. 3, pp. 23–45.

Cincotti, S., M. Raberto and A. Teglio (2010) 'Credit Money and Macroeconomic Instability in the Agent-based Model and Simulator EURACE', *The Open-Access, Open-Assessment E-Journal*, vol. 4 (2010-26).

Dawid, H., S. Gemkow, P. Harting, R. Kabus, M. Neugart and K. Wersching (2008) 'Skills, Innovation, and Growth: An Agent-based Policy Analysis', *Journal of Economics and Statistics*, vol. 228, nos 2–3, pp. 251–275.

Dawid, H., S. Gemkow, P. Harting and M. Neugart (2009) 'On the Effects of Skill Upgrading in the Presence of Spatial Labor Market Frictions: An Agent-based Analysis of Spatial Policy Design', *Journal of Artificial Societies and Social Simulation*, vol. 12, no. 4.

De Grauwe, P. (2010) 'The Scientific Foundation of Dynamic Stochastic General Equilibrium (DSGE) Models', *Public Choice*, vol. 144, nos 3–4, pp. 413–443.

Deaton, A. (1992) 'Household Saving in LDCs: Credit Markets, Insurance and Welfare', *The Scandinavian Journal of Economics*, vol. 94, no. 22, pp. 253–273.

Kahneman, D. and A. Tversky (1979) 'Prospect Theory: an Analysis of Decision under Risk', *Econometrica*, vol. 47(2), pp. 263–292.

Minsky, H. (1986) *Stabilizing an Unstable Economy* (New Haven, CT and London: Yale University Press).

Myers, S. and N. Majluf (1984) 'Corporate Financing and Investment Decisions when Firms have Information that Investors do not have', *Journal of Financial Economics*, vol. 13, no. 2, pp. 187–221.

Raberto, M., A. Teglio and S: Cincotti (2006a) 'A Dynamic General Disequilibrium Model of a Sequential Monetary Production Economy', *Chaos, Solitons and Fractals*, vol. 29, no. 3, pp. 566–577.

Raberto, M., A. Teglio and S. Cincotti (2006b) 'A General Equilibrium Model of a Production Economy with Asset Markets', *Physica A*, vol. 370, no. 1, pp. 75–80.

Raberto, M., A. Teglio and S. Cincotti (2008a) 'Integrating Real and Financial Markets in an Agent-based Economic Model: An Application to Monetary Policy Design', *Computational Economics*, vol. 32, nos 1–2, pp. 147–162.

Raberto, M., A. Teglio and S. Cincotti (2008b) 'Prospect Theory Behavioral Assumptions in an Artificial Financial Economy', *Lecture Notes in Economics and Mathematical Systems*, vol 614 (Berlin: Springer), pp. 55–66.

Taylor J.B. (1993) 'Discretion Versus Policy Rule in Practice', *Carnegie-Rochester Conference Series on Public Policy*, vol 39, no. 1, pp. 195–214. See also http://www.sciencedirect.com/science/article/pii/016722319390009L.

Teglio, A., M. Raberto and S. Cincotti (2009) 'Explaining Equity Excess Return by Means of an Agent-based Financial Market', in C. Hernández, M. Posada and A. López-Paredes (eds), *Artificial Economics* (Berlin and Heidelberg: Springer), pp. 145–156.

Teglio, A., M. Raberto, S. Cincotti (2010a) 'Balance Sheet Approach to Agent-based Computational Economics: The EURACE Project', in Combining Soft Computing and Statistical Methods in Data Analysis, *Advances in Intelligent and Soft Computing*, vol. 77 (Berlin and Heidelberg: Springer), pp. 603–610.

Teglio, A., M. Raberto, S. Cincotti (2010b) 'Endogenous Credit Dynamics as Source of Business Cycles in the EURACE Model', in: M. Li Calzi, M. Limone and P. Pellizzari (eds), *Progress in Artificial Economics*, Lecture Notes in Economics and Mathematical Systems, vol. 645 (Berlin and Heidelberg: Springer), pp. 203–214.

Tesfatsion, L. and K. Judd (eds) (2006) 'Agent-Based Computational Economics', *Handbook of Computational Economics*, vol. 2 (Amsterdam: North-Holland).

Tversky, A. and D. Kahneman (1992) 'Advances in Prospect Theory: Cumulative Representation of Uncertainty', *Journal of Risk and Uncertainty*, vol. 5, no. 4, pp. 297–323.

Part III
Social Norms

5
Aspects of Naturalizing the Social Contract

Brian Skyrms
University of California, Irvine and Stanford University, USA

> For they (philosophers) conceive of men, not as they are, but as they themselves would like them to be. Whence it has come to pass that, instead of ethics, they have generally written satire... (Spinoza, *Tractatus Politicus*, 1677)

5.1 Introduction

Spinoza's acerbic comment on moral and political philosophy is as relevant today as it was in his own time. It is not difficult to find contemporary targets not only in philosophy, but also in political theory and in economics. How are we to proceed if we want a naturalistic theory of the social contract? The main outlines of a plausible answer were drafted by David Hume in 1739. I quote from everyone's favorite passage:

> Nor is the rule concerning the stability of possession the less derived from human conventions, that it arises gradually and acquires force by a slow progression...

Much of human behavior is governed by habits, conventions and norms. These were themselves less a product of rational decision, rather than of a gradual adaptive process. The social contract evolved.

The appropriate theoretic tool for pursuing a naturalistic theory of the social contract was only suggested by Hume, but is now in full flower – *evolutionary game theory*. I take this in the inclusive sense that it has come to have, including interactions governed by all sorts of adaptive processes. These operate on different time scales, from biological evolution through cultural evolution to individual learning. Empirical evidence is required to identify the relevant dynamics and to deal with path-dependence and cultural and psychological diversity.

Modern Humeans, pursuing a naturalistic theory of the social contract, include my co-symposiasts Robert Sugden (*The Economics of Rights, Cooperation and Welfare*) and Ken Binmore (*Game Theory and the Social Contract I, II* and *Natural Justice*). Important empirical study of the evolution and functioning of small-scale social contracts can be found in the work of Elinor Ostrom (*Governing the Commons*).

Today, I will focus on two aspects of evolutionary game theory that distinguish it sharply from more traditional approaches to game theory: *dynamics* and *correlation*.

5.2 Dynamics

Why bother with dynamics? Many plausible evolutionary dynamics have Nash equilibria as their rest points (or close enough.) Why not just stick to equilibrium analysis? As discussed in the next section, when correlation enters the picture Nash equilibrium may not be even close to the relevant dynamical equilibrium. But leaving correlation to the side, there are still many reasons why to pay attention to dynamics.

There is the problem of *equilibrium selection*. Even if we postulate that an equilibrium will be reached, in games with many equilibria there is the question of which one will be reached. If anthropologists have taught game theorists anything, they have shown that any plausible model of the social contract must have multiple equilibria.

There is the question of whether we ever reach equilibrium. This has two aspects, a theoretical one and a practical one. On the theoretical side, across a spectrum of adaptive dynamics, we have examples where the dynamics never reaches equilibrium. Besides toy examples like replicator dynamics in the game of 'Matching Pennies,' we find cycles more serious examples like Michael Spence's job market signaling game from economics (Spence 1974; Noldeke and Samuelson 1997; Wagner 2010) and John Maynard Smith's 'Sir Philip Sydney game' from evolutionary biology (Huttegger and Zollman 2009).

Beyond cycles there is *chaos*: dynamical behavior that is both non-convergent and unpredictable. Chaos in one-population replicator dynamics was identified by Schnabl et al. (1991). I called attention to chaos as raising questions about the explanatory significance of equilibrium in 1993. Sato, Akiyama and Farmer (2002) found Hamiltonian chaos in two-population replicator dynamics. Wagner (2011) finds Hamiltonian chaos in a signaling game.

Replicator dynamics is the dynamics of differential reproduction, deriving from biology. It also arises from differential imitation in models of cultural evolution, and has strong connections with reinforcement learning. But there are other dynamics that incorporate more strategic rationality, such as 'fictitious play.' Here players optimize against an inductive estimate of other players' actions. A game that generates chaos with replicator dynamics need not do so with fictitious play. Do we find chaos in fictitious play?

We do. Cowan (1992) constructs an example chaos in fictitious play in his PhD thesis. As with replicator dynamics, it took some time for this early finding to be followed up by game theorists. But recently chaos in fictitious play has been studied by Sparrow and co-workers (Sparrow et al. 2008; van Strien et. al. 2011). The conclusion that cycles and chaos can be found in many game dynamics is reinforced by recent work by Hommes and Ochea (2012) that finds cycles and indications of chaos in smoothed best response dynamics.

We have to conclude that across a broad range of game dynamics we may simply not reach equilibrium. And even in cases where the dynamics eventually leads to a steady state, the waiting times may be so long that the result is irrelevant to practical affairs (for example, Pemantle and Skyrms 2004a).

Should this surprise us? As we look at the world – financial markets, international relations, social rebellions and revolutions – we do not see a steady state. For a theory of social interaction to rely on solely equilibrium analysis seems ludicrous.

5.3   Correlation

Biology has a second lesson for game theory. That is that correlation of encounters can make a difference in (some) game dynamics. Suppose that individuals are matched at random from an infinite population to play a two-person game, and that the relevant dynamics is the replicator dynamics. Consider the Prisoner's Dilemma. From any starting point where defectors are not extinct, the dynamics converges to the state where all defect. And, in general, the dynamic leads to iterative deletion of strictly dominated strategies.

The picture changes dramatically if encounters are correlated – if the probability of strategy S encountering strategy T depends on S:

$Pr[T|S]$ *unequal to* $Pr[T]$

Thus in Prisoner's Dilemma, sufficient positive correlation allows the evolution of altruism, since the payoff of C played against C is greater than the payoff of D played against D.

Table 5.1   Prisoner's dilemma

	Cooperate	Defect
Cooperate	3	1
Defect	4	2

Row's Payoff.

Table 5.2   Prisoner's delight

	Cooperate	Defect
Cooperate	4	2
Defect	3	1

Row's Payoff.

Table 5.3   Stag hunt

	Cooperate	Defect
Cooperate	3	1
Defect	2	2

And in Ken Binmore's 'Prisoner's Delight' negative correlation can explain the evolution of spite, since the payoff of D against C is greater than the payoff of C against D.

Best responders will, of course, defect in the Prisoner's Dilemma and cooperate in the Prisoner's Delight. But cultural evolution driven by differential imitation, or social learning driven by reinforcements can be influenced by positive and negative correlations. If individuals often act out of habit, or in accordance with conventions or social norms, and if these in turn arise from cultural evolution, then correlation must be taken into account.

All biological explanations of the evolution of altruism rely on correlation mechanisms. This was already understood by Hamilton and Price (Hamilton 1975).

It may take extremes of positive and negative correlation to favor cooperation in Prisoner's Dilemma or defection in Prisoner's Delight. But quite modest amounts of correlation can have significant impacts on equilibrium selection. Consider the Stag Hunt game.

If there is no correlation of encounters, the safe (risk-dominant) equilibrium, All Defect, has the greatest basin of attraction. But small amounts of positive correlation can increase the basin of attraction of cooperation in Stag Hunt games, so that cooperation then becomes the stochastically stable strategy.

Prisoner's Delight, Stag Hunt and Prisoner's Dilemma are not the only simple games that raise issues central to the social contract. We could separate the issues of cooperating to produce a public good, and deciding how that good is to be divided. The latter concern is the philosophers' problem of distributive justice, and it brings **bargaining games** to center stage.

Consider the simplest Nash Bargaining game. Two players have bottom line demands for a share of a common good. If the demands exceed the available good, agreement is impossible and players get nothing. Otherwise they get what they demand. We simplify radically by assuming that there are only three possible demands: one-third, one-half, and two-thirds.

Table 5.4 Mini-Nash demand game

	Demand 1/3	Demand 1/2	Demand 2/3
Demand 1/3	1/3	1/3	1/3
Demand 1/2	1/2	1/2	0
Demand 2/3	2/3	0	0

5.3.1 Mini-Nash demand game

Evolutionary dynamics in a large, random-encounter environment, with and without persistent random shocks, has been the subject of a substantial amount of analysis. Allowing differential reproduction to carry a population to equilibrium, there are two possibilities. The population may reach an egalitarian consensus, where all demand one-half. This has the greatest basin of attraction. Or it may reach a polymorphic state where half the population demands two-thirds and half the population demands one-third. Greedy players get their two-thirds half the time; modest players get their one-third all the time. This inefficient polymorphism wastes resources, but it is evolutionarily stable and has a significant basin of attraction. Persistent shocks can allow a population to escape from this polymorphic trap and favor the egalitarian norm in the very long run (Young 1993) but the inefficient polymorphism remains a possibility for medium-run behavior.

However, the effect of correlation mechanisms is rarely discussed in connection with Nash bargaining. If correlation plays an important role in producing a surplus to be divided, might it not also play an important role in deciding how the division takes place? Positive correlation of demand types obviously favors the egalitarian solution. Those who ask for equal shares do best when they meet each other. Negative correlation is more complicated. Greedy players who demand two-thirds do very well if paired with modest players who ask for one-third, but not well if paired with those who ask for half. But if negative correlation initially allows greedy players to out-reproduce all others, it cannot be maintained because they run out of modest players. On the other hand, if the negative correlation is of the kind that is sufficiently disadvantages the egalitarians, then a greedy-modest polymorphism is a real possibility.

So far, negative correlation has played a rather sinister role in this story. This is not always the case. In cooperating to produce a common good organisms sometimes discover the efficiency of the division of labor, and find a way to implement it. Modern human societies are marvels in their implementation of division of labor; so are the societies of cells in any multicellular organism. On the most elementary level, we can suppose that there are two kinds of specialists that an individual can become, A and B, and that these specialists are complementary. On the other hand, an individual might not specialize at all; instead

Table 5.5 Division of labor game

	Specialize A	Specialize B	Go It Alone
Specialize A	0	2	0
Specialize B	2	0	0
Go It Alone	1	1	1

they might, rather less efficiently, do the same as both specialists. This gives us a little division-of-labor game.

In a random encounter setting, specialists do badly. Positive correlation makes it worse.

What is required to get division of labor off the ground is the right kind of negative correlation. Not all the correlation mechanisms that we have discussed here do the trick. What works best is dynamic social network formation, where the network structure evolves quickly. Specialists quickly learn to associate with the complementary specialists, and then specialists outperform those who 'go it alone.' The effect of correlation depends on the nature of the interaction.

It is clear that correlation can have important theoretical consequences, but the empirical importance of this fact depends upon the actual extent of the correlation. Is correlation significant? I think that it often is. The world is full of correlation devices. Three that have been extensively studied, and that deserve special mention are (1) local interaction on a network (for example, Pollock 1989; Nowak and May 1992); (2) partner choice (for example, Eshel and Cavalli-Svorza 1982); and (3) signaling (for example, Robson 1990).

At a different level, we can see that many social institutions function as correlation devices: for a sample consider clubs, political parties, universities, religions, and this conference. Correlation devices can affect the evolution of habits, conventions, and norms, but correlation devices themselves also evolve.

5.4 Dynamic correlation

Correlation may not be fixed, but rather may itself evolve. I will discuss in some detail one example – *a dynamic model of social network formation* – from my work with Robin Pemantle.

5.4.1 Partner choice and network dynamics

A small group of individuals interact repeatedly, where the interactions have consequences for participants' well-being or utilities. Interactions could involve, for example, making friends, gift-giving, participating in a group enterprise such as cooperative hunting, bargaining how to split a payoff, trade, gossip, division of labor. In an interaction, individuals actualize some behavior and the behavior of the individuals jointly determines the outcome of the interaction. At a high level of abstraction, we can model interactions as games. The relevant behaviors of individuals in the interaction are the strategies of the game, and the strategies of the players jointly determine their payoffs.

Since the interactions are repeated, players can modify their behavior in the light of experience – they can learn. Agents can learn two things: *with whom to interact* and *how to act*. That is to say that adaptive learning dynamics operates both on network structure and on strategy. Evolutionary game theory models usually fix the network structure and concentrate on studying how strategies evolve. Most often the network structure is degenerate, simply assuming random encounters in a large population. Sometimes, but less often, it is assumed that individuals interact with neighbors on a circle, torus, or other fixed structure.

In Skyrms and Pemantle (2000) we first reverse the usual bias and investigate the evolution of network structure when strategies are held fixed. Then we move to the coevolution of structure and strategy where the respective learning dynamics may be of different kinds and may proceed at different rates. Relative rates of evolution are seen to make all the difference for the evolution of cooperation in the Stag Hunt game, with a fast network dynamics favoring cooperation.

The basic model admits of many realizations, depending on the interactions modeled and the forms of learning used for modification of network structure and of strategy, and – as I have just said – the relative rates of the structure and strategy dynamics. Some of these variations have been explored in subsequent work, but many others remain to be investigated. It is important in interpreting these models to pay attention not only to long-run limiting results, but also to medium-run transient behavior. In some cases limiting results are approached very quickly, but in others medium-run transient behavior can look very different from true limiting behavior even after millions of repetitions (Pemantle and Skyrms 2004a).

5.4.2 Making friends, Stag Hunt

We start by considering network dynamics by simple reinforcement learning of the kind found in Roth and Erev (Roth and Erev 1995; Erev and Roth 1998). In the basic model, individuals start with initial propensities to choose among various options, choose with probability proportional to the propensities, and update the propensity for the option chosen by the payoff (reinforcement) received.

Now we assume that on each day each of our individuals wakes up and decides to visit someone else according to some initial propensities for whom to visit. It will be assumed that the population is small enough so that there is plenty of time in the day for all choices to be satisfied. It is also assumed that all visits are received. If everyone else decides to visit Samantha, everyone else gets to visit Samantha. (Obviously each of these assumptions could be modified, and modification might well be appropriate in certain situations.) At the end of the day each individual updates her weights for visiting an individual by adding the payoffs gotten from that day from interactions with that individual (both as visitor and as host.)

As baseline models, consider two models of 'Making Friends.' In Friends I the visitor is treated well, for a payoff of 1, while the host gets a payoff of 0. In Friends II both visitor and host enjoy themselves equally, and each has a payoff of 1. These may be viewed degenerate games, where the visitor and host only have one available strategy, with payoff matrices:

Friends I	Host	Friends II	Host
Visitor	1,0	Visitor	1,1

We begin investigation of the network formation for these two interactions by starting ten individuals with equal initial weights of 1 for visiting each other individual. The initial network structure is one of random encounters. In this setting, it is easy to run computer simulations of the Friends I and Friends II processes, and it is a striking feature of such simulations that in both cases non-random interaction structure emerges rapidly. Furthermore, re-running the processes from the same starting point seems to generate a different structure each time. We see the emergence of structure without an organizer, or even an explanation in terms of payoff differences. The state of uniform random encounters with which we started the system does not persist, and so must count as a very artificial state. Its use as the fixed interaction structure in many game theoretic models should be suspect.

We can understand the behavior of the Friends I process if we notice that each individual's learning process is equivalent to a Pólya urn. We can think of him as having an urn with balls of different colors, one color for each other individual. Initially, there is one ball of each color. A ball is chosen (and returned), the designated individual is visited. Because visitors are always reinforced, another ball of the same color is added to the urn. Because only visitors are reinforced, balls are not added to the urn in any other way. The Pólya urn converges to a limit with probability one, but it is a random limit with uniform distribution over possible final probabilities. Anything can happen, and nothing is favored! *In Friends I the random limit is uniform for each player, and makes the players independent* (Theorem 1 of Skyrms and Pemantle 2000). All interaction structures are possible in the limit, and the probability that the group converges to random encounters is zero.

In Friends II, both visitor and host are reinforced and so the urns interact. If someone visits you, you are reinforced to visit him – or, to put it graphically, someone can walk up to your door and put a ball of his color in your urn. This complicates the analysis considerably. Nevertheless, the final picture is quite similar. *In Friends II the limiting probabilities must be symmetric, that is to say X visits Y with the same probability that Y visits X, but subject to this constraint and its consequences anything can happen* (Theorem 2 of Skyrms and Pemantle 2000).

The Making Friends games provide building blocks for analyzing learning dynamics where the interactions are games with non-trivial strategies. Consider the following two-person Stag Hunt. Individuals are either Stag Hunters or Hare Hunters. If a Stag Hunter interacts with a Hare Hunter no Stag is caught and the Stag Hunter gets zero payoff. If a Stag Hunter interacts with another Stag Hunter the Stag is likely caught and the hunters each get a payoff of one. Hare Hunting requires no cooperation, and its practitioners get a payoff of .75 in any case. It makes no difference who is visitor or who is host.

	Stag	Hare
Stag	1	0
Hare	.75	.75

The Stag Hunt game is of particular interest for social theory. Stag Hunting is both mutually beneficial and an equilibrium, but it is risky. Deciding to hunt Stag requires a measure of *trust* that the other player will cooperate. In a large population composed of half Stag Hunters and half Hare Hunters with random interactions between individuals, the Hare Hunters would get an average payoff of .75 while the Stag Hunters would only get an average payoff of .50. The conventional wisdom is that in the long run evolution will strongly favor Hare hunting.

But suppose that the players *learn to network*. We use exactly the same model as before, except that the payoffs are now determined by the individuals' strategies: Hunt Stag or Hunt Hare. We start with an even number of Stag Hunters and Hare Hunters. *In the limit, Stag Hunters always visit Stag Hunters and Hare Hunters always visit Hare Hunters* (Theorem 6 of Skyrms and Pemantle 2000). Simulation confirms that such a state is approached rapidly. Although on rational choice grounds Hare Hunters 'should not care' whom they visit, they cease to be reinforced by visits from Stag Hunters after Stag Hunters learn not to visit them. Hare Hunters continue to be visited by other Hare Hunters, so all the differential learning for Hare Hunters takes place when they are hosts rather than visitors. Once learning has sorted out Stag Hunters and Hare Hunters so that each group only interacts with its own members, each is playing

Friends II with itself and previous results characterize within-group interaction structure.

Once Stag Hunters have learned to network, they prosper. The disadvantage that they experienced in the random encounter situation has been overcome, and now their payoff is superior to that of non-cooperative Hare Hunters.

5.4.3   Coevolution of structure and strategy

So far, strategies have been fixed. Individuals were either Stag Hunters or Hare Hunters, and could not change their type. We now investigate the coevolution of network structure and strategies. The process now involves two interacting dynamic processes. The strategy revision dynamics might be qualitatively the same as the partner choice dynamics, or it might be qualitatively different. They might operate at different time rates, with one being fast and the other slow. The population might be heterogeneous with respect to the operative learning dynamics. Let us consider a few examples.

To the two-person Stag Hunt we add a strategy revision process based on imitation to get a *reinforcement-imitation* model of coevolution. With some specified probability, an individual wakes up, looks around the whole group, and if some strategy is prospering more than his own, switches to it. Individuals' probabilities are independent. If imitation is fast relative to structure dynamics, it operates while individuals interact more or less at random and Hare Hunters will take over more often than not. If imitation is slow, Stag Hunters find each other and prosper, and then imitation slowly converts Hare Hunters to Stag Hunters (who quickly learn to interact with other Stag Hunters).

Simulations show that in intermediate cases, timing can make all the difference. We start with structure weights equal to 1 and vary the relative rates of the dynamics by varying the imitation probability. With 'fast' imitation (pr $= .1$) 78 per cent of the trials ended up with everyone converted to Hare Hunting and 22 per cent ended up with everyone converted to Stag Hunting. Slower imitation (pr $= .01$) almost reversed the numbers, with 71 per cent of the trials ending up All Stag and 29 per cent ending up All Hare. Fluid network structure coupled with slow strategy revision reverses the orthodox prediction that Hare Hunting (the risk-dominant equilibrium) will take over. *Free association favors cooperation.*

The foregoing model illustrates the combined action of two different dynamics, reinforcement learning for interaction structure and imitation for strategy revision. What happens if both processes are driven by reinforcement learning? In particular, we would like to know whether in such circumstances the relative rates of structure and strategy dynamics still make the same difference between Stag Hunting and Hare Hunting. In this *Double Reinforcement* model (Skyrms 2004), each individual has two weight vectors, one for interaction propensities and one for propensities to either Hunt Stag or Hunt Hare. Probabilities for whom to visit, and what to do, are both gotten by normalizing the appropriate weights. Weights are updated by adding the payoff from an interaction to both the weight for the individual involved and to the weight for the action taken. Relative rates of the two learning processes can be manipulated by changing the magnitude of the initial weights.

In the previous models we started the population off with some Stag Hunters and some Hare Hunters. That point of view is no longer correct. The only way one could be deterministically a Stag Hunter would be to start out with zero weight for Hare Hunting, and then he could never learn to hunt Stag. We have to start out individuals with varying propensities to hunt Hare and Stag. There are various interesting choices that might be made here; we will report some simulation results for one. We start with a heterogeneous group of 10: 2 confirmed Stag Hunters (weight 100 for Stag, 1 for Hare), 2 confirmed Hare Hunters (weight 100 for Hare, 1 for Stag), and six undecided guys (weights 1 for Stag and 1 for Hare). Initial weights for interaction structure were all equal, but their magnitude was varied from .001 to 10, in order to vary the relative rates of learning structure and strategy. The percentage of 10,000 trials that ended up All Stag or All Hare (after 1,000,000 iterations) for these various settings are shown in Figure 5.1.

As before, fluid interaction structure and slow strategy adaptation favor Stag Hunting, while the reverse combination favors Hare Hunting. *Free association favors cooperation.*

However, a third possible strategy-revision dynamics – the Cournot dynamics – gives different results. Suppose that agents change their strategies by choosing the one which would have given the greatest payoff against the opponent's plays in the previous round. Suppose, as before, that network structure adapts quickly, and that players are sorted into Stag Hunters interacting with Stag Hunters and Hare Hunters interacting with Hare Hunters. Then the Cournot dynamics simply confirms everyone in their strategy choice, since Stag Hunters

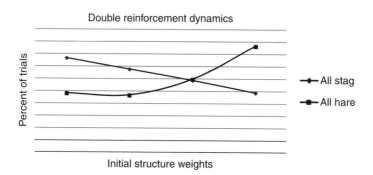

Figure 5.1 Stag Hunt with reinforcement dynamics for both strategy and structure

do better against Stag Hunters and Hare Hunters do better against Hare Hunters. We now have two non-interacting social classes. Stag Hunters cooperate and prosper, while myopic optimization locks Hare Hunters into an inefficient equilibrium.

In each of these models the dynamics of correlation is crucial. In the scenarios in which Stag Hunting takes over the population, correlation disappears in the limit, but transient correlation determines the limiting result.

5.5   Evolution and the social contract

An evolutionary theory of the social contract stands in some contrast to social contract theory as usually practiced in contemporary philosophy. Philosophers usually assume that everyone is, in some sense, rational. And they usually assume that in the relevant choice situation – perhaps behind a veil of ignorance – the relevant choosers are all basically the same. They all have the same rational choice rule, they all have the same basic values and, therefore, they all make the same choice. Correlation of types plays no part because it is assumed that there is only one relevant type.

Evolutionary game theory brings different types of individual into the picture from the beginning. Evolutionary game theory is full of contingency. There are typically many equilibria; there are many possible alternative social contracts. The population might never get to equilibrium; rather it might cycle or describe a chaotic orbit. Mutation, invention, experimentation and external environmental shocks add another layer of contingency.

Evolutionary game theory has strong connections with rational choice theory in the absence of correlation. This is modified when interactions are correlated. But correlation, positive and negative, is at the heart of the social contract. Correlation gets it started. Correlation lets it grow and develop more complex forms. Social institutions and networks evolve to enable and maintain correlation. Correlation explains much of what is admirable, and much of what is despicable in existing social contracts – what we would like to keep and what we would like to change. A better understanding of the dynamics of correlation should be a central concern for Darwinian social philosophy.

References

Binmore, K.G. (1994) *Playing Fair: Game Theory and the Social Contract vol. I* (Cambridge, MA: MIT Press).

Binmore, K.G. (1998) *Just Playing: Game Theory and the Social Contract vol. II* (Cambridge, MA: MIT Press).

Binmore, K.G. (2005) *Natural Justice* (New York: Oxford University Press).

Cowan, S.G. (1992) *Dynamical Systems Arising from Game Theory* PhD Thesis. University of California, Berkeley.

Erev, I. and A. Roth (1998) 'Predicting How People Play Games: Reinforcement Learning in Games with Unique Strategy Equilibrium', *American Economic Review*, vol. 88, pp. 848–881.

Eshel, I. and L.L. Cavalli-Sforza (1982) 'Assortment of Encounters and Evolution of Cooperativeness', *Proceedings of the National Academy of Sciences,* vol. 79, pp. 1331–1335.

Hamilton, W.D. (1975) 'Innate Social Aptitudes of Man: An Approach from Evolutionary Genetics', in R. Fox (ed.), *Biosocial Anthropology* (London: Maleby Press), pp. 133–153.

Hommes, C.H. and M.I. Ochea (2012) 'Multiple Equilibria and Limit Cycles in Evolutionary Games with Logit Dynamics', *Games and Economic* Behavior, vol. 74, no. 1,pp. 434–441.

Huttegger, S. and K. Zollman (2009) 'Dynamic Stability and Basins of Attraction in the Sir Philip Sydney Game', *Proc. Royal Society B*, vol. 277, pp. 1915–1922.

Noldeke, G. and L. Samuelson (1997) 'A Dynamic Model of Equilibrium Selection in Signaling Games', *Journal of Economic Theory*, vol. 17, pp. 118–156.

Nowak, M. and R. May (1992) 'Evolutionary Games and Spatial Chaos', *Nature*, vol. 359, pp. 826–829.

Ostrom, E. (1990) *Governing the Commons: The Evolution of Institutions for Collective Action* (Cambridge: Cambridge University Press).

Pemantle, R. and Skyrms, B. (2004) 'Time to Absorption in Discounted Reinforcement Models', *Stochastic Processes and Their Applications*, vol. 109, pp. 1–12.

Pemantle R. and Skyrms, B. (2004) 'Network Formation by Reinforcement Learning: The Long and the Medium Run', *Mathematical Social Sciences*, vol. 48, pp. 315–327.

Pollock, G.B. (1989) 'Evolutionary Stability of Reciprocity on a Viscous Lattice', *Social Networks*, vol. 11, pp. 175–212.

Robson, A.J. (1990) 'Efficiency in Evolutionary Games: Darwin, Nash and the Secret Handshake', *Journal of Theoretical Biology*, vol. 144, pp. 379–396.

Roth, A.E. and I. Erev (1995) 'Learning in Extensive Form Games: Experimental Data and Simple Dynamic Models in the Intermediate Term', *Games and Economics Behavior*, vol. 8, pp. 164–212.

Sato, Y., E. Akiyama and J.D. Farmer (2002) 'Chaos in Learning a Simple Two-Person Game', *Proceedings of the National Academy of Sciences*, vol. 99, pp. 4758–4761.

Schnabl, W., P.F. Stadler, C. Forst and P. Schuster (1991) 'Full Characterization of a Strange Attractor: Chaotic Dynamics in Low Dimensional Replicator Systems', *Physica D*, vol. 48, pp. 65–90.

Skyrms, B. (1992) 'Chaos and the Explanatory Significance of Equilibrium: Strange Attractors in Evolutionary Game Dynamics', in *PSA 1992 vol. 2* (Philosophy of Science Association), pp. 374–394.

Skyrms, B. (1996) *Evolution of the Social Contract* (Cambridge and New York: Cambridge University Press).

Skyrms, B. (2004) *The Stag Hunt and the Evolution of Social Structure* (Cambridge and New York: Cambridge University Press).

Skyrms, B. and R. Pemantle (2000) 'A Dynamic Model of Social Network Formation', *Proceedings of the National Academy of Sciences of the USA* 97: 9340–9346.

Sparrow, C., S. van Strien and C. Harris (2008) 'Fictitious Play in 3 x 3 Games: The Transition between Periodic and Chaotic Behaviour', *Games and Economic Behaviour*, vol. 63, pp. 259–291.

Spence, M. (1974) *Market Signaling: Informational Transfer in Hiring and Related Screening Processes* (Cambridge, MA: Harvard University Press).

Spinoza, B. (1677) *Tractatus politicus*. Edited with an Introduction by R. H. M. Elwes. Translated by A. H. Gosset (London: G. Bell & Son, 1883).

van Strien, D. and C. Sparrow (2011) 'Fictitious Play in 3x3 Games: Chaos and Dithering Behavior', *Games and Economic Behavior*, vol. 73, pp. 262–286.

Sugden, R. (1986) *The Economics of Rights, Co-operation and Welfare* (Oxford: Basil Blackwell).

Wagner, E. (2010) 'The Dynamics of Costly Signaling', IMBS Working Paper. University of California, Irvine.

Wagner, E. (2011) 'Deterministic Chaos and the Evolution of Meaning', *British Journal for Philosophy of Science*. Doi: 10.1093/bjps/axr039. First published online 16 December 2011.

Young, H. P. (1993) 'An Evolutionary Model of Bargaining', *Journal of Economic Theory*, vol. 59, pp. 145–168.

6

The Role of Salience in the Emergence and Reproduction of Norms*

Robert Sugden
University of East Anglia, UK

Decision and game theory engage with morality in at least two ways. The first kind of engagement occurs when moral philosophers, or economists playing the role of moral philosophers, use ideas from the theory of rational choice in describing systems of moral thought. Rational choice motifs can be found in many of the theories that moral philosophers discuss, including classical utilitarianism, egalitarianism, contractarianism, libertarianism, welfarism, John Rawls's theory of justice, and Amartya Sen's theory of capabilities. This philosophical tradition can be traced back to those Enlightenment thinkers who tried to ground morality in Reason. Some writers in this tradition may still see themselves as seeking to discover moral truths through the exercise of pure reason, but I think it is more useful to see this kind of philosophy as an attempt to systematize widely-held moral intuitions and to work out their implications. On this view, propositions about rational choice do not have substantive implications about the content of morality, but they impose conditions of internal consistency on the systematization that philosophers construct.

The second kind of engagement occurs when social scientists try to explain the moral beliefs that in fact are professed and upheld by ordinary people – people who are not thinking about morality as professional philosophers or moralists. One might think, as I do, that such beliefs *are* the 'moral intuitions' that it is the job of moral philosophy to systematize. (Could it be that by practising moral philosophy one can somehow gain access to a superior kind of intuition, and hence that moral philosophy might justifiably concern itself with systematization the intuitions *of moral philosophers*? I think Ken Binmore (2005: 1) is right to say that moral philosophers 'have no more access to some noumenal world of moral absolutes than the boy who delivers our newspapers.') Decision and game theory become relevant for this second kind of enquiry if one entertains the hypothesis that actual moral beliefs are shaped by people's experiences of recurrent interaction with one another. Very roughly, the hypothesis is that if the members of some population recurrently face problems of coordination and cooperation, conventions for resolving those problems will tend to emerge, and that those conventions will tend to acquire the aura of morality. This way of thinking about morality is fundamental to David Hume's (1739–40/1978) analysis of the principles of justice. Following the invention of game theory, it has become possible to see that important parts of Hume's analysis are game theory *avant la lettre*; more explicitly game-theoretic developments of the Humean approach have been made by, among others, David Lewis (1969), Brian Skyrms (1996), Peyton Young (1998), Binmore (2005), and me (Sugden, 2004).

If the explanation of people's actual moral beliefs is to be a genuine enterprise of empirical science, it is essential to start from an empirical concept of morality. The whole purpose of the research program would be defeated if we *defined* 'morality' in such a way that a belief could count as moral only if it were consistent with some pre-specified account of goodness and badness, rightness and wrongness. Thus, we need a theoretical framework which permits the possibility that slavery, rape, incest and genocide are believed to be moral. We might hope to show that, in the environments in which we now live, such possibilities are unlikely to be realized; but that must be treated as an empirical hypothesis in need of verification and explanation, not a proposition that can be made true by definition. The most useful starting point, I suggest, is that taken by Hume (1739–40/1978: 455–476, 574–591). It is to treat morality as *generalized approval*, where 'approval' is a particular kind of psychological sensation that is directed at whatever is approved and that is perceived as pleasurable. Hume argues that if some conventional rule of behavior becomes established in some social group, and if that rule allows people to solve coordination problems to their mutual advantage, then behavior in accordance with the convention will tend to be the object of generalized approval. In other words, a disposition to behave in accordance with the convention will be seen as a virtue. (In the modern literature, this feature of Hume's theory is developed particularly explicitly by Lewis and – using Lewis's analysis as a starting point – by me.)

The qualification 'generalized' makes a distinction between moral approval and mere preference. (If I enjoy gardening, I may feel a pleasurable sense of self-congratulation when I work in my garden; but for this sensation to be moral I must also feel a sense of approval when *you* work in *your* garden.) But what is in fact the subject of generalized approval may not be the sort of thing that features in the theories discussed by moral philosophers. (Indeed, it is quite plausible to suppose that keen gardeners *do* give generalized approval to gardening.) Of more serious import, what is in fact the subject of generalized approval may be the sort of thing that received moral theories treat as *im*moral. Suppose I am a slaveholder in eighteenth-centuryAmerica. If I not only approve of my own ownership of slaves but also approve of other people's ownership of them, then *for me* slavery is moral.

If we are to use the concept of 'generalization' to define an empirical research program, we should not think of generalization in terms of elaborate veil-of-ignorance thought experiments or consistency tests: to do that would be to impose too much pre-specification on moral beliefs. Thus, for the American slaveholder's beliefs to count as moral, he does not have to certify that he would approve of being kidnapped by a hypothetical slave trader and shipped off to slavery in a hypothetical African country. If he feels approval for the actual enslavement of Africans by Americans but disapproval for the hypothetical enslavement of Americans by Africans, one might want to say that his moral beliefs are inconsistent or arbitrary; but that does not mean that they are not moral beliefs at all.

This marks a significant difference between the moral philosopher's perspective on morality and that of the empirical social scientist. Because the moral philosopher is trying to *systematize* moral intuitions, she is entitled to treat consistency and non-arbitrariness as desirable properties of her systematizations. But the task of the empirical social scientist is to discover and explain the general properties of *actual* moral beliefs. Whether actual moral beliefs are consistent or inconsistent, arbitrary or non-arbitrary, are among the issues that a Humean research programme should investigate. If moral beliefs have grown up around conventions that are the products of spontaneous social evolution – if, as Binmore (1994: 145) puts it, they are what evolution has washed up on the beach – we must be willing to entertain the possibility that they are sometimes inconsistent or arbitrary, as viewed in the perspective of moral philosophy.

In particular, there are good reasons to expect this kind of arbitrariness in moral beliefs about the distribution of property rights. In the Humean perspective, property rights are conventional solutions to recurrent problems of conflict over valuable resources. Hume (pp. 501–13) argues that the process by which these solutions emerge is likely to favor conventions of property that make use of pre-existing and psychologically salient relations between claimants and disputed objects, and that among the most salient such relations are being the first possessor of the object (the principle of 'occupation') and having been in possession of the object for a long time ('prescription'). Thus, spontaneous social evolution will tend to induce moral beliefs about property which, seen from the viewpoint of moral philosophy, have an arbitrary conservative bias. In my own contributions to the Humean programme, I have endorsed Hume's conservative conclusions and have appealed to Thomas Schelling's (1960) theory of focal points to support the claim that salience plays an important role in the emergence of conventions (Sugden 2004: 91–107). However, this claim is controversial. Most evolutionary game theorists have not treated salience as a significant explanatory principle. In this paper, I explain why I believe the claim to be correct.

6.1   The Right Turn Problem

In understanding how moral beliefs can emerge as salient solutions to coordination problems, it is useful to think about such problems in ordinary life. Consider a coordination problem that is faced by road users: who should give way to whom in which circumstances? More specifically, consider the following problem.[1]

At most British road junctions, driving behavior is governed by priority rules that are designated by the highway authorities. Normally, one road through a junction is assigned priority; 'Give way' signs and road markings on the other routes signify that vehicles on those routes must yield priority to the traffic on the major road. This system works well at T-junctions, but has proved to be dangerous at crossroads – so much so that, outside towns, crossroads have progressively been replaced either by roundabouts or by pairs of slightly offset T-junctions. Where crossroads survive, drivers continually confront the Right Turn Problem. Consider a crossroads at which the east–west road has priority. Suppose this road is clear. One vehicle is approaching the junction on the minor road from the north, indicating the intention to go straight ahead; another is approaching on the minor road from the south, signalling to turn right. Since the UK drives on the left, their paths will cross. Which vehicle should give way to which? Failure to resolve this coordination problem can result in two stationary vehicles in the middle of the junction – a very dangerous outcome, since major-road drivers (who do not expect to have to give way to anyone) may be approaching the junction at speed.

Surprisingly, the Highway Code (the official codification of the rules of the road in Britain) provides no guidance on this question. A few years ago, I was driving my car near my home, approaching a crossroads which I knew to be an accident blackspot. I was flagged down by a police officer who said he was stopping drivers to warn them of how dangerous this crossroads was. I told him that I knew this already, and that the source of the danger seemed to be the Right Turn Problem: could he tell me the priority rule for this case? He said that as far as he knew, there was no rule; one should maintain eye contact with the other driver and (in effect) negotiate priority on a case-by-case basis. However, he added the unofficial advice that he thought there was a tendency for drivers to follow a certain unofficial convention, which I will explain later.

A game theorist would represent the Right Turn Problem as a two-player game that is played recurrently and anonymously in a large population. Table 6.1 represents a simplified version of the game in normal form, with what I stipulate to be its payoffs. This game has a Battle of the Sexes structure, except that I have assumed that both players have a slight preference for (*give way, give way*) over (*proceed, proceed*). The idea here is that either form of discoordination of initial intentions will lead to delay, because of the need for an on-the-spot negotiation

Table 6.1   The right turn problem (version 1)

		P2 (driver going straight on)	
		proceed	*give way*
P1 (driver turning)	*proceed*	0,0	10,9
	give way	9,10	2,2

of who goes first; but if both drivers move forward, this negotiation will take place in the path of vehicles on the main road.

If the game is presented in this form, it has two pure-strategy Nash equilibria, (*proceed, give way*) and (*give way, proceed*). Each of these equilibria can be interpreted as a putative convention for recurrent play; the first corresponds with the rule 'straight-on gives way to turn' and the second with the rule 'turn gives way to straight-on'. If one looks only at those features of the game that are recognised by conventional game theory – that is, those that are represented by the formal structure of strategies and payoffs – these two conventions are isomorphic with one another. They differ only in respect of the *labels* that are attached to the players and strategies.

Do such labels matter? It is now widely recognised that in real world *one-shot* games, players often *do* take account of the labels that feature in their own descriptions of those games, and that these labels can play an important role in equilibrium selection. As first hypothesized by Schelling (1960), players recognize (and expect their co-players to recognise) that, by virtue of differences in labeling, some equilibria are more 'prominent' or 'salient' than others; there is a systematic tendency for the most salient equilibrium (the 'focal point') to be selected. There is now a large body of experimental evidence which confirms this hypothesis in relation to pure coordination games (e.g. Mehta et al. 1994; Crawford et al. 2008), and some evidence that this result extends to coordination games with slightly asymmetric payoffs when these are framed in ways suggestive of real world bargaining (Isoni et al. 2011). If one considers the Right Turn Problem as a one-shot game, the labels do seem potentially relevant, although it is not immediately obvious which of the two ways of coordinating is more salient. If one thinks of the minor road as a continuous route across the junction, it may seem natural to give priority to the vehicle going straight ahead. However, that perception is weakened by the significance that has been assigned to the major road. An opposing thought, encouraged by experience of offset T-junctions and roundabouts, is that the right-turning vehicle is joining the major road, and so inherits the priority of major-road vehicles after it has turned.

But does labeling influence the emergence of conventions in *recurrent* games? Salience has received surprisingly little attention from evolutionary game theorists.[2] In standard evolutionary game-theoretic models, equilibria are reached by dynamic processes of experiential learning, such as replicator dynamics or fictitious play; and these processes are represented without reference to how strategies are labeled. If players' strategies and payoffs are completely symmetrical with one another, conventions are modeled as originating in symmetry-breaking perturbations. In a criticism of Lewis's (1969) use of salience in explaining the reproduction of conventions, Skyrms (1996: 93) appeals to a model of symmetry-breaking, arguing that which convention emerges is a matter of chance, not salience. Skyrms' discussion of the emergence of conventions is entitled 'Birds do it.' What Skyrms means by this is that some features of bird behavior are conventions in the game-theoretic sense. The suggestion is that perceptions of salience are beyond the cognitive capacity of birds, and hence that the existence of these conventions must be explained without reference to salience. And so (we are invited to think) the concept of salience might be redundant for the explanation of human conventions.

As a first step in arguing that salience *is* relevant to recurrent games, I return to the unofficial advice I received from the police officer. He thought that priority tended to be given to whichever of the minor-road vehicles reached the crossroads first. (He didn't elaborate, but on a natural application of this rule to the case of queues, a vehicle is deemed to have reached the junction only when it gets to the front of its queue; so if there are queues on both minor roads, drivers take turns to proceed.) My subsequent experience has persuaded me that this was good advice: there *is* a tendency for priority to be determined by order of arrival, even though that tendency is not strong enough to make crossroads safe.

For my present purposes, the point of this story is that there is an alternative representation of the Right Turn Problem – the one shown in Table 6.2. In one sense, the only differences between version 1 (in which P1 is the turning driver) and version 2 (in which P1 is the first arrival) are matters of labeling. So does it matter if some players think of the problem in terms of one set of labels and others think of it in terms of the other?

If every instance of the Right Turn Problem were exactly the same as every other, it might reasonably be argued that this difference of labeling would not affect a symmetry-breaking model of the emergence of conventions. In any given instance of the problem, one driver is turning and the other is going straight

Table 6.2 The right turn problem (version 2)

		P2 (second arrival)	
		proceed	*give way*
P1 (first arrival)	*proceed*	0,0	10,9
	give way	9,10	2,2

on; and one driver is the first arrival and one is the second arrival. If every instance really were exactly the same as every other, the connection between these two labeling features would remain constant: *either* it would always be the case that the first arrival was turning, *or* it would always be the case that the first arrival was going straight on. To keep the discussion concrete, I consider the first possibility. In this case, the rule 'straight-on gives way to turn' prescribes exactly the same behavior as 'first gives way to second' (and, correspondingly, 'turn gives way to straight-on' prescribes exactly the same behavior as 'second gives way to first'). The only difference between the two rules is a matter of labeling. To put this another way, there are only two possible conventions of behavior, even though each of these conventions can be described in two different ways.

Now consider the implications of this for a symmetry-breaking account of the emergence of conventions. Imagine a population of players of the Right Turn Problem in which some proportion, λ, of the players use the version 1 labels ('straight-on' and 'turn') and the rest use the version 2 labels ('first' and 'second'). Suppose that initially, no one conditions their behavior on the labels, and strategy choices are in mixed strategy equilibrium: *proceed* is played with probability 8/17). Now suppose that, as a result of random perturbations, there happens to be an interval of time in which the relative frequency with which *proceed* is chosen by turning drivers and with which *give way* is chosen by straight-on drivers is μ, where μ is greater than 8/17. Using a symmetry-breaking argument, suppose that individuals who use the version 1 labels recognise this pattern and begin to adapt to it. That is, they begin to switch to the strategy that is the best response to this pattern, namely the rule 'straight-on gives way to turn.' But, since all games are identical with one another by assumption, it must be the case that in the same interval of time, the relative frequency with which *proceed* is chosen by first arrivals (and with which *give way* is chosen by second arrivals) is also μ. So individuals who use the version 2 labels observe the same asymmetric pattern in other players' behavior, even though they describe it in different terms. They will begin to switch to the strategy that is the best response to this pattern, namely the rule that they describe as 'second gives way to first.' But this rule generates exactly the same behavior as 'straight-on gives way to turn.' Thus, if we (as analysts) are interested only in explaining how conventions *of behavior* emerge, we need take no account of differences in individuals' use of labels. In particular, there is no reason to expect that which convention is more likely to emerge will be systematically affected by the value of λ.

However, real world instances of the Right Turn Problem are *not* identical with one another. Consider how the symmetry-breaking argument presented in the preceding paragraphs would be affected if one made the much more realistic assumption that the turn/straight-on and first/second distinctions were completely uncorrelated.

Suppose, as before, that version 1 labels are used by a proportion, λ, of the population, and that we start from a mixed-strategy equilibrium in which *proceed* is played with probability 8/17. To keep the assumptions as close as possible to those used in the case of identical games, suppose that random perturbations produce an interval of time in which the relative frequency with which *proceed* is played by both first arrivals and turning drivers, and with which *give way* is played by both second arrivals and straight-on drivers, is μ, where $\mu > 8/17$.[3] Individuals who use version 1 labels will tend to switch to 'straight-on gives way to turn,' while those who use version 2 labels will tend to switch to 'second gives way to first.' But (in contrast to the case of identical games) these rules do *not* prescribe the same behavior: each rule helps individuals to coordinate with, but only with, those individuals who use it. If the labels used by each individual are fixed, and if λ is not too close to 0 or 1,[4] two parallel conventions will emerge, and full coordination will not be achieved. Since average payoffs will be greater for players who follow the convention that is followed by the majority of the population, one might expect a long-run (and self-reinforcing) tendency for individuals who initially follow the minority convention to learn to recognize the labeling asymmetry that the majority use and to switch to their convention.

The implication is that when different instances of a recurrent coordination problem are similar but not identical to one another, which convention is more likely to emerge depends on which labels are more commonly used in the population. To put this more generally: other things being equal, we should expect the conventions by which coordination problems are resolved to be based on labeling asymmetries that are particularly salient.

6.2   Labels and similarity

To help to explain what it means to say that a labeling asymmetry is salient, I now present a stylized model of the Right Turn Problem which allows a much more general representation of individuals' different perceptions of labeling.

In this model, a game with the symmetric payoff matrix that is common to Tables 6.1 and 6.2 is played recurrently and anonymously in a large population; players are randomly re-matched between games. *As viewed by the modeler*, each game is an interaction between two drivers at a crossroads, one going straight on and the other turning right. However, I do not assume that players conceptualize the interaction in these terms. Instead, the mechanism of labeling is as follows.

In any given instance of the game, each of the two players sees the same *image*. This can be thought of as a photograph or video of the relevant interaction, prior to the point at which each player has to decide whether to proceed or to give way. It shows features of the interaction that would be visible to both drivers but which are not represented in the payoff matrix – which driver is turning, which driver arrived first, what kinds of vehicle are being driven, the landscape surrounding the crossroads, the time of day, the state of the weather, and so on. Each image has two *orientations*, corresponding with the viewpoints of the two drivers; one player sees the image in one orientation, the other sees it in the other. For example, one player might see an image showing a first-to-arrive Ford van turning right and a second-to-arrive Volkswagen car going straight on, with an orientation that showed him that he was driving the van; the other player would see exactly the same image, but with an orientation showing her that she was driving the car. Having seen the relevant *orientated image* (that is, the image and its orientation in relation to her), each player chooses *proceed* or *give way*, knowing that the consequences of the two players' choices will be as shown in the payoff matrix. To keep things simple, I assume that there is a very large finite set G of images. Each image g is a set $\{g^+, g^-\}$, where g^+ and g^- are the two orientations of g. For each instance of the game, an image is drawn at random from G; which orientation is seen by which player is determined at random.

As modelers, we can define objective properties that orientated images may or may not possess. Some such properties have perfect negative correlation, that is, if one orientation of any image has the property, the other orientation does not. Among these properties are *first* (the relevant driver is the first arrival), *second* (equivalent to 'not *first*'), *turn* (the relevant driver is turning) and *straight-on* (equivalent to 'not *turn*').[5] Other properties have perfect positive correlation (for example, 'it is raining'); yet others may be uncorrelated (for example, 'the relevant driver is in a red car'). I do not assume that players consciously recognise every (or even any) objective property, but merely that they have subjective perceptions of the degree of similarity between one orientated image and another. Formally, for each individual i there is a *similarity function* which assigns a real-valued index to every pair of orientated images. This index measures the degree of similarity between the two images, as subjectively perceived by i.

A natural way of modeling experiential learning in this version of the Right Turn Problem is suggested by Itzhak Gilboa and David Schmeidler's (1995) *case-based decision theory*. The essential idea is that when an individual faces a new decision problem, he recovers from memory other problems that he perceives as similar to it and in which he chose actions that led to satisfactory results; he then chooses the action in the new problem that is most similar to those previously successful actions. I now offer a very rough sketch of how this approach might be applied to the Right Turn Problem.[6]

In the context of the Right Turn Problem, the basic unit of memory for any given individual is a description of a previous instance of the game played by that individual. This description, which I will call an *episode*, is specified by the individual's orientated image, the individual's chosen strategy (*proceed* or *give way*), and the co-player's chosen strategy. An episode has a satisfactory outcome if and only if the two players choose different strategies, thereby achieving coordination (and giving the individual a payoff of at least 9); such an episode is a *success*. Each individual's *memory* is defined as the set that contains the N most recent cases (or the set of all previous cases, if there are no more than N of these); $N \geq 1$ is a parameter of the model. As a very simple model of similarity-based learning, assume that when an individual faces a new instance of the game, he retrieves from memory the episode which, of all successful episodes in memory, has the orientated image that he perceives as most similar to the orientated image of the new instance. He then chooses whichever strategy he chose in the retrieved episode. (If his memory contains no successful episode, he chooses at random.) This model defines a dynamic process of experiential learning in which strategy choices at any time t are stochastically determined by strategy choices made in previous periods. I now discuss some very general properties of this process.

From the perspective of the modeler, conventions are most naturally described in terms of objective properties of orientated images. For example, consider the convention that is described by the rule 'straight-on gives way to turn.' We might say that this convention is in operation over some extended time interval if, over that interval, the relative frequency with which *proceed* is chosen is greater than 0.5 for turning players (that is, players whose orientated images have the property *turn*) and less than 0.5 for straight-on players.[7] How might such a convention reproduce itself?

The mechanism of reproduction has two components. The first is that if a convention is in operation, strategy choices that are consistent with the relevant rule (for example, 'straight-on gives way to turn') are over-represented in players' memories of successful episodes. For example, suppose that up to some time t, turning players have chosen *proceed* with probability μ and straight-on players have chosen *give way* with the same probability μ, where $0.5 < \mu < 1$; I will say that μ is the *reliability* of the convention. And suppose that the choices of straight-on and turning players are stochastically independent. Aggregating over all instances of the game prior to t, the relative frequency of cases in which the turning player chose *proceed* and the straight-on player chose *give way* is μ^2; the relative frequency of cases in which coordination was achieved in the opposite way is $(1 - \mu)^2$. Thus, aggregating over all successful episodes in each player's memory, and ignoring the effects of random noise, the proportion of episodes that are consistent with the rule 'straight-on gives way to turn' is $\mu^2/[\mu^2 + (1 - \mu)^2]$, which is not only greater than 0.5 but also greater than μ.

The effect of this asymmetry in players' memories on behavior at time t depends on the second component of the reproduction mechanism. Consider a representative player i who, at time t, faces an instance of the game and sees the orientated image $g^\#$ (where $\# \in \{+, -\}$). Suppose that $g^\#$ has the property *turn*. (The analysis is exactly symmetrical if it has the property *straight-on*.) Whether i chooses *proceed* (that is, acts in accordance with the rule) or *give way* depends on which strategy was chosen in the episode that she retrieves from memory.

The assumption that is most favorable to the reproduction of the convention is that similarity perceptions are fully determined by the *straight-on/turn* property, so that with probability 1 the orientated image of the retrieved episode has the property *turn*. Under this extreme assumption, the convention is clearly self-amplifying: the probability with which i chooses in accordance with the rule is $\mu^2/[\mu^2 + (1 - \mu)^2] > \mu$. But it would be more plausible to assume that similarity perceptions are influenced by many different properties, of which *straight-on/turn* is only one. Let $h^\#$ be the orientated image in i's memory of successful episodes that she perceives as most similar to $g^\#$. It would be natural to assume that the probability that $h^\#$ has the property *turn* is greater than 0.5. (By virtue of the symmetry properties of the model, successful episodes in memory are equally likely to be *straight-on* or *turn*. Other things being equal, one would expect a given orientated image to be perceived as more similar to $g^\#$ if it is *turn* than if it is *straight-on*.) But this assumption is not enough to ensure that the convention retains its degree of reliability μ as it is reproduced. It implies only that, at t, individuals choose in accordance with the rule with a probability greater than 0.5, while what is needed is that this probability is greater than or equal to μ.

The implication of all this is that, in order for a convention to reproduce itself without losing reliability, the labeling asymmetry that it exploits must have a sufficiently close correspondence with players' subjective perceptions of similarity. In other words, the labeling asymmetry must have a sufficient degree of psychological salience.

6.3   Conclusion

I conclude that salience *does* play a significant role in the emergence and reproduction of conventions. If game theorists are to explain which conventions are followed in a population, they must be prepared to take account of individuals' subjective perceptions of similarity between labels, even if this requires game theory to deal with ideas that have traditionally been thought of as the preserve of psychology or cultural history. And if one accepts the Humean hypothesis that repeated experience of the operation of a convention tends to induce moral approval for the behavior that the convention requires, one must recognize that people's actual moral beliefs will inherit the arbitrariness of whatever similarity judgments underlie the emergence and reproduction of conventions.

I end with a speculation about biology. Could my conclusion about salience apply not only to human conventions, but also to conventions observed in the behavior of other animals? As Skyrms might phrase the question: Can birds do it? It is difficult to imagine how any animal could learn from its experiences of a complex environment unless it was capable of recognising similarities between non-identical decision problems. Without such perceptions of similarity, a heuristic of repeating previously satisfactory actions and avoiding previously unsatisfactory ones would have little or no application. The learning model I have sketched in this paper is based on an extremely simple heuristic of this kind, combined with a basic ability to perceive similarities. My tentative conclusion, then, is that birds *can* do it.

Notes

* This paper builds on joint work with Federica Alberti, Shaun Hargreaves Heap and Kei Tsutsui. It is based on the talk I gave at the 'Social Norms' session of the 16th World Congress of the International Economic Association held at Tsinghua University, Beijing. I thank participants in this session for their comments.
1. The description of the Right Turn Problem is taken from Alberti et al. (2011).
2. One exception (in addition to my own work) is Binmore and Samuelson's (2006) evolutionary analysis of games in which it is costly to 'monitor' labels.
3. This asymmetry can be generated by assuming: (i) that in the 50 per cent of games in which the turning driver is the first arrival, *proceed* is played by the turning driver (and therefore also by the first arrival) with probability $\varphi > 8/17$, and *give way* is played by the straight-on driver (and therefore also by the second arrival) with the same probability φ; and (ii) that in other 50 per cent of games, *proceed* is played by both drivers with the equilibrium probability 8/17. Then $\mu = (\varphi + 8/17)/2$.
4. If λ is sufficiently close to 1 (that is, almost everyone uses version 1 labels), and if everyone who uses these labels follows the rule 'straight-on gives way to turn', the best response for a player who recognises only version 2 labels is *give way*, irrespective of whether she is first or second. A corresponding argument applies for version 1 players if λ is very close to 0.
5. For simplicity, I ignore the case in which two drivers arrive at exactly the same instant. The definition of the Right Turn Problem entails that there is always one and only one turning driver.
6. With two colleagues, I have proposed a specific similarity-based learning mechanism – the 'replication heuristic' – which requires only a one-period memory. We have examined its implications for a class of pure coordination games that can be implemented in a laboratory experiment (Alberti et al., 2011).
7. Some readers may ask why this definition uses a critical relative frequency of 0.5 rather than 8/17 as in the analysis in section 6.1. The explanation is that the case-based learning mechanism does not take account of expected payoffs except in so far as it distinguishes between 'satisfactory' and 'unsatisfactory' outcomes. Thus, it treats *proceed* and *give way* as isomorphic.

References

Alberti, Federica, Robert Sugden and Kei Tsutsui (2011) Salience as an Emergent Property. Unpublished paper, University of East Anglia.

Binmore, Ken (1994) *Game Theory and the Social Contract,* Volume I: *Playing Fair* (Cambridge, MA: MIT Press).

Binmore, Ken (2005) *Natural Justice* (Oxford: Oxford University Press).

Binmore, Ken and Larry Samuelson (2006) 'The Evolution of Focal Points', *Games and Economic Behavior,* vol. 55, pp. 21–42.

Crawford, Vincent P., Uri Gneezy, and Yuval Rottenstreich (2008) 'The Power of Focal Points is Limited: Even Minute Payoff Asymmetry May Yield Large Coordination Failures', *American Economic Review,* vol. 98, no.4, pp. 1443–1458.

Gilboa, Itzhak, and David Schmeidler (1995) 'Case-based Decision Theory', *Quarterly Journal of Economics,* vol. 110 no. 3, pp. 605–639.

Hume, David (1739–40/1978) *A Treatise of Human Nature* (Oxford: Oxford University Press).

Isoni, Andrea, Anders Poulsen, Robert Sugden and Kei Tsutsui (2011) Focal Points in Tacit Bargaining Games. CBESS Working Paper 11–13, University of East Anglia.

Lewis, David (1969). *Convention: A Philosophical Study* (Cambridge, MA: Harvard University Press).

Mehta, Judith, Chris Starmer and Robert Sugden (1994) 'The Nature of Salience: An Experimental Investigation of Pure Coordination Games', *American Economic Review,* vol. 84, no. 3, pp. 658–673.

Schelling, Thomas C. (1960) *The Strategy of Conflict* (Cambridge, MA: Harvard University Press).

Skyrms, Brian (1996) *Evolution of the Social Contract* (Cambridge: Cambridge University Press).

Sugden, Robert (2004). *The Economics of Rights,Cooperation and Welfare,* second edition (Basingstoke: Palgrave Macmillan; first edition 1986).

Young, H. Peyton (1998). *Individual Strategy and Social Structure: An Evolutionary Theory of Institutions* (Princeton, NJ: Princeton University Press).

7

Fairness as an Equilibrium Selection Device

Ken Binmore*
University College London, UK

7.1 Evolution of fairness

The vampire bat is an exotic example of a food-sharing species. The bats roost in caves in large numbers during the day. At night, they forage for prey, from whom they suck blood if they can, but they are not always successful. If they fail to obtain blood for several successive nights, they die. The evolutionary pressure to share blood is therefore strong.

The biologist Wilkinson (1984) reports that a hungry bat begs for blood from a roostmate, who will sometimes respond by regurgitating some of the blood it is carrying in its own stomach. This would not be too surprising for related roostmates, but the bats also share blood with roostmates who are not relatives. Such behavior can nevertheless be evolutionarily stable if the sharing is done on a *reciprocal* basis, so that bats are more likely to help out roostmates that have helped them in the past. Bats that refuse to help their fellows therefore risk not being helped themselves in the future.

Vampire bats have their own way of sharing, and we have ours. We call our way of sharing 'fairness.' If the accidents of our evolutionary history had led to our sharing in some other way, it would not occur to us to attribute some special role to our current fairness norms.

7.2 The original position

How do our fairness norms work? My thesis is that all the fairness norms that we actually use in daily life have a common deep structure (Binmore 2005, 1994, 1996). John Rawls (1972) refers to this deep structure as the *original position*.

Rawls uses the original position as a hypothetical standpoint from which to make judgments about how a just society should be organized. Members of a society are asked to envisage the social contract to which they would agree *if* their current roles were concealed from them behind a 'veil of igno-rance.' Behind this veil, the distribution of advantage in the planned society would seem determined as though by a lottery. 'Devil take the hindmost' then becomes an unattractive principle for those bargaining in the original position, since you yourself might end up with the lottery ticket that assigns you to the rear.

However, I do not follow Rawls in talking about the major coordination prob-lems faced by a nation state. Our sense of fairness did not evolve for use on such a grand scale. Nor do I follow Rawls in regarding the original position as an operationalization of Immanuel Kant's categorical imperative. The idea of the original position certainly hits the spot with most people when they first hear of it, but I do not believe this is because they have a natural bent for meta-physics. I think it is because they recognize a principle that matches up with the fairness norms that they actually use every day in solving the equilibrium selection problem in the myriads of small coordination games of which daily life largely consists.

The sort of coordination problems I have in mind are those that we commonly solve without thought or discussion. Who goes through that door first? Who moves how much in a narrow corridor when a fat lady burdened with shopping passes a teenage boy with a ring through his nose? Who gets that parking space? Whose turn is it to wash the dishes tonight? These are picayune problems, but if conflict arose every time they needed to be solved, our societies would fall apart.

Most people are surprised at the idea that there might be something problem-atic about how two people pass each other in the corridor. In such situations, our fairness program usually runs well below the level of consciousness, as with our internal routines for driving cars or tying shoelaces. Like Molière's Mon-sieur Jourdain, who was delighted to discover that he had been speaking prose all his life, we act morally in small-scale coordination problems without know-ing that we are moral. Just as we only take note of a thumb when it is sore, we tend to notice moral rules only when they are applied in situations for which they are not adapted. We are then in the same position as Konrad Lorenz when he observed a totally inexperienced baby jackdaw go through all the motions of taking a bath when placed on a marble-topped table. By triggering such instinctive behavior under pathological circumstances, Lorenz learned a great deal about what is instinctive and what is not when a bird takes a bath. But this vital information is gained only by avoiding the mistake of supposing that bath-taking behavior confers some evolutionary advantage on birds placed on marble-topped tables.

Similarly, one can learn a lot about the mechanics of moral algorithms by triggering them under pathological circumstances – but only if one does not make the mistake of supposing that the moral rules are adapted to the coordination problems they fail to solve. However, it is precisely from such sore-thumb situations that I think traditional moralists (and some modern behavioral economists) derive their ethical claims. We discuss these and only these situations endlessly, because our failure to coordinate successfully brings them forcefully to our attention.

7.3   Justice as fairness

Rawls (1972) reduces justice to fairness. I think our traditional personification of justice as a blindfolded matron bearing a pair of scales in one hand and a sword in the other provides some support for this reduction. Her blindfold can be identified with Rawls' veil of ignorance, but what of her scales and her sword?

Justice needs her scales behind the veil of ignorance to weigh up the relative well-being of different people in different situations. The issue of how interpersonal comparisons are to be made is often treated as a side issue of no great importance by traditional moral philosophers, but it is clearly necessary for people to be able to make such comparisons in order for it to be possible for them to use the original position to make fairness judgments. If we were not able to say whether we thought it preferable to be Adam in one situation as opposed to being Eve in another, we would be helpless to say anything at all behind the veil of ignorance.

Under mild conditions, John Harsanyi (1977) showed that such empathetic preferences – preferences requiring us to put ourselves in the position of another to see things from their point of view – can be summarized by naming a rate at which Adam's units of utility are to be traded off against Eve's units. But how do we acquire such standards of interpersonal comparison to which we implicitly appeal every time we make a fairness judgment?

Modern philosophers typically pay even less attention to the sword carried by our blindfolded matron. They neglect the enforcement question because they commonly take for granted that fairness exists to trump the unbridled use of power that they think would otherwise reign supreme. However, I shall be arguing that fairness evolved as a means of *balancing* power rather than as a *substitute* for power. Without power being somehow exercised in her support, our blindfolded matron would be no more than a utopian fancy. As Thomas Hobbes put it: covenants without the sword are but words.

John Mackie (1977) is an exception to the current philosophical orthodoxy. His book *Ethics: Inventing Right and Wrong* first debunks the standard metaphysical arguments for absolute moral systems, and then proposes that scientific alternatives need to be based on anthropological data to be analyzed using game theory as a conceptual framework. What anthropological data does he have in mind?

7.4   Pure foraging societies

There is no shortage of cultural differences between Kalarahi bushmen, African pygmies, Andaman islanders, Greenland eskimos, Australian aborigines, Paraguayan indians, and Siberian nomads, but the consensus is strong among modern anthropologists that these and other pure hunter-gatherer societies that survived into the twentieth century all operated social contracts without bosses or social distinctions in which food, especially meat, was shared on a markedly egalitarian basis. Even Westermarck, a leading anthropologist who was once infamous for his moral relativism, agreed that the Golden Rule – 'do as you would be done by' – was universally endorsed in such societies.

Two caveats are important here. The first is that it really matters that we are talking about *pure* foraging societies, in which the economic means of production remained the same as among our ancestors before the agricultural revolution of ten thousand or more years ago. The evidence is strong that a society's social contract evolves in tandem with its economy. I suspect that one would look in vain for universal principles underlying the social contracts that cultural history generated in different times and places after the agricultural revolution.

The second caveat is that one needs to put aside the idea that the egalitarianism of pure foraging societies makes them pastoral idylls of noble savages. Infanticide and murder are common. So is selfishness. Citizens of foraging societies do not honor their social contract because they like giving up food when they are hungry. They will therefore cheat on the social contract by secretly hoarding food if they think they can get away with it. The reason they comply with the norm most of the time is because their fellows will punish them if they do not.

Nor need there be anything nice about how food and other possessions are shared. In some societies, a fair allocation is achieved through 'tolerated stealing.' Eve may grab something of Adam's because she thinks he has more than his fair share. If everybody else agrees, Adam is helpless to resist. Even when possessions are voluntarily surrendered to others, the giver will sometimes explain that he or she is only complying with the norm to avoid being the object of the envy that precedes more serious sanctions.

There is therefore squabbling and pettiness aplenty in pure foraging communities, but there is also laughter and good fellowship. In brief, human nature seems much the same in foraging societies as in our own. I therefore think the strong parallels that anthropologists have uncovered between the social contracts of geographically distant groups living in starkly different environments have important implications for us. If their nature includes an instinctive disposition to use fairness norms that all share the deep structure of the Rawlsian original position, is it not likely that the same disposition is built into our nature too?

7.5 Game theory

A game is any situation in which people or animals interact. The plans of action of the players are called strategies. A Nash equilibrium is any profile of strategies – one for each player – in which each player's strategy is a best reply to the strategies of the others.

Nash equilibria are of interest for two reasons. If it is possible to single out the rational solution of a game, it must be a Nash equilibrium. For example, if Adam knows that Eve is rational, he would be stupid not to make the best reply to what he knows is her rational choice. The second reason is even more important. An evolutionary process that adjusts the players' strategy choices in the direction of increasing payoffs can only stop when it reaches a Nash equilibrium.

Because evolution stops working at an equilibrium, biologists say that Nash equilibria are evolutionarily stable (usually ignoring the fact that their formal definition includes further small print). Each relevant locus on a chromosome is then occupied by the gene with maximal fitness. Since a gene is just a molecule, it cannot *choose* to maximize its fitness, but evolution makes it appear as though it had. This is a valuable insight, because it allows biologists to use the rational interpretation of an equilibrium to predict the outcome of an evolutionary process, without following each complicated twist and turn that the process might take. This standard methodology in evolutionary game theory need not be confined to biology. In this paper, it needs to be applied to both biological and cultural evolution.

7.6 Coordination games

I think that fairness evolved as Nature's answer to the equilibrium selection problem in the human game of life. What is an equilibrium selection problem?

The Driving Game that we play each morning when driving to work provides the simplest example. The two-player version has three Nash equilibria. The two efficient equilibria require that both players either drive on the left, or both drive on the right.

In the inefficient equilibrium, both choose the side of the road on which to drive at random. If all the players care about is avoiding an accident, then there is no rational way of distinguishing between the two efficient equilibria. As Hume (1978) first explained, we need a generally understood social convention to select one of these equilibria on our behalf. Schelling (1960) famously referred to such conventions as focal points.

In Britain and Japan, the accidents of social history have made it conventional to drive on the left. In the USA and China, the convention is to drive on the right. I guess we have all driven in countries where the third equilibrium seems to be the norm. It would obviously be better for everybody in such countries to switch their convention to one of the efficient equilibria of the Driving Game, but such switches from one equilibrium to another are not necessarily easy to achieve in practice, especially when the Driving Game is replaced by an alternative (like the famous Battle of the Sexes) in which the players are not indifferent between the efficient equilibria, but each prefers a different convention favoring a different equilibrium.

Fortunately, our infant species was not faced with a game of life with such a difficult equilibrium selection problem as the Battle of the Sexes. Evolution needed to solve the equilibrium selection problem in some kind of *repeated* game.

7.7 Reciprocity

It is traditional to refer to the way a society organizes itself as its social contract. For me, this means regarding a social contract as the set of common understandings that allow the citizens of a society to coordinate on one of the many equilibria of their game of life. Game theorists think that only equilibria are viable in this role, because, when each citizen has independent goals which sometimes conflict with each other, only equilibria can survive in the absence of an external enforcement agency. In brief, only equilibria are self-policing.

The suggestion that a social contract is no more than a set of common understandings among players acting in their own enlightened self-interest commonly gets a skeptical reaction. How can anything very sturdy be erected on such a flimsy foundation? Surely a solidly built structure like the modern state must be based firmly on a rock of moral certitude, and only anarchy can result if everybody just does what takes their fancy?

I believe such objections to be misconceived. There are no rock-like moral certitudes that exist prior to society. To adopt a metaphor that sees such moral certitudes as foundation stones is therefore to construct a castle in the air. Society is more usefully seen as a dynamic organism, and the moral codes that regulate its internal affairs are the conventional understandings which ensure that its constituent parts operate smoothly together when it is in good health. Moreover, the origin of these moral codes is to be looked for in historical theories of biological, social and political evolution, and not in the works of abstract thinkers no matter how intoxicating the wisdom they distill. Nor is it correct to say that anarchy will necessarily result if everybody 'just' does what they want. Adam would be stupid in seeking to achieve a certain end if he ignored the fact that what Eve is doing may be relevant to the means for achieving that end.

Intelligent people will *coordinate* their efforts to achieve their individual goals without necessarily being compelled or coerced by real or imaginary bogeymen.

The extent to which simple implicit agreements to coordinate on an equilibrium can generate high levels of cooperation among populations of egoists is not something that is easy to appreciate in the abstract. That *reciprocity* is the secret has been repeatedly discovered, first by the ancient Chinese philosopher called Confucius in the West, and most recently by the biologist Trivers (1971) and the political scientist Axelrod (1984).

However, David Hume (1978: 521) had already put his finger on the relevant mechanism three hundred years before:

> I learn to do service to another, without bearing him any real kindness: because I foresee, that he will return my service, in expectation of another of the same kind, and in order to maintain the same correspondence of good offices with me or others. And accordingly, after I have serv'd him and he is in possession of the advantage arising from my action, he is induc'd to perform his part, as foreseeing the consequences of his refusal.

In spite of all the eighteenth-century sweetness and light, one should take special note of what Hume says about foreseeing the consequences of refusal. The point is that a failure to carry out your side of the arrangement will result in your being *punished*. The punishment may consist of no more than a refusal by the other party to deal with you in future. Or it may be that the punishment consists of having to endure the disapproval of those whose respect is necessary if you are to maintain your current status in the community. However, nothing excludes more active forms of punishment. In particular, the punishment might be administered by the judiciary, if the services in question are the subject of a legal contract.

At first sight, this last observation seems to contradict the requirement that the conventional arrangements under study be *self-policing*. The appearance of a contradiction arises because one tends to think of the apparatus of the state as somehow existing independently of the game of life that people play. But the laws that societies make are not part of the rules of this game. One *cannot* break the rules of the game of life, but one certainly can break the laws that man invents.

Legal rules are no more than particularly well-codified conventions. And policemen, judges, popes and kings do not exist outside society. Those charged with the duty of enforcing the laws that a society formally enacts are themselves only players in the game of life. However high-minded a society's officials may believe themselves to be, the fact is that society would cease to work in the long run if the duties assigned to them were incompatible with their own incentives. I am talking now about corruption. And here I do not have so much in mind the conscious form of corruption in which officials take straight bribes for services rendered. I have in mind the long-term and seemingly inevitable process by means of which bureaucracies gradually cease to operate in the interests of those they were designed to serve, and instead end up serving the interests of the bureaucrats themselves.

7.8 The folk theorem

Game theorists rediscovered Hume's insight that reciprocity is the mainspring of human sociality in the early 1950s when characterizing the outcomes that can be supported as equilibria in a repeated game. The result is known as the *folk theorem*, since it was formulated independently by several game theorists in the early 1950s. The theorem tells us that external enforcement is unnecessary to make a collection of Mr Hydes cooperate like Dr Jekylls; it is only necessary that the players be sufficiently patient and that they know they are to interact together for the foreseeable future. The rest can be left to their enlightened self interest, provided that they can all monitor each other's behavior without too much effort – as, for example, must have been the case when we were all members of small hunter-gatherer communities.

What outcomes can be sustained as Nash equilibria when a one-shot game is repeated an indefinite number of times? The answer provided by the folk theorem is very reassuring. Any mixture of outcomes in the one-shot game can be sustained as a Nash equilibrium outcome in the *repeated* game, provided that each player gets a payoff at least as large as the worst punishment that can be inflicted on him in the one-shot game if he knows how he is going to be punished.

Repeated games satisfying the conditions of the folk theorem therefore normally have an infinity of Nash equilibria, both efficient and inefficient. So they pose the equilibrium selection problem in an acute form. Our current convention might perhaps require us to operate an inefficient equilibrium, but the folk theorem tells us that any efficient outcome that we all prefer to the status quo can also be sustained as a Nash equilibrium – and hence we could all be made better off by changing our convention. Axelrod's (1984) computer simulations go on to suggest that we should expect evolution to organize such a reform spontaneously on our behalf if given long enough to operate in a stable environment.

Space does not allow a discussion of the difficulties that arise when seeking to see how far the folk theorem extends to a modern society in which each player's past history of play is often anything but an open book (Mailath and Samuelson 2006; Ostrom 2000). On the other hand, the theorem does provide the beginnings of an explanation of how cooperation is possible in societies without any need to postulate some real or invented source of external enforcement.

In practice, very few of the punishments that sustain a social contract are administered through the legal system. Indeed, nearly all punishments are administered without either the punishers or the victim being aware that a punishment has taken place. No stick is commonly flourished. What usually happens is that the carrot is withdrawn a tiny bit. Greetings are imperceptibly gruffer. Eyes wander elsewhere. These are all warnings that your body ignores at its peril.

The accounts that anthropologists offer of the higher stages of punishment observed among pure hunter-gatherer societies are particularly telling, since they mirror so accurately similar phenomena that the academic world uses to keep rogue thinkers in line. First there is laughter. If this does not work – and who likes being laughed at – the next stage is boycotting. Nobody talks to the offending party, or refers to their research. Only the final stage is maximal: a persistent offender is expelled from the group, or is unable to get his work published at all.

7.9   Selecting equilibria

The folk theorem says that indefinitely repeated games – including those markets that are repeated on a daily basis – usually have very large numbers of equilibria amongst which a choice must somehow be made. The response that only efficient equilibria need be considered does not help with this equilibrium selection problem, because efficient equilibria are also usually present in large numbers. But two facts do help. If disagreement arises over which of two equilibria should be adopted as conventional, there are always equilibria in between to serve as possible compromises. There is also always a payoff-enhancing path through intermediate equilibria from any inefficient equilibrium to any efficient equilibrium that everybody prefers.

One way of selecting an equilibrium is to delegate the task to a leader or an elite, but our foraging ancestors had no leaders or elites. Another equilibrium selection device was therefore necessary. Fairness is our name for the device that evolution came up with. In spite of our dressing this device up in fancy language, the unflattering truth is that our ancestors were fair for the much the same reason that the Chinese drive on the right and the Japanese on the left. Any solution to the equilibrium selection problem is better than none.

7.10   Deep structure of fairness

Recognition of the Golden Rule seems to be universal in human societies. Is there any reason why evolution should have written such a principle into our genes? Some equilibrium selection devices are obviously necessary for social life to be possible, but why should something like the Golden Rule have evolved?

Insuring against hunger. If the Golden Rule is understood as a simplified version of the device of the original position, I think an answer to this question can be found by asking why social animals evolved in the first place. This is generally thought to have been because food-sharing has survival value.

The advantages of sharing food among vampire bats are particularly strong – so strong that evolution seems to have taught even unrelated bats to share blood on a reciprocal basis. By sharing food, the bats are essentially *insuring* each other against hunger. Animals cannot write insurance contracts in the human manner, and even if they could, they would have no legal system to which to appeal if one animal were to hold up on his or her contractual obligation to the other. But the folk theorem tells us that evolution can get round the problem of external enforcement if animals interact together on a *repeated* basis.

By coordinating on a suitable equilibrium in their repeated game of life, two animals who are able to monitor each other's behavior sufficiently closely can achieve whatever could be achieved by negotiating a legally binding insurance contract. It will be easier for evolution to find its way to such an equilibrium if the animals are related, but the case of vampire bats shows that kinship is not necessary if the evolutionary pressures are sufficiently strong.

What considerations would Adam and Eve need to take into account when negotiating a similar mutual insurance pact? Imagine a time before cooperative hunting had evolved, in which Adam and Eve foraged separately for food. Like vampire bats, they would sometimes come home lucky and sometimes unlucky. An insurance pact between them would specify how to share the available food on days when one was lucky and the other unlucky.

If Adam and Eve were rational players negotiating an insurance contract, they would not know in advance who was going to be lucky and who unlucky on any given day on which the contract would be invoked. To keep things simple, suppose that both possibilities are equally likely. Adam and Eve can then be seen as bargaining behind a *veil of uncertainty* that conceals who is going to turn out to be Ms Lucky or Mr Unlucky. Both players then bargain on the assumption that they are as likely to end up holding the share assigned to Mr Unlucky as they are to end up holding the share assigned to Ms Lucky.

Original position. I think the obvious parallel between bargaining over such mutual insurance pacts and bargaining in the original position is no accident. To nail the similarity down completely, we need only give Adam and Eve new names when they take their places behind Rawls' veil of ignorance. To honor the founders of game theory, Adam and Eve will be called John and Oskar.

Instead of Adam and Eve being uncertain about whether they will turn out to be Ms Lucky or Mr Unlucky, the new set-up requires that John and Oskar pretend to be ignorant about whether they will turn out to be Adam or Eve. A move to the device of the original position then only requires that the players imagine themselves in the shoes of somebody else – either Adam or Eve – rather than in the shoes of one of their own possible future selves. If Nature wired us up to solve the simple insurance problems that arise in food-sharing, she therefore also simultaneously provided much of the wiring necessary to operate the original position.

Of course, in an insurance contract, the parties to the agreement do not have to *pretend* that they might end up in somebody else's shoes. On the contrary, it is the reality of the prospect that they might turn out to be Ms Lucky or Mr Unlucky that motivates their writing a contract in the first place. But when the device of the original position is used to adjudicate fairness questions, then John knows perfectly well that he is actually Adam, and that it is physically impossible that he could become Eve. To use the device in the manner recommended by Rawls (and Harsanyi), he therefore has to indulge in a counterfactual act of imagination. He cannot become Eve, but he must pretend that he could. How is this gap between reality and pretence to be bridged without assuming that Nature can jump from the simple to the complex in a single bound? As Linnaeus explained, Nature tinkers with existing structures rather than creating hopeful monsters *de novo*. To make a naturalistic origin for the device of the original position plausible, it is therefore necessary to give some account of what tinkering she might have done.

Expanding circles.   In Peter Singer's (1980) *The Expanding Circle*, the circle that expands is the domain within which moral rules are understood to apply. For example, Jesus sought to expand the domain of the principle that you should love your neighbor by redefining a neighbor to be anyone at all. How might evolution expand the domain within which a moral rule operates?

My guess is that the domain of a moral rule sometimes expands when players misread signals from their environment, and so mistakenly apply a piece of behavior or a way of thinking that has evolved for use within some inner circle to a larger set of people, or to a new game. When such a mistake is made, the players attempt to play their part in sustaining an equilibrium in the inner-circle game without fully appreciating that the outer-circle game has different rules. For example, Adam might treat Eve as a sibling even though they are unrelated. Or he might treat a one-shot game as though it were going to be repeated indefinitely often.

A strategy profile that is an equilibrium for an inner-circle game will not normally be an equilibrium for an outer-circle game. A rule that selects an equilibrium strategy in an inner-circle game will therefore normally be selected against if used in an outer-circle game. But there will be exceptions. When playing an outer-circle game as though it were an inner-circle game, the players will sometimes happen to coordinate on an equilibrium of the outer-circle game. The group will then have stumbled upon an equilibrium selection device for the outer-circle game. This device consists of the players behaving *as though* they were constrained by the rules of the inner-circle game, when the rules by which they are actually constrained are those of the outer-circle game.

I guess that nobody questions Aristotle's observation that the origins of moral behavior are to be found in the family. A game theorist will offer the explanation that the equilibrium selection problem is easier for evolution to solve in such games. The reason why is to be found in Hamilton's Rule, which explains that animals should be expected to care about a relative in proportion to their degree of relationship to the relative. For example, if Eve is Adam's full cousin, it makes evolutionary sense for him to count her fitness as worth one-eighth of his own fitness (because the probability is one-eighth that a newly mutated gene in his body responsible for modifying some relevant behavior is replicated in her body). Family relationships therefore provide a natural basis for making the kind of interpersonal comparison of utility that is necessary to operate the device of the original position.

The circle was then ready to be expanded by including strangers in the game by treating them as honorary or fictive kinfolk, starting with outsiders adopted into the clan by marriage or co-option. Indeed, if you only interact on a regular basis with kinfolk, what other template for behavior would be available?

The next step requires combining these two developments so that the original position gets to be used not just in situations in which Adam and Eve might turn out to occupy the role of Ms Lucky or Mr Unlucky themselves, but in which they proceed as though it were possible for each of them to turn out to occupy the role of the other person. To accept that I may be unlucky may seem a long way from contemplating the possibility that I might become another person in another body, but is the difference really so great? After all, there is a sense in which none of us are the same person when comfortable and well fed as when tired and hungry. In different circumstances, we reveal different personalities and want different things.

To pursue this point, consider what is involved when rational players consider the various contingencies that may arise when planning ahead. To assess these, players compute their expected utility as a weighted average of the payoffs of all the future people – lucky or unlucky – that they might turn out to be after the dice has ceased to roll. When choosing a strategy in a family game, players similarly take their payoffs to be a weighted average of the fitnesses of everybody in their family. In order to convert our ability to negotiate insurance contracts into a capacity for using fairness as a more general coordinating device in the game of life, all that is then needed is for us to hybridize these two processes by allowing players to replace one of the future persons that a roll of the dice might reveal them to be, by a person in another body. The empathetic preferences that are needed to assess this possibility require nothing more than that they treat this person in another body in much the same way that they treat their sisters, their cousins or their aunts.

Social indices.   It should be emphasized that I follow Harsanyi (1977) here in identifying the standard of interpersonal comparison necessary to make fairness judgments with the empathetic preferences with which Adam and Eve enter the original position. I follow the psychology literature in specifying this standard by assigning positive numbers to Adam and Eve, but I refer to these positive numbers as *social indices* rather than worthiness coefficients.

The social indices we use when discounting the fitnesses of our partners in a family game are somehow obtained by estimating our degree of relationship to our kinfolk from the general dynamics of the family and our place in it. But how do the social indices with which we discount a stranger's utils get into our own empathetic utility functions?

I do not think that we acquire the social indices we apply to different people at different times and in different contexts through any process of conscious reflection. Still less do we consult the works of moral philosophers. We pick up the appropriate social indices in much the same way as we pick up most of our social behavior; we unconsciously imitate the behavior of those of our fellow citizens whom we admire or respect. That is to say, I attribute our standard of interpersonal comparison of utility in dealing with folk outside our intimate circle of family and friends to the workings of social or cultural evolution.

7.11   Enforcement

The previous section offers a putative evolutionary explanation for why we personify Justice as a blindfolded matron bearing a pair of scales. But what of the sword that represents her powers of enforcement?

Harsanyi or Rawls?   The answer makes all the difference between whether the use of the original position leads to a utilitarian or an egalitarian conclusion. Space does not allow a review of the argument, but if we follow Harsanyi in assuming that the hypothetical deal reached in the original position is enforced by some outside agency, then the outcome will be utilitarian (Binmore 2005: chapter 10). On the other hand, if we admit no external enforcement at all, then the outcome is egalitarian (Binmore 2005: chapter 11).

Harsanyi (1977) invents an agency called 'moral commitment' that somehow enforces the hypothetical deal reached in the original position. Rawls (1972) similarly invents an agency called 'natural duty' for the same purpose. My own view is that we are not entitled to invent anything at all. If we treat the government of a modern state as an omnipotent but benign power whose function is to enforce the decisions made by the citizens under fair conditions, then Harsanyi's analysis provides a reason why the government should make decisions on a utilitarian basis. However, if there is no real (as opposed to invented) external enforcement agency, then Harsanyi's argument fails. In particular, it fails if the officers of a government are themselves treated as people with their own personal interests, just like any other citizen.

How come that Harsanyi is led to a utilitarian conclusion and Rawls to an egalitarian conclusion, given that they begin with the same assumptions? Game theorists trace the reason to Rawls' decision to deny orthodox decision theory. Without this iconoclastic expedient, he too would have been led to a utilitarian conclusion – although his *Theory of Justice* was explicitly written to provide a reasoned alternative to utilitarianism. My own view is that Rawls' purposes would have been better served if he had taken more seriously the concerns he refers to as the 'strains of commitment' in the third and longest part of his book. Taken to their logical extreme, these stability considerations require that everything involved in operating the original position must be self-policing. But then we are led to an egalitarian position not so very different from that he defends in his *Theory of Justice* without any need to throw orthodox decision theory out of the window.

Modern equity theory. There is some empirical support for the kind of egalitarian sharing to which one is led by analyzing the result of bargaining in the original position when all the arrangements must be self-policing (Wagstaff 2001). In this psychological literature, the theory is usually called 'modern' equity theory, although it goes all the way back to Aristotle's dictum that 'What is just ... is what is proportional.'

The theory says that people decide what is fair using the principle that each person's gain over the status quo should be proportional to the appropriate social index for that person in the relevant context. The fair outcome generated by such an egalitarian norm will generally be very different from the outcome generated by a utilitarian norm. The latter is determined by *dividing* each player's gain by the appropriate social index and then maximizing the sum of the corrected payoffs. Aside from other significant differences, a player gets more from the egalitarian norm if his social index is increased, but less from the utilitarian norm.

7.12 Moral relativism

Long ago, Xenophanes made an empirical observation which says everything that needs to be said about the supposedly universal character of the various supernatural entities that have been invented down the ages, 'The gods of the Ethiopians are black and flat-nosed, and the gods of the Thracians are red-haired and blue-eyed.' However, the fact that we all belong to the same species surely implies that some of our natural properties must be universal.

I think that one of these universal natural properties is the deep structure of fairness. If I am right, then all the fairness norms we use successfully in solving the small-scale coordination problems of everyday life are rooted in Rawls' original position. Space precludes giving the arguments, but a testable consequence is that we should expect all fairness norms that are actually used in all well-established societies to respond in the same way to changes in contextual parameters like need, ability, effort, and social status (Binmore 2005: chapter 11).

Although I believe that the deep structure of fairness is probably universal in the human species, the same cannot be true of the standard of interpersonal comparison that is needed to operate the device of the original position. This must be expected to vary, not only between cultures, but between different contexts in the same culture. Otherwise it would not be possible to explain the substantial differences in what is regarded as fair observed in different places and times.

If I am right, the analogy with language is therefore close. All our fairness norms share the same deep structure, but just as the actual language spoken varies between cultures and contexts, so does the standard of interpersonal comparison that determines who gets precisely how much of a surplus that is divided fairly. For example, my theory suggests that it will always be regarded as fair for a person with high social status to get a smaller share than a less exalted individual, but the exact amount by which their shares differ will depend on the cultural idiosyncrasies of the society in which they live.

7.13   Reform

My theory of fairness is an attempt at a descriptive theory; it seeks to explain how and why fairness norms evolved. Karl Marx might respond that it is all very well seeking to understand society, but the point is to change it, and I do not disagree. I hope very much that the scientific study of how societies really work will eventually make the world a better place for our children's children to live in, by clarifying what kind of reforms are compatible with human nature, and which are doomed to fail because they are not.

As an example, consider the pragmatic suggestion that we might seek to adapt the fairness norms that we use on a daily basis for settling small-scale coordinating problems to large-scale problems of social reform. This is one of the few things I have to say that traditional moralists find halfway acceptable. But they want to run with this idea without first thinking hard about the realities of the way that fairness norms are actually used in solving small-scale problems. In particular, they are unwilling to face up to the fact that fairness norms did not evolve as a substitute for the exercise of power, but as a means of coordinating on one of the many ways of balancing power.

This refusal to engage with reality becomes manifest when traditionalists start telling everybody how they 'ought' to make interpersonal comparisons when employing the device of the original position. But if I am right that the standards of interpersonal comparison we actually use as inputs when making small-scale fairness judgments are culturally determined, then these attitudes will necessarily reflect the underlying power structure of a society. One might wish, for whatever reason, that these attitudes were different. But the peddling of metaphysical arguments about what would be regarded as fair in some invented ideal world can only muddy the waters for practical reformers who actually have some hope of reaching peoples' hearts. Nobody is going to consent to a reform on fairness grounds if the resulting distribution of costs and benefits seems to them unfair according to established habit and custom, whatever may be preached from the pulpit.

It is true that facing up to such facts requires recognizing that it is sometimes pointless or counterproductive to urge reforms for which a society is not ready. What would anyone have gained by urging the abolition of slavery in classical times, when even Aristotle thought that barbarians were natural slaves? What of the emancipation of women at a time when even the saintly Spinoza took time out to expound on their natural inferiority? Instead of tilting at such windmills, I think reformers need to make a hard-nosed assessment of the nature of the current social contract, and all the possible social contracts into which it might conceivably be transformed by pushing on whatever levers of power are currently available. Only when one has seriously thought through this feasibility question is there any point in asking what is optimal.

This pragmatic attitude mystifies traditional moralists, who pretend not to understand how a naturalist like myself can talk about optimality at all. How do I know what is best for society? What is my source of authority? Where are my equivalents of the burning bush and the tablets of stone?

The answer is that I have no source of moral authority at all – but I think everyone else is in precisely the same boat. I know perfectly well that my aspirations for what seems a better society are just accidents of my personal history and that of the culture in which I grew up. If my life had gone differently or if I had been brought up in another culture, I would have had different aspirations. But I nevertheless have the aspirations that I have – and so does everyone else.

The only difference between naturalists and traditionalists on this score is that naturalists do not try to force their aspirations on others by appealing to some invented source of absolute authority. We do not need a source of authority to wish that society were organized differently. If there are enough people with similar aspirations sufficiently close to the levers of power, we can get together

and shift the social contract just because that is what we want to do – and for
no other reason.

Note

* I am grateful to the British Arts and Humanities Council for funding this work through
  grant AH/F017502/1.

References

Axelrod, R. (1984) *The Evolution of Cooperation* (New York: Basic Books).
Binmore, K. (1994) *Playing Fair: Game Theory and the Social Contract I* (Cambridge, MA:
  MIT Press).
Binmore, K. (1996) *Just Playing: Game Theory and the Social Contract II* (Cambridge, MA:
  MIT Press).
Binmore, K. (2005) *Natural Justice* (New York: Oxford University Press).
Harsanyi, J. (1977) *Rational Behavior and Bargaining Equilibrium in Games and Social
  Situations* (Cambridge: Cambridge University Press).
Hume. D. (1978) *A Treatise of Human Nature,* second edition (Oxford: Clarendon Press;
  first published 1739).
Mackie, J. (1977*) Ethics: Inventing Right and Wrong* (London: Penguin Books).
Rawls, J. (1972) *A Theory of Justice* (Oxford: Oxford University Press).
Schelling, T. (1960) *The Strategy of Conflict* (Cambridge, MA: Harvard University Press).
Singer, P. (1980) *The Expanding Circle: Ethics and Sociobiology* (New York: Farrar, Strauss and
  Giroux).
Trivers, R. (1971) 'The Evolution of Reciprocal Altruism', *Quarterly Review of Biology*, vol.
  46, pp. 35–56.
Wagstaff, G. (2001) *An Integrated Psychological and Philosophical Approach to Justice* (Lam-
  peter, Wales: Edwin Mellen Press)
Wilkinson, G. (1984) 'Reciprocal Food-sharing in the Vampire Bat', *Nature*, vol. 308. pp.
  181–184.

Part IV
Corporate Governance and Organization

8

A Shapley-Value Parable of Corporations as Evolutive Systems of Associational Cognition*

Masahiko Aoki
Stanford University, USA

8.1 Introduction: why corporations as systems of associational cognition

Orthodox economic and legal theory views the business corporation as the nexus of contracts in which the shareholders are endowed with residual claimant status (Jensen and Meckling 1976) as well as residual rights of control (Hart 1995), while the contracts are enforced by the state. However, the legal notion of 'corporations' as permanent entities historically emerged prior to the birth of modern nation states and business corporations. Although the legal concept of corporations is arguably said to have originated in the Roman era, it was in medieval Europe that the incorporation was initiated for various social functions and started to flourish in a variety of domains: religion, learning, politics, philanthropy, trades and crafts. Needless to say, contemporary business corporations are a highly developed form of the corporation that is both historically unparalleled and also still evolving. Their special features, such as the pooling of a large sum of financial capital and the transferability of its shares through markets, the capital market control of management, limited liability, and the organization of operational activities through various types of contracts, need to be understood in their own light and indeed understanding has been sought through the disciplines of economics, jurisprudence, finance theory, business studies and areas stuides. At the same time, however, business corporations share some generic features with other species of corporations that pursue different objectives than business and perform diverse social functions. This point is so obvious that it may appear not worthwhile mentioning. But reflecting a little on the generic features of corporations may help to shed light on some of the aspects of business corporations that are often left behind in specialized professional inquiries.

One common characteristic of corporations that is often emphasized is the generic nature of corporations as a 'permanent' entity or as having perpetual life. Indeed, it is obvious that corporations can do what individuals with limited biological longevity cannot do. For one thing, the corporate ability to own property, backed up by the institution of shared ownership and share transferability, makes the permanence of business corporations secure. However, what an individual cannot do but corporations can is not limited to owning and using physical assets. Actions, physical and cognitive, are also relevant. Corporations can organize by distributing cognitive and physical actions among members. Corporations as corporate bodies can cognize and store what a mere collection of individuals cannot. From this perspective, it is telling that the first prominent types of corporations that emerged in the early medieval period and became legal models preceding latter-day business forms of corporations were those 'founded *ad studendum et orandum* [for study and prayer], for the encouragement and support of religion and learning' (Blackstone 1765–9/2005).

The primary functions of these types of corporations were to understand or interpret the world, accumulate, theorize, and bestow knowledge for future uses and advancement, sustain culture as common knowledge and so on – although property ownership issues were not unimportant for them either. On the other hand, the primary purpose of business corporations is to make money, not to learn. But even for them, the reasons why incorporation is vital for religious and learning activities are not entirely irrelevant. As knowledge use and creation (that is, innovation) becomes an increasingly important resource for the competitiveness of business corporations, this point cannot be overlooked. Production and other activities taking place within the corporate firm may appear on the surface as a mere assemblage of individual physical actions, with physical externalities among them (for example, congestion in the use of corporate physical assets, the common use of digital files, and so on). However, all these individual human physical actions are coordinated by cognitive actions, while the physical actions and physical production assets provide extended resources for the latter. But the orthodox economic theory of contracts is implicitly premised on the idea that cognition can take place only within the mind of individuals. Thus people may hide their intentions, information, and so on to their individual advantage, unless they are provided with proper incentives to reveal them. This presumption indeed lies at the heart of microeconomics (the economics of information) that theoretically supported the shareholder-oriented view of business corporations in past decades. However, the recent development of experimental cognitive science, social brain science, and related areas increasingly provides evidence and theories that human cognition also takes place at the group level in some contexts.[1] Therefore, the way in which business corporations are organized as *group-level systems of cognition* deserves no less attention than the financial aspects of the corporation. Therefore, by business corporations I refer below to *organizations 'incorporating' systems of associational cognition for business purposes.*

Conceptualizing business corporations in that way does not imply, however, we should ignore incentive and governance issues that have constituted a focal attention of the orthodox economics. Within corporate organizations, cognitive activities are systematically distributed between the management and the workers, as well as among the workers, while the shareholders in effect supply cognitive tools to them based on their own cognitive judgment as regards the potential values of such internal cognitive linkages. However, the management, the workers and the shareholders certainly have different payoff functions and different cognitive skills (assets). In spite of these fundamental differences, under what conditions can they cooperate in their cognitive activities (and hence also in physical activities) as if they have a common quasi-identical objective and thus can in effect form a de facto 'team'? Section 8.2 discusses this fundamental issue by applying a recent achievement of potential game theory. In this discussion, the vital role of a fairness norm embedding the members of business corporations is to be clarified, without specifying its form. Section 8.3 turns attention more explicitly to the nature of cognitive assets of the management and the workers in their mutual relationships vis-à-vis physical assets as cognitive tools. These three-way relationships define the notion of essentiality/non-essentiality of the respective assets in a manner coherent with, and amplifying, discussions in the preceding section. Using this notion, section 8.4 narrates simple parables of varied forms of corporate architecture as systems of associational cognition connected with particular norms and governance. Then section 8.5 discusses how, as cognitive environments of corporations become increasingly complex, those corporate forms tend to evolve into modular systems of associational cognition incorporating reciprocal essentialities of the corporate stakeholders. This discussion logically clarifies the increasingly problematic nature of the orthodox premise of shareholder sovereignty. Section 6 concludes by discussing the implications of preceding discussions for the role of corporate law in corporate evolution.

8.2   The Shapley value payoffs allow individually-rational agents to form a team of associational cognition

The Nobel laureate Herbert Simon characterized the organization as

> the complex pattern of communications and other relations in a group of human beings. This pattern provides to each member of the group much of the information, assumptions, goals, attitudes that enter into his decisions, and provides him also with a set of stable and comprehensive explanations as to what the other members of the group are doing and how they will react to what he says and does (Simon 1957: xvi).

In this perspective, the nature of the organization as a system of associational cognition is clearly recognized. But how do individual members come to accept such a specified pattern and follow it as their own cognitive frame? In other words, under what kind of conditions can individually rational agents behave as if they have a common organizational purpose? A branch of theory called team theory is often invoked to design an 'optimal' informational structure of the organization (that is, an ideal system of associational cognition by distributing cognition among its members), contingent on organizational environments (Marschak and Radner 1972). But how can such design be implemented by organizational participants who may not have identical payoff functions?

A somewhat related question is raised by the orthodox principal–agent theory from an incentive perspective. In this framework, agents' tasks are supposed to be prescribed, while agents' preferences and information are supposed to be hidden from the principal as well as from each other. Under this situation, an agent's behavior is to be aligned with the principal's objective in the second-best sense through the principal's design of incentive contracts. Because of its individualistic approach characterized by the premise of hidden information, the only factor that is assumed to be public knowledge prior to a contract design is the so-called 'participation constraints' which are assumed market-conditioned.

Exploring what could be behind individual contracts seems to be the key to find a way to reconcile the information-system-design-oriented team theory and the incentive-contract-design-oriented principal–agency theory. Is it not that the emergence of group identity among 'individually-rational' agents playing an organizational game could be founded on, and mediated through, some deep structure of social contract? Indeed, a branch of game theory, that is, the potential game theory, suggests that such conjecture may make a sense, which then provides an information-incentive-integrated approach to comparative corporate organizations. The essence of its contributions can be simply stated as follows.

Suppose that N agents consider whether or not to join in an organizational collaborative venture. It can produce transferable value $F(x_1, \ldots x_i, \ldots x_N)$ with the effort contribution of the i-th agent represented by x_i, where $i = 1, \ldots N$. Suppose that the payoff of the i-th agent is represented by the form:

$$u^i(x_i) = G^i(F(x_1, \ldots x_i, \ldots x_N)) - c^i(x_i), or = 0 \text{ if } x_i = 0, \text{ for all } i.$$

This organizational game $\boldsymbol{u}$ is a potential game if there exists a single function $P(x_1, \ldots x_i, \ldots x_N)$ such that

$$P(x_1, \ldots x_i', \ldots x_N) - P(x_1, \ldots x_i'', \ldots x_N) = u^i(x_i') - u^i(x_i'')$$

for all $x_i', x_i'' (i = 1, \ldots, N)$ and for all $x_j (j \neq i)$. Namely, the individual payoff difference due to his/her own choice variation, given others' actions fixed, is equal to the value difference in P. P is then called a potential function. If a potential function exists, the set of Nash equilibrium of the organizational game $\boldsymbol{u}$

coincides with that of an identical interest game P in which every agent has the identical payoff function P (Monderer and Shapley 1996).[2] In other words, a potential game maximizer is identical with the equilibrium constellation of $x = (x_1, \ldots x_i, \ldots x_N)$ that would be selected by payoff-maximizing individuals in the organizational game u. That is to say, organizational participants act as if they form a team. When does it become so? The answer is: the organizational game u becomes a potential game (and thus a team) if and only if $G^i(F(.))(i = 1, \ldots .N)$ is the Shapley value on the organizational game u where collaboration helps but never hurts anyone (Ui 2000).

As is well known, the Shapley value is the unique solution arising in the game u viewed as a cooperative game that satisfies the conditions of symmetry (the labeling of the agents does not play any role in the assignment of their gains), marginalism (only the marginal contributions of each agent come in as determinants), and efficiency (there is no waste in distributing total value). As Binmore (2005: see also chapter 7 in this volume) argued and illustrated for the case of two-person game, this solution may be considered as corresponding to the only agreement that would emerge in the original position under the Rawlsian veil of ignorance. It is the situation in which positions of members of a society are not yet assigned, but they have to agree on a social contract prior to their actual assignments. As such, it may be considered to represent the 'deep structure of the fairness nor' that everyone actually uses in daily life. If such a fairness norm is shared by members of a society prior to the formation of individual organizations and believed to prevail within organizations to which they choose to join, then games within organizations that are voluntarily formed may become potential games. However, a precise form of the fairness norm is not unique, and depends on the characteristics of the game as discussed below in more concrete contexts.

Now consider more explicitly an aspect of organizations as systems of associational cognition. Namely, cognitive tasks are distributed among participating members so as to produce transferable value not possible by the mere aggregates of their independent cognitive (and physical) actions. Each member is a Bayesian rational agent who collects information and makes decisions under uncertain environments to maximize their individual payoff. Even so, if the value that they would create together is believed to be distributed according to the fairness norm implicit in the Shapley value, the system of associational cognition can be architected to maximize a single potential function. The assignments of specialized information-processing tasks and associated decision rules to each member thus derived can provide 'the pattern of communications.' Following it becomes consistent with individual members' self-interests.[3] In other words, Bayesian rational agents reason and behave as if they have group minds, when they are actually pursuing their own goals (Ui 2010).

With this in the background, we move to discuss how potential maximizers can be implemented in situations where agents with potentially varied characteristics are assigned to actual positions in corporate systems of associational cognition. The next section conceptualizes a notion of essentiality/non-essentiality of individual agent' cognitive assets in the system of associational cognition. This notion will play a crucial role in determining agents' bargaining powers in varied systems of associational cognition, and thus their governance structure.

8.3   Whose cognitive assets are essential in associational cognition, and how?

Saying that the sharing of a potential fairness norm could be an important condition for business corporations to be coherent and efficient does not necessarily mean that there is a universal norm that prevails over time and across economies. On the contrary, its substance may be varied, depending on the type of associational cognition and characteristics of agents who may participate in it. Let us single out one factor that is crucial for determining the substantive nature of the Shapley value. To simplify our argument, first we explicitly consider only two types of agents as the explicit members of corporate associational cognition, the management and the workers (the owner of physical assets will be introduced later in more concrete contexts). The management and the workers are assumed to be distinct in terms of their position in associational cognition: the former is primarily responsible for cognizing the systemic and common environment (the world, so to speak) of the corporation and envisioning its position in it – that is, corporate strategy – while the latter is responsible for the local environment in which their tasks take place to implement corporate strategy. Their cognition can be connected in various ways that will be specified below. The management and the workers each possess a particular cognitive skill characterized by a certain orientation, attributes, disposition and so on to do its assigned cognitive tasks. Those skills also serve as sources for their holders to derive shares (Shapley value dividends) in the organizational gain. Therefore I refer to them as (human) *cognitive assets*. There are two reasons for adopting this term.

Needless to say, human actions in the context of the organization involve not only mental activities (e.g. perceiving, imaging, guessing, theorizing, deciding, etc.) but also physical ones (e.g. operating machines, uttering speech, typing an e-mail, etc.). However, physical activities are not possible without being under control (conscious or unconscious) by mental activities, while they serve as important resources for mental activities. Thus cognitive and physical actions are inseparable. The cognitive scientist Andy Clark views the workings and states of the mind broadly in terms of the complex, continued interplay of brain, body and world (which includes social and institutional 'scaffolding'), and points out that 'the traditional divisions among perceptions, cognition, and action look increasingly unhelpful. . . . [R]eal world actions often play precisely the kinds of functional roles more usually associated with internal processes of cognition and computation' (Clark 1997: 221). Secondly, the human skills required in an organizational context, including those of bodily actions, may not be entirely invariable, apart from the specific context of associational cognition, but may be conditional on the ways in which individuals relate to each other in that context. In order to emphasize this aspect of human skills in the context of associational cognition, the unconventional term 'cognitive assets' is proposed here instead of the customary 'human capital.' While the notion of human capital usually (albeit not necessarily) refers to skills invested by individuals and portable through the labor market, I focus below on the quasi-collective nature of the respective skills of the management and the worker in the context of particular modes of associational cognition. Human cognitive skills are certainly embodied in individuals, but their characteristics and values are fully determined and expressed only in that context. The source of the so-called firm-specificity of human assets may be traced perhaps to their cognitive relationships with each other in a particular system of associational cognition and I want to make this point more explicit.

Further, the attributes and values of management's and workers' cognitive assets may not be determined solely by their mutual cognitive relationships. Corporate associational cognition uses a system of various non-human, physical assets as well, such as office buildings, computers, information networks, robotic machines, digitally stored files, and so on, as cognitive tools in common or for individual uses. Then, it may be the three-way relations among those three categories of assets that specify the varied modes of organizational architecture of associational cognition. In order to make this point clear, let me adopt the classical distinction of three kinds of rights related to non-human physical assets: rights to decide on their supply to corporate organizations as well as their withdrawal from them (ownership rights); rights to derive returns from the deployment and use of the assets (income rights); and rights to decide on how to use them in a specific way in associational cognition (use-control rights). I refer to the integrated holders of the first and second rights as the *investors*. The third type of rights may be integrated with the first and second rights in some cases (as in the case of owner-managed firms), but they can be separated from those and entrusted to another agent (say to the management, but also in some cases partly to the workers). Ownership and income rights are certainly important for defining the basic attributes of any form of corporate governance. However, as I am about to show, to whom the use-control rights are de facto accrued becomes highly relevant to the nature of associational cognition within business corporations and thus to productivity, incentives, and the bargaining power of the holders of cognitive assets (the management and the worker) vis-à-vis the owners of physical assets in corporate governance structure. Somewhat surprisingly, a single concept – to be introduced below – can lead us closer to such reality. What can such a concept be?

Let us adopt the following notion of cognitive assets essentiality defined in terms of a three-way relationship among management's cognitive assets (MCA), workers' cognitive assets (WCA) and non-human, physical assets (PHA). Below, the acronyms MCA, WCA, and PHA (or simply M and W when there cannot be misunderstanding) are used to refer to the respective assets as well as their personification, that is, the holders/owners, depending on context. First, recall the Edgeworth notion of complementarity between either of a specific pair of MCA or WCA on one hand and the use-control rights over PHA on the other (not between MCA and WCA as usually discussed in the theory of the firm). That is, if the marginal product of either MCA or WCA is increased by the assignment of use-control rights over PHA to it, then PHA is said to be complementary to MCA or WCA respectively. Let us further ask a specific question in a particular context of associational cognition: Can PHA remain complementary to either, or both, of MCA and WCA, even if they are separated from each other in associational cognition (and replaced by possible others)? If it cannot remain complementary to MCA, then the departing partner (i.e. WCA) proves to be indispensable for associational cognition and we say WCA are *essential* to this particular system of associational cognition. The symmetrical definition applies to MCA. To repeat this more formally, let $V = F(M, W : R)$ where $R \in [1.0]$ is the relative degree of use-rights control of PHA by MCA ($R = 1$ is the full control by MCA). If $\partial^2 F / \partial M \partial R = 0$ (respectively > 0) at $W = 0$, then W is essential (respectively, not essential), and if $\partial^2 F / \partial W \partial R = 0$ (respectively < 0) at $M = 0$, then M is essential (respectively). This concept of assets essentialities is originally due to Hart (1995: 45). Hart applied this concept primarily to the human assets held by division managers as the determinant of the boundary of the firm. I apply it to understanding the roles and positions of MCA and WCA in associational cognition.

According to this definition, either, neither, or both forms of cognitive assets can be essential. Intuitively, MCA may appear to always be essential in any associational cognition as the workers are not likely to increase their marginal products merely by controling the use of PHA without management strategy or direction, unless they are self-employed operators. But, as will be seen below, the degree to which MCA is essential may vary depending on the mode of associational cognition, and if it is rather weak in terms specified below, I will refer to such MCA as quasi-essential. On the other hand, WCA may, or may not, be essential (or quasi-essential in the same sense as mentioned above). Then, we may have six, and only six, generic modes of associational cognition as

discussed in next section, depending on the combination of essentiality properties of MCA and WCA. Before that, let us make a generic remark on the role
of the essentiality property in determining a substantive characteristic of the
Shapley value, or, more specifically, that of the Nash bargaining solution in the
two-person game context.

The extent to which MCA and WCA are essential can condition the relative
bargaining power of their holders over the distribution of organizational gains
available to them (after the payment to PHA taken as fixed at this moment),
and accordingly their incentives to invest in their own cognitive assets. For, if
only one of them is essential, then the holder of those assets can still increase
potential organizational gains by acquiring the use-control rights over PHA even
if the other party is replaced by any other available in markets. This indicates
a potential of this party's unique contribution to the value associational cognition. Therefore, it is not also bad news for the other party who participate in the
sharing of the value, even though their relative share becomes smaller. Therefore they may consent to yield the use-control rights to the holder of essential
cognitive assets as a fair deal, in which case the latter will be motivated to invest
in, and use, its own cognitive assets. Then a Shapley value distribution (a Nash
bargaining solution in this two-person game) is likely to emerge, and if indeed
it does, both parties can cooperate in associational cognition from their respective interests. Conversely, in order for them to be able to do so, a Shapley value
distribution needs to be expected to hold. However, if both cognitive assets are
bilaterally essential, then the assignment of the use-control rights over PHA to
either party may cease to be a defining factor for efficiency and a shared sense of
fairness. In the next section, we will illustrate these varied cases by introducing
a modicum of reality.

8.4   Three evolutionary parables of corporate associational cognition

Table 8.1 exhibits six possible modes of combination between WCA and MCA
based on their essentiality characteristics. These characteristics are defined in
terms of their potential value derived from controling the use-rights of PHA.
Thus, each of the modes may dictate the best allocation of the use-control rights
that maximizes the potential of their association, which leads to a particular
mode of corresponding governance. As some of these modes are well known,
we will discuss them only in the context of three possible evolutionary paths
from one mode to another.

(i) *From* (A) *to* (C), *via* (B) *and* (E): In the theoretical literature, mode (A) is
the most prominently discussed, notably in Hart's property rights theory of
the firm (Hart 1985). In this mode MCA is unilaterally essential, as it can be
associated with any WCA employed from the market by a contract. Only it can

Table 8.1   Modes of associational cognition

M \ W	Non-essential	Quasi-essential	Essential
Essential	(A) Classical hierarchy	(B) Delegated hierarchy	(C) Integrated modularity
Quasi-essential		(Dα) Embedded in bilateral collective essentialities (Dβ) Cognitive assimilation	(E) Competitive modularity
(Non-essential)			(F) Self employment

then enhance the organizational potential by controling the use of PHA, contingent on evolving events that are not specified *ex ante* in the contract. Therefore, MCA is to be combined with the use-control rights of PHA. If MCA has financial resources to own PHA, then MCA becomes nothing but the entrepreneur identifiable with the neoclassical 'firm.' If MCA does not have own resources to do so, then separation between the ownership of PHA and MCA results. As the implications of this separation to corporate governance and behavior have been extensively debated in the literature over decades, we do not dwell upon them. We only posit that the residual after contractual payments to WCA is divided between PHA and MCA according to their bargaining power.[4] We move on to narrate on possible evolution of this mode in the direction of (B) and then (C), possibly via (E), motivated by now well-known Silicon Valley folklore (for example, Baldwin and Clark 2000).

As the technological possibility progresses so that cognitive loads on associational cognition increases, it become imperative to decompose tasks performed by MCA into a hierarchical order, while a part of WCA becomes quasi-essential through firm-specific training. As a result firms come to incorporate large internal organizations à la Chandler as a system of associational cognition (mode B). Suppose further that a corporation internalizing such delegated hierarchy attempts to develop a product system of considerable complexity. To do so, MCA decomposes the design of the potential system into quasi-independent modules and only specifies interface rules that the design of each module needs to follow. Once the design of an entire system is completed in this way, a further improvement in the design of each module need no longer be under the control of a single MCA, as far as the interface rules are made open. Suppose that WCA indispensable for the design of a module thus become autonomous modules of associational cognition by being externally financed. Let us call them the modular firms. These quasi-independent WCA compete with each other for improvement, substitution, addition and transformation of modules to innovate the system further. Their performances are evaluated and evolutionarily selected for innovation-generating recombinations by external financiers. Such competitive process provides incentives for each modular firm to encapsulate its associational cognition within itself to win competition in innovative modular design. On the other hand, open interface rules that connect modular cognitive activities may be evolving through the strategic mediation of the financier who selects, terminates and/or refinances competing modules for system innovation. However, the financier's MCA may be characterized as at most quasi-essential, because financial assets (PHA) managed by them can yield profitable returns only through successful modular design by some modular firms that it finances. On the other hand, WCA at modular firms can be only potentially essential at the start-up stage. Their potentiality can selectively be actualized only when their modular designs are integrated together into a larger technological system. Thus we have mode (E): the competitive modular architecture of associational cognition. The value realization of potential essentialities of successful modular firms (for example, in the form of capital gains in the Initial Public Offering (IPO) or, acquisitions by larger corporations) may be legitimized by their creative entrepreneurship.

Under the high degree of uncertainty and complexity involved in the development of a product system, the tournament-like governance of the above process is known to have two important performance characteristics: (1) it can create option value by running parallel development efforts (experiments) among multiple modular firms (Baldwin and Clark 2000); and (2) it can provide greater incentives for modular firms to invest in potentially essential cognitive assets than under an integrated mode of architecture (Aoki and Takizawa 2002). These two attributes make mode (E) particularly appropriate to the development of a large system to be formed by *ex post* combinations of selected modularized products. This is particularly the case in the ICT industry where the nature of digital technology makes the commercialization of design implemented on various material devices and media (for example, wireless, fiber optics, copper cables, discs, and so on) so that the design and the manufacturing can be completely separable. However, WCA encapsulated in successful modular firms are to be reconnected under a single MCA exercising strong strategic direction for the evolution of system. The resulting architecture is then characterized as reciprocal essentialities between MCA and WCA, which is (C) mode. As discussed in the next section, this mode may be thought of as an emergent aspect of the contemporary corporate landscape. However, the path we have described may not be the only one to that mode. For one thing, mode (B) corporations may gradually transit to that mode, as their internal WCA become more and more indispensable to associational cognition within them. Leaving aside this obvious case, we now turn to two other parables.

(ii) *From* (Dα) *to* (C): Let us begin with mode (F), where WCA operate autonomously through their own control over specific PHA (tools) as self-employed individuals or via an occupational association (based on, say, craft skills). Imagine that as manufacturing knowledge develops, some would-be entrepreneurs attempt to set up factory organizations by recruiting WCA from among them. Suppose that, in parallel, there have developed occupational solidarity and common interests within WCA along types of skills related to the use of PHA of a specific type, and they are willing to offer services to any employer under the same employment conditions.[5]

Then, the following situation emerges: workers' investment in occupation-specific WCA, along with their participation in the (partial) control over the use of specific PHA, enhances their marginal satisfaction and/or productivity even without relational association with *any particular* MCA. On the other hand, the potential benefit that individual entrepreneurs can derive from retaining (at least partial) use control over PHA is invariant under the turnover of WCA with the same occupational qualifications. If we literally apply the theoretical definition of essentiality to this situation, the first statement implies that 'individual' MCA are not essential, while the second implies that 'individual' members of WCA are not essential. From the industrial perspective, however, neither MCA nor WCA, as collective entities, can gain by mere accessibility to the (partial) use-control rights over PHA without the other party's cooperation. That is to say, they are both essential at the industrial level. Therefore, it may be said that MCA and WCA are both quasi-essential by being embedded in the industrial frame of bilateral essentialities. The bilateral essentiality at the industrial level implies the allocation of use-control rights over PHA does potentially affect the initial bargaining positions of both parties. Technically speaking, this is the case of endogenous threat point in bargaining theory. Given the symmetric positions of both parties, therefore, a basic agreement on the sharing of the use-control rights over PHA, or co-determination, can be a logical outcome. It provides an embedding norm to the bargaining at the level of the individual corporation. Its sharing and implementation provide the glue to cement MCA and WCA in spite of possible fluidity of their association at the individual corporate level.

As in the case of (A) mode, the bifurcation of integrated MCA-PHA can logically take place in two ways: the investor (the owner of PHA) hires MCA, or MCA are financed by outside investors. But, logically or historically, the commitment of the MCA to the sharing of use-rights control over PHA with WCA can be transplanted to this evolutionary development. There must be three-way governance relationships in which WCA may be in direct relationship with the owner of PHA, not via MCA as in the (B) mode, in order to secure their participation in the partial use-control rights over PHA. It may be institutionalized, for example, in the form of traditional German co-determination. If the investors are interested in keeping their dominant ownership position, as well as restraining management's rent seeking and excessive risk-taking behavior, they would prefer additional financing to be in the form of long-term lending rather than equity financing. In this way their interests may become congruent with those of the workers.[6]

However, as technology develops, some occupational skills may become relatively obsolete, while new WCA emerge as essential cognitive assets. This will lead to the weakening of industrial-level norm of co-determination embedding individual corporations. In reaction to this situation, competitive corporations may transit to mode (C), incorporating a system of associational cognition involving reciprocal essentiality. However, ways by which such a system is governed may be diverse. Some corporate firms may adapt the institutional arrangement of co-determination (for example, into that of the works council) in a path-dependent manner, while some others may move to experimenting on a new governance arrangement as discussed below.

(iii) *From* (Dβ) *to* (C): Let us turn to the third parable on an evolutionary path to mode (C). Suppose that a manufacturing firm was formed by MCA who borrowed capital funds from financiers to finance PHA and recruited WCA from those with similar social backgrounds and sharing similar behavioral norms of cooperation. WCA is less mobile from one firm to another because of such social bondage, while future MCA is expected to be selected from among WCA. In this case associational cognition may involve a high degree of information assimilation rather than differentiation between MCA and WCA. Then the cognitive contributions of MCA and WCA to the organizational goal appear inseparable in the sense that their marginal products are not individually distinguishable and thus remain ambiguous. This situation may be considered as corresponding to the 'team' property of organizational architecture originally conceptualized by Alchian and Demsetz (1972). Both MCA and WCA become symmetrically quasi-essential to each other in that their (unobservable) marginal products cannot be enhanced by unilateral control by either party of use-control rights over PHA without mutual cooperation. For this system of associational cognition, it can be shown that the following type of governance is the second-best governance arrangement in the sense of Shapley value (Aoki 1994; 2001: 291–305, 422–423).

The individual investors who are unable to form a coalition with either MCA or WCA finance through a bank and delegate the monitoring of the joint use-control of PHA by MCA and WCA to the bank as a relational monitor. If the collective performance of the team is expected to exceed a certain threshold point, the relational monitor allows the team of MCA and WCA to be residual claimants after contractual interest payments to the holder of PHA. MCA and WCA divide the residual between them through internal bargaining, organizational rules, or conventions (such as seniority rules). When the collective performance of the team falls below the critical point, however, the delegated monitor is expected to bail out the team if the continuation value of the team is judged to be worth preserving, or withdraw PHA from the team and punish the team by dissolving it if not. The threat of a withdrawal of PHA in the worst event enforces some discipline on the members of the team as a whole, while the expectation of a bailing-out option can help preserve the value of the cognitive assets of the team in the event of a relatively minor problem, perhaps caused by temporal external shocks for which the team is not responsible. Since the use-control rights and residual claimant status shift, contingent on the value state of the corporation, this governance structure may be called relational contingent governance. Contractual distribution between the insiders and the outside investors is *ex ante* determined by their relative bargaining power conditioned by the potential value of the insider's cognitive assets and market power of the investors. The relational monitor obtains a fixed rate of rents from the services to the investors in the normal state. However, it becomes a residual claimant (actually loss-bearer) in the event of the bailing-out or liquidation of the team, which provides an incentive for earnest monitoring by the relational monitor.

This model is reminiscent of some stylized features of traditional Japanese corporations before the 1990s. The role of a relational monitor was borne by a so-called main bank that has relational associations with client corporations. The power of contingent relational monitoring by the bank is enhanced if WCA and MCA is less mobile because of their relational association. Thus, the main bank system and the firm-as-quasi-community norm complement each other in this governance structure. However, if demands for bank financing decline, or if the main bank becomes less competent in monitoring, the incentives of MCA and WCA may become compromised due to the lack of external discipline and their moral hazard behavior may become less easy to control. On the other hand, as technological complexity increases and competitive positions of corporations in global markets require more intricate directing, increases in the respective sophistication of WCA and MCA may become called for. This situation lessens the role of the shared quasi-community norm of cognitive assimilation and requires a clearer bifurcation of cognitive assets between MCA and WCA in associational cognition, which may eventually lead some competitive corporations to mode (C).

Three parables were told, each departing from a different initial condition but evolving to a similar mode (C) of associational cognition through (*i*) recombination, (*ii*) emergence, or (*iii*) bifurcation taking place between MCA and WCA. These evolutions take place under the pressure of competitive markets and technological complexity arising as endogenous outcomes of an evolutionary path, which require the accumulation of mutually specific and refined MCA and WCA at the individual corporate level. Table 8.2 summarizes the preceding discussion on governance structure corresponding to each mode of associational cognition as an institutional representation of possible Shapley value in it. We

Table 8.2 Governance forms as Shapley value implementation

W M	Non-essential	Quasi-essential	Essential
Essential	(A) Entrepreneurial control combining MCA and PHA	(B) Bargaining between PHA and MCA	(C) Mutual commitment
Quasi-essential		(Dα) Codetermination, (Dβ) Contingent relational governance plus quasi-community norm	(E) Tournament among modular firms (WCA) refereed by the financier as MCA-PHA
Non-essential			(F) Self-employment

will further discuss the meaning and implication of the entry in mode (C) in the next section.

8.5   An implication of emergent reciprocal essentialities: the investors are not sovereign

The cognitive tasks of the management and the workers in corporate associational cognition are, in practice, mutually complementary and there must also be some degree of information assimilation between the two in any architecture. Yet, a situation may arise such that both the overall environment of the corporate organization facing the management (for example, general market conditions, technological trends, political situations, social tenors and so on) and the idiosyncratic environment facing each of the operational tasks (for example, task-specific technology, specific market conditions, and so on) become so complex that scarce cognitive assets, both MCA and WCA, are to be used in a focused, innovative manner. Then, an appropriate type of organizational architecture may become more modular than under (B) and (D). But, distinct from under the competitive modular mode (E), MCA provides a more specific cognitive frame and interface rules in the forms of corporate strategy and integrated-organizational design. Suppose that such a situation is characterized as follows: both MCA and WCA cannot increase their respective marginal products merely by controling the use-rights to PHA in the absence of other's cooperation. Namely, in order for them to use PHA productively, the management needs to be associated with WCA that are particularly fit for the implementation of its unique strategy, while the workers need MCA's strategy to be fit for the productive use of their WCA. Then MCA and WCA become reciprocally essential at the individual corporate level. Although both MCA and WCA may be highly specialized in their respective cognitive actions in order to make a good use of the power of modularity, the holder of each cannot dispense with the other. Reciprocally indispensable human relationships become of primary importance, while the control over PHA becomes secondary. This is the defining characteristic of mode (C). How, then, can this kind of relationship be governed? Can the owner's control (the shareholder sovereignty) of overall corporate affairs be derived endogenously in the sense of Shapley value as in the case of mode (A)?

From the purely theoretical point of view, Hart argued that the reciprocal essentialities of human assets imply that 'the ownership structure does not matter since neither party's investment [in its own human assets] will not pay off in the absence of agreement with the other' (Hart 1995: 48). By the phrase 'the ownership structure' Hart is referring to the assignment of the residual rights of control over PHA (that is, the rights to use-control integrated with the ownership right that cannot be specified *ex ante* in contracts) between the division managers of an organization, while I am dealing with the assignment of use-control rights over PHA between MCA and WCA. But Hart's argument may also basically apply here: ways in which the assignment of use-control rights over PHA is made would not directly affect either party's initial bargaining position nor consequently their incentive for investment in cognitive assets without mutual commitment to cooperation in associational cognition. Thus, one important implication of the reciprocal essentiality can be a diversity of organizational architecture and associated governance structure implied by Shapley value at the corporate level.

A corollary to the 'irrelevance' of the allocation of use-control rights to PHA is that there may not be a particular reason for productive gains to arise from exclusive coalition between PHA and MCA vis-a-vis WCA as in mode (A) or (B). However, saying so does not imply that the share market plays only a secondary role in this case. It would perform the even more important information function as autonomously evaluating the relative effectiveness of reciprocally essential relationships between MCA and WCA across corporations. To the extent that the share market is informative, the share price may be formed as a summary statistic of diverse opinions regarding the future values of specific internal relationships between MCA and WCA. If the board of directors is entrusted to effectively replace or appoint top management of the corporation contingent on the (expected) long-term share value prospect, the management can be disciplined to create and sustain the valuable internal relationship with the workers, while the workers are motivated to invest in their specific WCA. On the other hand, the shareholders themselves may be motivated to do a better monitoring job if they can benefit from making good judgments in selecting their own portfolios. Therefore, complementarities may arise between the creation and sustenance of reciprocally essential relationships at the individual corporate level, on one hand, and the efficient stock market evaluation of their values, on the other. In such a model, the board of directors ought to act not as the agent of the value-maximizing shareholders but as the 'trustees' for the stakeholders, including MCA and WCA who are the source of value creation of the corporation as an associational cognitive system. The board should not force the management to increase the share value at the expense of the workers and/or through a collusive arrangement with the management, because it would be likely to destroy the valuable internal relationship of the MCA and the WCA.

Obvious examples of reciprocal essentialities may be found in knowledge-intensive, professional organizations, such as law firms, consulting companies, and so on, as well as in teams of creative talents directed by heavyweight leaders in the fields of arts, sports, researches, and other areas. However, as the above parable suggests and empirical evidence submitted in Aoki (2010, chapter 5) supports, reciprocal essentialities of MCA and WCA are evolving as conspicuous features of some well-run business corporations in various path-dependent forms. In particular, corporations of this type may become competitive in industries facing complex technology, highly uncertain markets and natural environments and the like, such as information and communications, health, and nuclear power.[7]

8.6   Concluding remarks: law does not originate corporations, but coevolves with them

We have focused on the aspect of business corporations as 'incorporating' systems of associational cognition for business purposes. This focus differs from an orthodox premise in economics and law that corporations are the property of the shareholders and, therefore, their objective ought to be the uncompromised pursuit of the share price maximization. Rather, we have derived the orthodox model as one possible equilibria (A) of the potential game for forming business corporations as a coalition for associational cognition. There can be other equilibria as summarily exhibited in Tables 8.1 and 8.2. The equilibrium notion we have adopted is the Shapley value. Thus, the architectural and governance modes respectively displayed there satisfy the efficiency criteria, together with corresponding notions of (fairness) norm such as classical and innovation-driven entrepreneurship (respectively, A and E), legacy of artisanship (Dα), or the firm-as-quasi-community norm (Dβ). However, as technology becomes more complex and markets become more competitive on the global scale, which themselves are nothing but endogenous outcomes of corporate associational cognition, some corporate firms have evolved to incorporate reciprocally essential managerial and operational cognitive assets (C). Evolutionary paths to this model could be diverse so that associated fairness norm can also be partially path-dependent and thus diverse.

One of the salient points implied by our Shapley value approach is that business corporations can be generically self-governing entities rather than the direct product of law or polity, as long as some norms are shared among corporate participants. These norms may evolve together with competitive systems of associational cognition. Having said that, however, we may briefly refer to a possible role of law in the sustenance and evolution of corporate systems that is consistent with our approach. We have distinguished different modes of corporate systems as Shapley value representations and accordingly as Nash equilibria of potential games. More generally, we can conceptualize an institution as a salient feature of equilibrium of any societal game that everyone cognizes and believes to be recurrently played. However, how can such common belief be formed among the players of the game that would in turn induce them to play the equilibrium play? By individual observations of stable repeated plays? But then how are stable plays created? A way to escape from the trap of logical infinite regression would be to think as follows: there ought to be some public representations that mediate between the equilibrium play of a societal game and individual belief formations. Such external media or artifact may linguistically represent salient features of equilibrium plays and be available to individuals as extended cognitive resources (Aoki 2010: Chapter 4; 2011). They may take various substantive forms such as signs, norms, rules, organizations of known types, and laws.

Then the final question relevant to our current concern is how corporate laws are written.[8] Forms of law could be various, and statutory laws may be considered as outcomes of strategic play in the political domain complementary to equilibrium play of economic games (Aoki 2010: Chapter 3). However, common laws cannot be explained in this way. More broadly then, we may consider a specific domain of societal interactions played by legislators, administrators, judges, prosecutors, attorneys and other private agents, which may be called the legal domain. This domain may be conceptualized as a distinct domain characterized by unique strategic features and orientations such as 'legal (public) discourse,' 'legal minded' and the like. Yet the legal domain itself has the same recursive structure as in other domains of societal games as noted above. Namely, based on common legal consciousness inherited from the past as a common prior, the players are strategically engaged in discourses and may arrive at an agreed, or socially acceptable, legal notion, which in turn mediates further discourses. This legal process is however not isolated, but 'strategically linked' to other domains of societal games such as economic, political and social exchanges. The uniqueness of the legal domain is to perform an important linguistic function for other domains to provide explicit public representations (laws) of their evolving states. This may be the reason why the notions such as fairness and justice are also mobilized in domains other than the legal one (cf. Shapley value). Thus, we may posit that the legal domain and the corporate domain are mutually autonomous, but they are strategically and linguistically linked. More specifically, an implication of this is that corporate laws, either common or statutory, co-evolve together with corporate practices of associational cognition and its governance, but it does not dictate the latter as the legal origin theory appears to claim.

Notes

* This paper draws on chapter 2 in a recent book of mine, *Corporations in Evolving Diversity: Cognition, Governance, and Institutions* (Aoki 2010) with some new material in sections 2 and 5. In preparing this paper, I benefited from discussions with Simon Deakin, Takeshi Fujitani, Carsten Herrmann-Pillath, Rolenzo Sacconi and Takashi Ui.
1. For references, see footnotes on Aoki (2010: 22).
2. If a potential function P is continuously differentiable and strictly concave, then a potential maximizer is a unique correlated equilibrium of a potential game (Neyman 1997).
3. In this sense, potential games allow a natural extension of the cooperative game concept of the Shapley value to non-cooperative games.
4. The orthodox theory posits that, if the separation occurs, then MCA is ought to be treated as if it were WCA, namely as the agent of the owner of PHA as the principal. There have been unsettled debates between this orthodox view, on one hand, and the managerialist and stakeholder-society views, on the other, as regards the (normative and positive) objective, behavior, and governance of the corporation. However, these different views may be subsumed under the bargaining view in which the relative weights of bargaining strength are allowed to be variable between PHA and MCA (Aoki 1984: Part III; 2001: 36–39).
5. In practice, such alignment historically evolving out of the legacy of artisanship may be sustained and formalized in the context of modern industry by a system of public training programs, occupation qualification certificates, industrial unions based on occupational categories and so on, as was the case in Germany.
6. See Aoki (2010: 289–290. These observations are consistent with well-known, stylized features of traditional German practices, such as the historical role of banks in perpetuating a concentration ownership through inter-corporate shareholding and long-term lending, as well as associated conflicts of interests with market-oriented minority shareholders.
7. See Aoki and Rothwell (2012) for the value of the integrative modularity based on reciprocal essentialities in the nuclear power industry.
8. I benefit from conversations with Professors Takeshi Fujitani and Simon Deakin in what follows. See Deakin (2011).

References

Alchian, A. and H. Demsetz (1972) 'Production, Information Costs, and Economic Organization', *American Economic Review,* vol. 62, pp. 777–795.

Aoki, M. (1984) *The Co-operative Game Theory of the Firm* (Oxford: Clarendon Press).

Aoki, M. (1994) 'The Contingent Governance of Teams: Analysis of Institutional Complementarity', *International Economic Reviews,* vol. 35, pp. 657–676.

Aoki, M. (2001) *Toward a Comparative Institutional Analysis* (Cambridge, MA: MIT Press).

Aoki, M, (2010) *Corporations in Evolving Diversity: Cognition, Governance, and Institutions* (Oxford, UK: Oxford University Press).

Aoki, M. (2011) 'Institutions as Cognitive Media between Strategic Interactions and Individual Beliefs', *Journal of Economic Behavior and Organizations*, vol. 79, pp. 20–34.

Aoki, M. and G. Rothwell (2012) 'A Comparative Institutional Analysis of the Fukushima Nuclear Disaster: Its Lessons and Policy Implications', http://papers.ssrn.com/sol3/papers.cfm?abstract_id=1940207.

Aoki, M. and H. Takizawa (2002) 'Information, Incentives, and Option Value: The Silicon-valley Model', *Journal of Comparative Economics*, vol. 30, pp. 759–786.

Baldwin, C. Y and K. B. Clark. (2000) *Design Rules: The Power of Modularity*, vol. 1 (Cambridge, MA: MIT Press).

Binmore, K. (2005) *Natural Justice* (New York: Oxford University Press).

Blackstone, W. (1765–9/2005) *Commentaries on the Laws of England*, www.LawMart.com.

Clark, A. (1997) *Being There: Putting Brain, Body and World Together Again* (Cambridge, MA: MIT Press).

Deakin, S. (2011) 'Legal Evolution: Integrating Economic and Systemic Approaches', Centre for Business Research, University of Cambridge Working Paper no. 424.

Hart, O. (1995) *Firms, Contracts, and Financial Structure* (Oxford: Clarendon Press).

Jensen, M. and W. Meckling (1976) 'Theory of the Firm: Managerial Behavior, Agency Costs, and Capital Structure', *Journal of Financial Economics*, vol. 3, pp. 305–360.

Marschak, J. and R. Radner (1972) *Economic Theory of Teams* (New Haven, CT: Yale University Press).

Monderer, D. and L.S. Shapley (1996) 'Potential Games', *Games and Economic Behavior*, vol. 14, pp. 124–143.

Neyman, A. (1997) 'Correlated Equilibrium and Potential Games', *International Journal of Game Theory*, vol. 26, pp. 223–227.

Simon, H. (1957) *Administrative Behavior*, second edn (New York: Free Press).

Ui, T. (2000) 'Shapley Value Representation of Potential Games', *Games and Economic Behavior*, vol. 31, pp. 121–135.

Ui, T. (2010) 'Bayesian Potentials and Information Structures: Team Decision Problems Revisited', *International Journal of Economic Theory*, vol. 5, pp. 271–291.

9
On the Plasticity of the Corporate Form

Katharina Pistor
Columbia Law School, Columbia University

9.1 Introduction

Comparative law and corporate governance scholarship emphasizes differences in law across countries and legal systems. Opinions vary, however, as to what amounts to important differences: the organization of corporate management into one- or two-tier boards; the extent to which corporate stakeholders can opt out of the law and determine critical features of the corporation by contrast; or specific legal guarantees of shareholder 'property rights.' Indeed, the focus of the academic debate has shifted over time, reflecting changes in the dominant economic and social theories and ideologies. In the 1970s, much emphasis was placed on structural features (two-tier vs one-tier management boards) and the representation of diverse stakeholder interest on these boards. In the 1980s and early 1990s the contractual nature of corporate law and the ability of company promoters and shareholders to design the corporate form in accordance with their interests and needs gained prominence. Since the mid-1990s, the bulk of attention has shifted to the protection of shareholder/investor rights as the company 'owners.'

This chapter proposes a different approach. It suggests that differences in corporate law across time and space notwithstanding, the corporate form's core features have remained remarkably stable and are compatible with different social, political and economic conditions. The ability of the corporate form to adapt to different environments without altering its generic features is referred to as its 'plasticity.' Such adaptability would be less striking if there was only one way to organize a business entity. Yet the corporation is only one form among many others that have emerged in different countries at different points in time – including, to name just a few, partnerships, limited partnerships, the traditional 'joint stock' company, and consumer or supplier cooperatives. Yet it is the corporation that has become the dominant mode for organizing large businesses in countries around the globe, and which has been celebrated as one of the most important institutional innovations in the development of modern market economies.

The plasticity of corporate law holds important lessons for the nature of legal ordering. Differences over time and between countries are frequently attributed to evolving or differing political or cultural preferences. The constancy of core features of the corporate form and its adaptability to a changing social, economic, and political environment, in contrast, emphasizes the durability and predictability of legal ordering beyond changing fads in politics or economic and social theories. It also suggests that the corporate form as such is much less determinative of economic outcomes than is often assumed; instead it can promote a diverse range of social and economic objectives. Whether this is a virtue or vice depends on the economic theory to which one subscribes. For those who believe in equilibrium models, rational expectation and efficient capital market hypotheses, there tends to be only one optimal model of legal design: that which emphasizes the rights and interests of shareholders and effectively deals with the agency problems they face. For those who are either skeptical of this model, or more fundamentally disagree with the theoretical premises on which it rests, the plasticity of the corporate form is more likely to be virtuous. It facilitates the adaptation of the generic form to a changing environment and to the changing assessment of that environment by lawmakers and market participants alike.

The remainder of this chapter is organized as follows. Section 9.2 explains the meaning of plasticity as used in this chapter and illustrates the corporate form's remarkable plasticity. Section 9.3 delineates the argument developed here from contemporary debates about convergence and divergence in corporate law. Moreover, it situates the argument about the plasticity of corporate law within economic theories that emphasize uncertainty and imperfect knowledge as opposed to efficient equilibrium outcomes. Section 9.4 analyzes the implications of the plasticity of law for the nature of legal ordering. Section 9.5 concludes.

9.2   The corporate form's plasticity

Definitions of the term plasticity abound, ranging from malleability and formability to the notion of deformation. The definition used in this paper is derived from biology, where plasticity means the ability of an organism to change its phenotype in response to changes in the environment. The genotype of the organism is retained, but changes in its phenotype enhance its ability to survive in different and changing environments. Transposed to the area of law and legal ordering, plasticity refers to the ability of basic forms of legal ordering to adapt to a changing environment without requiring alterations to their core features. This requires a delineation of features that are deemed core, and others that are variable.

The line between core and variable features of the corporate form is not absolute and requires some judgment calls. This can, however, be corroborated by real world evidence of organizations that share the corporate form's core features but differ along many other dimensions. I consider the following features to be core features of the corporation: Legal personhood, asset partitioning, and a designated legal agent to act on behalf of the corporation (Eisenberg 2000). These features distinguish the corporate form from other forms of business organizations, such as partnerships, while at the same time being fully compatible with many variations in corporate form. Table 9.1 contrasts the corporation with the simple partnership along these dimensions.

Legal personhood means that a business organization has its own legal identity. While decried as legal fiction by some, legal personhood has important real world implications. The corporate form can change its business purpose, capital structure, owners, management, even its name, and yet still own the same assets and retain rights and obligations from contractual commitments entered into prior to such change. The notion that the corporation is a nexus of contract fails to capture these critical aspects of the corporate form: Contracts are temporal and limited in time; they are terminated with the accomplishment of its goals or in the event that one of the parties to the contract ceases to exist. In contrast, the corporate form is immune from such changes.

Legal personhood is also the foundation for the second generic feature of the corporate form, asset partitioning (Hansmann and Kraakman 2000). Without attributing independent legal personality to the corporation, the delineation of assets belonging to it rather than its owners makes little sense. Conversely, asset partitioning helps sustain an organization as an independent legal person. It limits creditors of the organization to enforce their claims against assets of

Table 9.1   Core features of corporations vs partnerships

Core features/ organizational form	Legal personhood	Asset partitioning	Designated agent
Partnership	Entity is dissolved when one partner withdraws	Creditors have choice between partnership's and partner's assets	Each partner can represent and bind the partnership
Corporation	Entity exists in perpetuity	Creditors have access only to entity assets	Corporation is represented by authorized management

Source: Author's own compilation.

that organization, and creditors of the organization's owners to their personal assets. Otherwise, the bankruptcy of a shareholder could trigger the dissolution of a business organization in the event that that shareholder's debt exceeded the assets of the corporation. A derivative of the principle of asset partitioning is limited liability. It means that shareholders are protected against liability for the corporation's debt. They may lose their initial capital contribution in the event of insolvency, but they cannot be forced to make good for the company's debts. Finally, while the corporation may be a person, it is a legal, rather than a natural one. It thus requires an agent to act on its behalf. This agent is not just anybody – for example, any of the shareholders as would be the case in a partnership – but a specifically designated agent who is recognized by law as the legally authorized representative of the corporation.

The emphasis on these legal attributes will strike some as formalistic. Economists and legal scholars schooled in the economic analysis of law in particular tend to focus on the voluntary nature of business associations, their ability to pool assets through a variety of mechanisms, including equity and debt, and the allocation of control rights and enuing agency problems among various stakeholders in a joint enterprise. These are all important issues, but they affect, in principle, any business organization and are not specific to the corporate form.

With these core principles in place, the corporation can be organized in many different ways, fitted with many additional features, and adapted to different needs and circumstances. Shares can be tradable or non-tradable; corporations can have one- or two-tier board structures; and the protection of shareholders and other stakeholders in the corporation can take many different forms, including voting and information rights, the right to sue, or the right to exit. These add-ons to the core features of the corporation are, as suggested by Aoki (2010), adaptations to the broader environment in which it operates, its cultural, social and political ground rules. Metaphorically speaking, they can be said to enhance the survival of the corporate form in radically different environments, as they don't affect its genotype.

To illustrate, consider the use of the corporate form to organize business organizations in different sectors, from manufacturing to financial services, hedge funds to sovereign wealth funds; with different ownership structures, whether concentrated or dispersed, public or private, institutional or personal; and its operation and survival in countries that ascribe to variant models of capitalism, such as the USA vs France, Japan vs the UK, or China vs Norway, or that belong to different legal systems, whether the common law or the civil law system (La Porta, Lopez-de-Silanes and Shleifer 2008).

Despite its plasticity, the corporate form is not compatible with just any environment. The generic attributes of the corporate form identified above require tolerance for a minimum amount of plurality and autonomy in economic decision-making. Not surprisingly, the corporate form made headway in the former socialist world only in its final years, when the deep flaws of a system that relied on central planning and decision-making became increasingly apparent. Attempts to fix the system included reforms that gave greater autonomy to state-owned enterprises, triggering the 'corporatization' of many entities that hitherto had been centrally controlled well before they were slated for privatization. Nonetheless, the Hungarian and Yugoslav reform experiences suggest that the corporate form is also compatible with variants of socialism. Similarly, in countries where a clear separation between the state apparatus and the ruling elite, state budget and the personal purse, are underdeveloped, the corporate form is used less frequently. While many sovereign wealth funds, for example, have been organized as limited liability companies, in Saudi Arabia they continue to operate largely as discretionary funds of the ruling elite without clear organizational boundaries that would indicate the existence of an independent entity with its own governance structure and decision-making autonomy (Hatton and Pistor 2011).

In sum, the corporate form's generic features facilitate the delineation of assets and autonomy in economic decision-making. Beyond these core attributes, the corporation can adopt many variable features, some of which may benefit some stakeholders more than others, or strike different compromises between the corporation's autonomy and social interests. It may well be that some of these variable features are more conducive to certain outcomes – that is, the development of financial markets, as has been suggested by a voluminous literature on law and finance. The importance and desirability of these outcome variables, however, is a matter of social choice, and, not surprisingly, varies over time and across space.

9.3 The corporate form's plasticity in light of contemporary corporate law and governance scholarship

Much of contemporary scholarship on comparative corporate law and governance is rooted in equilibrium models of markets and the efficient capital market hypothesis (ECMH). Markets are presumed to self-organize and to achieve Pareto-efficient outcomes. From this vantage point it is indeed puzzling why not all economic relations are market-based and why, instead, firms exist. The discovery of the firm in neoclassical economics has spurred a huge literature to explain its existence. The most widely accepted explanations include transaction costs, agency costs or incomplete contracts. An alternative perspective on the relation between markets and firms, the one pursued in this paper, is to start with firms and use differences in the organization and governance of firms to explain different markets. This has been the vantage point of the literature on varieties of capitalism, research which starts from the assumption that markets are institutionally structured.

Comparative corporate governance scholarship is more deeply rooted in the former approach. The basic premise about market efficiency has led this literature to emphasize shareholder value and attributes of corporate law that enhance shareholder value. After all, shareholders control the capital without which the corporation cannot operate. Only corporations that can attract sufficient capital will survive in the marketplace. The most successful corporations are therefore the ones that allocate capital to achieve the highest returns for their shareholders. As it turns out, the best firms are said to be those that mimic efficient markets – notwithstanding the fact that the very existence of firms has been explained by market inefficiencies in the first place (Black 1990). Another loop in this circular analysis is that market pressure will lead to the convergence of corporate law and corporate governance around the world. As companies that are subject to a superior governance structure outperform others with inferior governance, lawmakers responsible for the latter will be pressured to adopt the most efficient legal rules or at least facilitate functional convergence (Gilson 2001). While there have been dissenters to this proposition, their reservations are based on institutional path-dependency, not the paradoxical nature of an argument that explains the existence of firms with market inefficiency only to suggest that these very markets will determine the optimal governance structure of firms.

The quest to optimize markets by optimizing corporate law has gained much credence in policy circles and has produced rankings of countries and legal systems along those lines. Surprisingly little attention has been paid to the fact that the very attributes that put corporate law in the service of making financial markets more efficient than they are *in natura* are not associated with greater economic growth and development. Instead, the efficiency paradigm has become an end in itself.

The ECMH and efficiency models of financial markets appear to be losing ground in economic theory (Frydman and Goldberg 2011), although the field for theories that might replace it is currently wide open, and many defenders still abound. This debate will most likely be resolved largely within the discipline of economics. The purpose of this chapter is, instead, to make a modest contribution to the debates on corporate law and corporate governance by returning to the concept of plasticity of the corporate form and its core attributes.

As suggested above, the corporate form's generic features facilitate the delineation of assets and their autonomous management. They thereby contribute to the up-scaling and down-scaling of economic activities: Up-scaling by supporting the accumulation of assets under one roof and managed by an autonomous decision-maker; and down-scaling by fostering the de-centralization and dispersion of economic decision-making among many such autonomous actors that have the capacity to accumulate and delineate assets. Viewed in this light, the corporate form is critical for constituting markets. Autonomous decision-making is a prerequisite for markets; and while individuals are autonomous decision-makers they cannot separate their personal assets from those risked in a business venture without a law that authorizes such separation. This is why the corporate form has been hailed as such an important 'invention' for the development of modern market economies. The type of market economy – whether liberal or coordinated, to borrow a distinction from the varieties of capitalism literature – is shaped by the variable attributes of corporate law and governance institutions. They affect corporate decision-making by giving different stakeholders more or less voice in the corporation and thus determine, if only indirectly, the interests that bear on the selection of corporate strategies and their effects on markets.

In contrast, contemporary corporate governance scholarship in the law and economics tradition holds that the only relevant criteria for corporate decision-making is and should be the maximization of shareholder value. Introducing other objectives is said to result in inefficiencies and to encourage abuse of power by corporate decision-makers. The major objection is that greater discretion increases agency costs and thus leads to a weakening of accountability. This line of reasoning assumes that markets are efficient; and that any inefficiencies, such as transaction costs and information asymmetries, can be patched up with legal and regulatory interventions that protect investors' property rights and/or enhance access to information. With these bandages in place markets will approximate efficiency, and any other form of legal intervention based on normative considerations should take place outside corporate law, that is, in labor law or by using taxes to redistribute wealth.

If, however, markets are not efficient and are fundamentally beset by imperfect knowledge, as argued by Frydman and Goldstein (2011), forcing corporate decision-makers to focus on share value as the single benchmark for determining corporate strategies makes little sense; indeed it can create more harm than good. The reason is that this benchmark may be determined by factors that have little to do with the earning potential of the corporation in question. Instead, changes in share prices may be affected by other factors, such as changes in oil prices, inflation, or 'exogenous' shocks like natural and man-made disasters. These factors may affect a given corporation's earning potential, but if and how is not a matter revealed in the fluctuating share price. Instead, it can be discerned only from carefully weighing many different factors, and – given that knowledge about the future is inherently imperfect – a substantial amount of guesswork. Focusing single-mindedly on share prices does not make sense for another reason. Corporate decision-makers simply cannot forecast with precision which factors will be deemed critical for securities analysts and traders in the future. This changes over time as market actors correct their perception of what matters in response to dynamic market developments. Nor should this necessarily determine the choice of corporate strategies, which should be geared toward corporate performance, not the demands of securities traders whose own actions are determined by multiple factors and can change course in ways that are difficult to predict *ex ante*. Share prices therefore cannot perform the role of a reliable guideline for corporate decision-making even though they may be one of many benchmarks to assess corporate performance in the short to medium term. Even if the informational content of share price was a reliable indicator for the firm's past and present performance, this leaves much guesswork to be done about what the future might hold in a dynamic environment.

A potential counter argument to this analysis is that shareholder value maximization does not necessarily require a single-minded focus on share prices. Instead, corporate actors should enhance the intrinsic value of a firm, which is not always fully captured by markets. This may well be true, but this argument concedes that corporate decision-making is complex and requires the exercise of substantial discretion by corporate decision-makers. It thus poses the same governance challenges as other models that deviate from the notion that firms should serve and be guided by efficient markets.

Once the idea of a single reliable objective for corporate decision-makers is put to rest, the issue of corporate governance appears in a different light. Most importantly, it demands recognition that corporate decision-making involves the exercise of discretion, the possibility of mistakes, and the need, nonetheless, to hold decision-makers accountable. Forcing decision-makers to focus on a single parameter, such as share price, will have one of two effects under conditions of uncertainty and imperfect knowledge. It may force them down a single path to cover their backs vis-à-vis the shareholder constituency, even if at the expense of unclear benefits for the long-term interests of the corporation and its core stakeholders. Alternatively, it will induce them to fudge the books to pretend that they are complying with the need to maximize share value, while in fact pursuing a different strategy. Fudging the books may, of course, also be the result of dishonesty. The point is that even honest, well-intentioned corporate decision-makers will have to engage in such practices, if they are bound by shareholder value, yet doubt that the strategy derived from share price alone will enhance corporate value.

Contrary to advocates of agency theory, discretion is not a bad thing: under conditions of uncertainty and imperfect knowledge discretion is indispensable. Recall that one of the core attributes of the corporate form is autonomy in the management of a pool of assets that can be delineated from its owners and other pools of assets as well. This helps diversify economic activities by ensuring that a plurality of actors pursues multiple goals and adopts different strategies to succeed. Under conditions of imperfect knowledge, it is not clear which goal/strategy combination will enhance success and ensure the survival of a given corporation at a given point in time – given the past is not necessarily a recipe for future success. Having flexibility to change goals and/or strategies in response to a changing environment is therefore likely to improve, not hinder, a firm's survival chance. Moreover, the diversification of goals and strategies among corporate entities may well be beneficial from a social welfare perspective, because it increases experimentation and reduces the probability that exogenous shocks affect all economic agents in the same way.

Because of its plasticity, the corporate form is not only compatible with but even conducive to such diversity of response strategies. This leaves the question of how to hold corporate decision-makers accountable who by definition have to exercise substantial discretion in the determination of the corporation's goals and strategies. One possible strategy is to enhance the decision-makers' accountability to a single constituency. This avoids collective action problems associated with allowing directors to consider the interests of multiple constituencies, the heterogeneity of whose interests, however, impedes effective collective governance. By the same token it limits discretion of corporate decision-makers who are likely to pay greater heed to the one constituency that can effectively hold them accountable. Yet a compromise can be struck if the law nonetheless recognizes competing objectives, because it raises the threshold for legal challenges. Directors who are legally empowered to protect the interests of shareholders and creditors cannot easily be held liable for taking actions that are more beneficial for creditors, even if shareholders have to bear the costs. Alternatively, governance arrangements can be designed to enhance accountability to multiple stakeholders. A potential danger of such a system is that corporate decision-makers may play different stakeholders off against one another. By designing institutions that reduce the costs of coalition building or create the possibility that competing views are voiced in a single forum, these dangers can be mitigated. Finally, law enforcement agents, such as courts or regulators, can be given greater discretion in reviewing corporate decision-makers to minimize abuse of powers.

Of the three strategies outlined above, the UK arguably pursues the first, Germany the second, and the USA the third. None of the three countries' corporate laws subscribes to the notion that maximizing shareholder value is the only criterion for assessing corporate decision-makers. Instead, company law in the UK emphasizes shareholder voice in the form of voting and agenda setting over *ex post* judicial monitoring. At the same time, the UK regime holds fast to the notion that directors are *not* agents of the shareholders, but act in the interests of a broader corporate community. Shareholders can replace them, but cannot dictate their actions. Germany has instituted multi-stakeholder governance in the form of co-determination. By bringing workers into corporate decision-making at the board level the law sought to counter the dominance of controlling shareholders and collusion between them and management. The term co-determination notwithstanding, the system at most provides workers direct access to information about corporate strategies and a right to be heard; not, however, a substantive veto right. While in actual practice the shareholder and employee benches of the supervisory board tend to make decisions at separate meetings, the joint board creates at least the potential for the consideration of a broader range of options. Finally, US/Delaware corporate law recognizes great latitude for corporate decision-makers, but as a corollary, courts exercise much more discretion in monitoring these decisions than in other jurisdictions. Entry barriers to litigation are substantially lower than in other countries and procedural devices, such as derivative actions and class action suits, further reduce the costs of litigation. Moreover, courts have substantial power to forge the contours of fiduciary duties, the major prism through which corporate decisions are reviewed (Coffee 1989). Courts have exercised their oversight powers not at all times with the same vigor; there is also evidence that reducing entry barriers to litigation creates possibilities for abuse by lawyers and litigants alike. Nonetheless, the basic features of the regime can be characterized by discretion cum judiciary oversight.

More generally, not every system has been able to strike the right balance between discretion and accountability. The point is that designing governance regimes that balance these competing objectives is not a simple design question aimed at optimizing the pursuit of a single corporate goal, but requires experimentation and learning over time. This in turn requires a re-conceptualization of corporate governance from a narrow perspective that focuses on maximizing investors' returns to one that recognizes alternative goals and strategies and finds governance solutions for ensuring that they are implemented to the degree possible. It places a normative debate about corporate goals front and center.

Using indicators of stock market development – as conventionally done in empirical analysis about the merits of different corporate governance regimes – assumes that stock market criteria are and ought to be the primary criteria for assessing corporate performance and the laws that shape corporate decision-making. Other criteria might include the diversity of corporate goals, strategies and industries; the inclusiveness of economic growth and development; or the sustainability of a particular growth model. Such a normative debate has been sidelined by assumptions about market efficiency, but needs to be invigorated in light of the limited explanatory powers of this theory and the havoc it has arguably caused in the real world.

The plasticity of the corporate form suggests that the corporate form is compatible with many different goals and outcome measures. This is manifested in the variable components of the corporate form. The normative debate is thus only partly a debate about comparative corporate law and governance in the narrow sense. Good governance is not about whether all variable components of one model are mimicked by all countries around the globe. Instead, the major task of corporate law and corporate governance is to assess whether the choice of institutions that govern corporate decision-making adequately reflects the normative goals and preferences of a given society, not to assume a single goal and use it as a benchmark for the merits of alternative regimes.

9.4 Implications for theories of legal ordering

The distinction between core and variable attributes of the corporation is important not only for the comparative analysis of corporate law and governance. It also has potential implications for theories about legal ordering of economic life more generally. The most widely accepted conceptualization of law or legal institutions is that institutions establish the rules of the game. That, however, misses a fundamental function of law, namely identifying or framing the game that can be played in the first place. If markets are presumed to be the wide-open field within which economic organizations and transactions arise spontaneously, the previous sentence makes little sense. It can be understood only if markets are conceptualized as being constituted by institutional arrangements without which they simply would not exist (other than in economic textbooks). The corporate form is one of such institutions that are critical for the operation of modern market economies. A 'nexus of contracts' conception of corporate forms suggests that they simply reflect basic market transaction – that is, contracts. Many attempts have been made to demonstrate that most features of the corporation could be contracted by its stakeholders and as such do not depend on state intervention. Yet the core features of the corporate form identified above require more than just a contract among interested participants. They need legal authority to be recognized beyond this narrow circle and to enable the corporation to exist in perpetuity.

The functions of law can thus be restated as follows. Law is constitutive of markets and organizations that populate them in general terms; and law provides a normative guide for structuring relations in social and economic life. Making the corporate form available – that is, creating an 'off-the-shelf' form for organizing business with the specific features of independent legal personality, asset delineation and effective legal representation – is an example of the constitutive function of law in relation to markets. The specific allocation of decision-making powers, rights and obligations among different stakeholders within the corporation sets the normative parameters that govern their relations.

The recognition of the normative aspects of allocating rights and responsibilities among corporate stakeholders differs from conventional views associated with the Coase Theorem (Coase 1960). It states famously that the initial allocation of property rights is irrelevant, because markets will reallocate them to the most efficient user. As Coase himself was quick to point out, this assumes efficient markets, or at least the possibility to simulate market efficiency with appropriate legal fixes. If, however, markets are not efficient and cannot be easily patched up to simulate efficiency due to more fundamental problems, such as imperfect knowledge, then one can no longer ignore the normative implications of how rights and responsibilities are allocated or the implied distributional effects.

The distinction between the constitutive and normative functions of law is not hard and fast. The choice whether to make the corporate form available in general or to require additional conditions, such as minimum capital requirements, is ultimately a normative choice. Conversely, the allocation of rights and responsibilities associated with a particular legal form may determine whether it is viable at all. Differences in tax treatment, registration or capital requirements, for example, tend to affect the choice of the corporate form over alternative organizations, such as limited partnerships, or limited liability companies.

The proposed distinction between the constitutive and normative functions of law may also help address some confusions in debates about law's functions in economic ordering. Much of the current debate about differences between the common law and the civil law systems focuses on whether a legal system is more or less market friendly, or instead favors state intervention. A different way to look at this is to ask when and why society should subsidize certain arrangements by lending the enforcement powers of the state to them. When the law recognizes private arrangements – a contract, or a particular form of business organization – as legally enforceable, it grants an institutional subsidy to those arrangements and the stakeholders whose interests they serve. It may well be the case that these arrangements generate positive effects well beyond the narrow interests of the parties involved, but that cannot be assumed simply on the grounds that these arrangements can be rationalized as the product of 'spontaneous self-ordering.' Put differently, the basic, constitutive function of law has private as well as social costs and benefits. The balancing between these interests is an immanent political process, as recognized in the legal origin literature. Yet the issue is not whether the law is market or state friendly, but which interests receive institutional support and which do not, and what effects this has on social welfare.

The corporate form can serve as an example to illustrate this point: The recognition of an organization's independent personality, asset partitioning, and autonomous management enhances the prospect of amassing wealth in the hands of these organizations. The same attributes that can create not only private, but, indirectly, social wealth, can also generate substantial social loss. Independent legal personality paired with asset delineation allows individuals and company promoters to limit their exposure to the risk of some undertakings, which they can conveniently incorporate in a separate entity that is spun off or bankrupted in case things go wrong. This implies that they don't have to internalize these risks and are therefore likely to over-invest in ventures that can also create substantial harm to others. Prominent examples include the production of hazardous products, or pollution. One might also point to the effect the incorporation of many financial intermediaries that previously operated as partnerships, such as investment banks, has had not only on their profitability, but also for the risks they have taken on and the effect this has had on the stability of the financial system. Corporate law has made this game possible – and subsequent legal change that facilitated the use of the corporate form by these intermediaries has expanded it well beyond its original scope.

The constitutive aspects of corporate law do indeed create the rules of the game. They can either re-enforce or seek to offset the dynamics set in motion by the creation of the game in the first place. Couching this in terms of market vs state misses the point that the game itself is dependent on law's constitutive function in creating the game. It disguises as market friendly measures that further define, or seek to redefine a game that is not the outcome of spontaneous development, but results from active legal construction. Whether the particular take on this reconstruction is desirable or not will depend on preferences, points of view, and normative aspirations.

Law's constitutive function might be best illustrated by turning the clock back to the early statutes on corporate law. Two hundred years ago, in 1811, the state of New York became one of the first jurisdictions to create a statute that provided for the registration of corporate entities without need of state authorization on a company-by-company basis. The latter procedure was the norm in many countries until the mid-nineteenth century: The UK moved towards free incorporation in 1844, France and Germany only in the second half of the century. New York introduced the notion that certain legal benefits could accrue to a company without the legislature adopting a specific decree to authorize such benefits. The law thereby constituted a new game – the entry of new firms that altered the relation among various stakeholders; first between the state and entrepreneurs; and second between shareholders and creditors. The game had certain characteristics, some of which may strike us as strange today, but that is precisely the point: Only manufacturing companies were allowed to play it, and financial intermediaries were explicitly ruled out; a corporation could raise a *maximum* of US$ 100,000 in corporate capital, but not more; and it faced a sunset provision 20 years down the road. The statute thus reflects concerns about the rise of economically powerful entities with resources and time horizons well beyond the scope of democratically elected state legislatures. It is worth imagining how the continuation of this particular game might have played itself out in practice.

Pressures to open up the game for many more players and purposes ultimately prevailed, at least in the West. More and more countries allowed the free incorporation without specific state approval, opened the corporate form for all kinds of businesses and required additional licenses only for systemically important

undertakings such as finance. Moreover, increasingly corporate doctrine and
legal rules that limited the corporation to specific business activities that were
stated in its statutes, or required supermajority vote for any change in corporate
capital, were abolished or made more flexible. Countries in other parts of the
world have followed this trend with a lag effect.

Even in the West, however, the question as to where to draw the line between
constitutive and normative features of the corporation remains a lively one.
Many US states prohibited corporations from owning shares in other corporations until the 1890s. That created an effective stopgap against empire building
through company groups. Germany allowed an individual to set up a corporation and thus operate in parallel as a natural and a legal person only in the 1980s;
and the New York Stock Exchange changed its rules to allow the public listing of
investment banks only in the 1980s, thus paving the way for the reorganization
of these firms from partnerships into corporations with the benefits of limited
liability and the possibility to raise capital by issuing shares and operating with
'other people's money' on a far grander scale than before. Each of these steps
was a game changer in the relation of different stakeholders in the respective
societies in which they took place, rather than the reversion to a natural market
that pre-existed the regulations that came before it.

A similar dynamic has unfolded with respect to the specific rules of the game.
Recognizing the corporation as an independent legal entity with its own assets
and management is only a first step. Creating the rules that determine who
decides, who is accountable to whom, and how to resolve competing interests inside the corporation and between it and the society in which it operates
is yet another one. Early corporate statutes had little to say about that. They
focused on constituting the game – that is, on the conditions for allowing entities to benefit from the corporation's core features by choice rather than explicit
authorization. Governance and accountability issues became more important
only after these essential features had been resolved and the game had opened
up. As it turned out, the normative function expressed in the detailed governance arrangement of corporate law is highly complementary to its constitutive
function. Viewed in this light, these arrangements are not constraints placed on
a dynamic, self-organizing market, but part of the figuration of a game in light
of competing objectives and normative considerations in a changing world.

9.5   Conclusion

This paper has sought to present an alternative approach to comparative corporate law and governance. Rather than emphasizing differences in specific, static
features of law and governance between countries or legal systems, it notes the
remarkable constancy of some as opposed to other features of the corporate
form. The paper uses the concept of 'plasticity' to suggest that the success of the

corporate form can be attributed largely to its ability to combine certain core features that have remained constant with variable add-ons that reflect different norms and preferences over time and across different societies.

The concept of plasticity stands in contrast to a widely held assumption that there is a single optimal way of organizing the corporation, and that countries around the globe should aspire to this one form (or will be pushed to do so by market forces). The belief in an optimal model of business organization is intellectually wed to the notion of efficient markets. Yet, the efficient capital market hypothesis has been called increasingly into question with regard to its predictive powers and normative implications. If relaxed or even abandoned, corporate law and governance appears in a different light. If markets are not efficient, share prices cannot give clear signals about optimal corporate strategies. This opens the door for recognizing the complexity and inherent uncertainty of corporate decision-making. The bottom line is that corporate decision-makers do, indeed ought to, exercise substantial discretion. Monitoring and governing how they use their discretion is a complex task – for which there is not a single optimal solution. The merits of these solutions should be assessed based on the normative goals they are said to achieve. For cross-country and cross-system comparisons it makes little sense to presume a single goal. This is not meant to preclude comparative analysis, but to encourage a different type: comparing different systems against a range of goals; in terms of their ability to devise governance regimes that fit these goals, and more generally, their ability to constitute governance frameworks within which decision-making under uncertainty can take place in a relatively orderly and cohesive fashion.

Finally, the paper suggests that the distinction between core and variable features of the corporation, which lies at the heart of the plasticity concept, can also illuminate the role of law in ordering economic affairs. This distinction highlights the extent to which law is not only creating the rules of a game, which is presumed to take place even in the absence of law, but is creating or constituting that very game.

References

Aoki, M. (2010) *Corporations in Evolving Diversity: Cognition, Governance, and Institutions* (Oxford: Oxford University Press).

Black, B.S. (1990) 'Is Corporate Law Trivial?: A Political and Economic Analysis', *Northwestern University Law Review*, vol. 84, no. 2, pp. 542–597.

Coase, R.H. (1960) 'The Problem of Social Cost', *Journal of Law and Economics*, vol. 3, no. 1, pp. 31–44.

Coffee, J.C., Jr. (1989) 'The Mandatory/Enabling Balance in Corporate Law: An Essay on the Judicial Role', *Columbia Law Review*, vol. 89, no. 7, pp. 1618–1691.

Eisenberg, M.A. (2000) *Corporations and Other Business Organizations*, eighth edition (New York: Foundation Press).

Frydman, R., and M.D. Goldberg (2011) *Beyond Mechanical Markets: Asset Price Swings, Risk, and the Role of the State* (Princeton, NJ: Princeton University Press).

Gilson, R.J. (2001) 'Globalizing Corporate Governance: Convergence of Form or Function', *American Journal of Comparative Law*, vol. 49, no. 2, pp. 329–357.

Hansmann, H., and R. Kraakman (2000) 'The Essential Role of Organizational Law', *Yale Law Journal*, vol. 110, no. 2, pp. 387–475.

Hatton, K., and K. Pistor (2011) 'Maximizing Autonomy in the Shadow of Great Powers: The Political Economy of Sovereign Wealth Funds', *Columbia Journal of Transnational Law*, vol. 50, no. 1, pp. 1–81.

La Porta, R., F. Lopez-de-Silanes and A. Shleifer (2008) 'The Economic Consequences of Legal Origin', *Journal of Economic Literature*, vol. 46, no. 2, pp. 285–332.

10

An End to Consensus? The Selective Impact of Corporate Law Reform on Financial Development

Simon Deakin
Prabirjit Sarkar
Ajit Singh
University of Cambridge, UK

10.1 Introduction

The view that a strengthening of shareholder and creditor rights is a precondition for financial development has been a mainstay of global policy initiatives and national law reform programmes since the early 1990s. Underpinning this policy has been the 'legal origins' hypothesis (see La Porta et al. 2008 for a recent restatement). This claims that legal institutions have a long-run impact on the pattern of economic growth. Countries whose legal systems derive from the common law are said to place a greater emphasis on freedom of contract and the protection of private property than those with civil law roots, which tend to favor an activist role for the state. The common law/civil law divide is reflected in economic outcomes. Quantitative indicators have been developed to chart the extent of cross-national variation in the content of laws governing the business enterprise and to establish correlations between legal and economic variables. These show that common law systems have a higher degree of dispersed share ownership and more liquid and extensive capital markets, together with more highly developed systems of private credit, than civil law ones. In part through the *Doing Business* reports of the World Bank, these findings have come to influence policy reform in 'dozens of countries' over the past decade (La Porta et al. 2008: 326). Over this period, changes to corporate and insolvency law became a core component of the Washington Consensus view on the importance of legal and institutional reform in promoting economic development.

Important and influential as it is, the legal origins literature is radically incomplete at the theoretical level. The claim that legal origin is exogenous to the long-run pattern of economic development carries with it the implication that

189

the nature of a country's legal infrastructure is fixed at the point when it first adopts or has imposed upon it a particular type of legal system. This is a very strong claim. An alternative hypothesis is that, over time, legal systems interact with economic and political structures at national level, and in addition to influencing them, may be altered by them. National legal orders are also subject to external pressures from harmonization and regulatory competition. These aspects of the dynamics of legal change are not currently well captured by legal origins theory.

The empirical side of the legal origins literature also suffers from significant limitations. The datasets used to substantiate the legal origins hypothesis provide mostly cross-sectional evidence on the state of the law as it stood in the late 1990s and early 2000s. It is highly problematic to draw firm conclusions on the long-run relationship between legal change and economic development on the basis of cross-sectional data of this kind, although this is precisely what many papers do, including some of the most highly cited in the law and finance field (for example, La Porta et al. 1998).

In this paper we synthesize the results of an emerging body of work, both theoretical and empirical, which provides a critique of the legal origins approach. This work draws on newly constructed longitudinal measures of cross-national legal variation which make it possible to reassess the relationship between legal and economic variables, using time series and panel-data techniques. Section 10.2 discusses legal origins theory and identifies a number of core hypotheses to emerge from that body of work and associated new-institutional analyses of legal systems. Section 10.3 provides an account of methodological issues arising from the coding of legal change over time and provides evidence from longitudinal datasets concerning the nature and direction of legal reforms since the mid-1990s in a range of developed, developing, and transition countries. Section 10.4 presents econometric analysis concerning the relationship between legal reforms and economic outcomes in the area of financial development in these countries. In addition to summarizing some earlier research using longitudinal datasets, we present new findings for a sample of 25 countries over the period 1995 to 2005. Section 10.5 concludes.

10.2   Legal origins theory: refining the core hypotheses

The theoretical foundation of the interdisciplinary field of law and finance lies in new institutional economics, and specifically in the claim that the quality of legal and other institutions makes a difference to economic development and growth (North, 1990). Within this general framework, legal origins theory, which has been extremely influential among researchers and policymakers since the mid-1990s, has generated two central hypotheses (La Porta et al., 1998,

2008). The first of these is that the content of the law affects the nature of economic growth: countries with laws that protect contract and property rights, and in particular those which seek to foster financial development through norms of shareholder and creditor protection, should experience a pattern of market-driven, financially-orientated economic growth. The second version of the claim is that countries with a common law origin (that is to say, a system derived ultimately from the English legal system) are more likely to have market-friendly laws in the sense just described, than those with their origins in one of the civil law families (the French, German and Nordic legal systems).

La Porta et al.'s early work focused on the first of these claims. Their landmark 'law and finance' paper (La Porta et al. 1998) showed that countries whose laws gave shareholders extensive rights to hold boards and senior managers to account, thereby reducing agency costs associated with the separation of ownership and control in listed firms, had more dispersed share ownership and a higher level of stock market capitalization relative to GDP than countries with weaker laws. In this early work, La Porta et al. used the common law or civil law origin of national laws as an instrumental variable for the purposes of demonstrating that the direction of causation ran from the content of the law to financial outcomes, rather than vice versa. In their more recent work, La Porta et al. (2008) have come round to the view that legal origin should be regarded as a causal variable in its own right. They argue that because nearly all countries in the world inherited their legal systems by conquest or colonization (the 'parent' systems of England, France and Germany are almost the only exceptions) prior to industrialization in the course of the nineteenth and twentieth centuries, legal origin must operate as an exogenous influence on the economy (La Porta et al., 2008).

It should be noted that La Porta et al. (2008) do not claim that there is empirical evidence in favor of the view that legal origin, as such, is causally linked to differences in the level of economic growth across national systems. They provide evidence that legal origin is linked to the availability of external finance through capital and credit markets. Because other studies suggest that legal support for external finance promotes growth at the level of the firm (Levine, 1999), it is tempting to conclude that legal origin is also linked to overall economic growth. However, empirical studies have generally failed to find evidence of a direct link between legal origin and the rate of growth of national GDP (see La Porta et al. 2008: 301–2). This suggests that there are aspects of the relationship between the legal system and national economic performance which have yet to be unraveled.

The two versions of the legal origins hypothesis are to some degree at odds with one another. The 'law matters' claim implies that a particular, market-orientated configuration of legal rules can be expected to foster financial development (and possibly economic growth more generally) in more or less all countries. The second, the legal origins claim in its more specific sense, implies that the approaches of common law and civil law systems to the governance and regulation of financial markets are fundamentally distinct. If this were the case, we would not expect 'one size to fit all' in the case of law reform; rather, law reform should be tailored to local business and institutional conditions.

The legal origins literature tends to the view that the common law model is not just different from the civil law alternative, but superior to it: if not 'always' superior, the common law generally provides more efficient solutions because the right regulatory response is often 'simply less government' (La Porta et al. 2008: 309). However, if the common law truly offered a superior model, we should expect all systems to gravitate to the basic features of that model over time, as barriers to convergence are removed as a result of the expansion of global trade and the removal of formal restrictions on cross-border capital flows (Gugler et al., 2004). This interpretation is consistent with certain policy applications of the legal origins approach, for example those of the World Bank's *Doing Business* reports (World Bank, various years), which have actively promoted convergence of this kind. An alternative interpretation of legal origins theory, however, is that attempts to bring about convergence through law reform based on a single model of assumed best practice are misplaced, since they amount to the external imposition of a common law model on legal and business systems unsuited to that approach.

The legal origins literature began with a striking empirical finding about the relationship between law and finance, to which a theory was later applied. The legal origins field has arguably remained somewhat undertheorized. A reassessment of the legal origins approach in terms of first principles may help clarify its central hypotheses. The comparative institutional analysis approach (Aoki 2001, 2010) models institutions as routines, conventions and norms of varying degrees of formality, which serve to coordinate the behavior of agents in environments characterized by uncertainty. In this approach, institutions are seen as evolved, emergent solutions to collective action problems. More formal institutions, such as those of the legal system, contain mechanisms for storing and transmitting information about solutions which have been shown to work in particular contexts (Deakin and Carvalho 2011). Formality may enable more information to be retained in the system, but at the expense of limiting its capacity for variation. Thus, legal institutions may be broadly adaptive in the sense of reflecting features of their environments, without being optimal. Complementarities across institutions will tend to lock in particular configurations of norms and practices. An implication of lock-in is that an institution's effectiveness depends on the context in which it is placed, and on the presence of complementary mechanisms of governance. Such institutions which may not work effectively when transplanted out of context.

Figure 10.1 Legal origin as an exogenous influence on legal rules and the economy

Source: Armour et al. (2009c).

The idea that legal rules are endogenous to particular economic and political contexts is to some degree recognised by legal origin theory. According to La Porta et al. (2008: 288), legal rules in a given country can be expected to have 'changed, evolved and adapted to local conditions' over time. However, they draw a distinction between the content of substantive rules of law, which can be adaptive to local contexts in this sense, and what they call 'legal infrastructure', by which they mean the more deeply embedded rules and practices which determine the role of the legal system in shaping social and economic behavior. In this deep sense, legal origin is concerned not just with individual rules and principles, but also with different 'styles of social control of economic life'; civil law 'style' is 'associated with a heavier hand of government ownership and regulation than the common law' which, by contrast, 'is associated with lower formalism of judicial procedures and greater judicial independence than civil law', and hence with 'greater contract enforcement and greater security of property rights' (La Porta et al. 2008: 286). While there may be feedback between the economic context and particular rules governing (in this context) finance and enterprise, the core legal infrastructure is, by contrast, relatively unchanging: 'the legal system provides the fundamental tools for addressing social concerns and it is that system, with its codes, distinctive institutions, modes of thought and even ideologies, that is very slow to change' (La Porta et al. 2008: 308). Figure 10.1 captures this approach.

A more thoroughgoing coevolutionary approach would argue that even legal infrastructure, in the sense referred to by La Porta et al. (2008), is susceptible to influence from the economy, and cannot be regarded as an entirely exogenous force shaping economic growth. The supposed pro-market orientation of the English common law may be just as much the result of early industrialization, which created the conditions within which influential groups lobbied for rules which were broadly protective of property rights and placed constitutional limits on the role of government, as its cause (Ahlering and Deakin 2007).

A coevolutionary perspective need not imply that legal rules are *perfectly* matched to their environment; the evolution of the law is to a certain degree determined by the internal conceptual forms and language of legal process (Deakin and Carvalho 2011). However, the economic and political context can be thought of as providing the environment within which certain legal rules are selected over others, and hence persist over time. The relationship between the

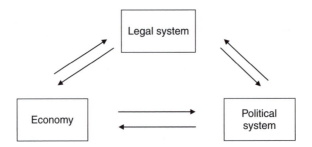

Figure 10.2   Coevolutionary model of the legal, economic and political systems

Source: Armour et al. (2009c).

legal system on the one hand and the economic and political systems on the other is one of dynamic interaction: no single system has priority, with each one exerting an indirect, environmental pressure on the evolution of the others (see Figure 10.2).

In the context of law and finance, the coevolutionary approach suggests a number of linked propositions concerning the functionality, diversity and transmissibility of legal norms. Firstly, rules of corporate law can be thought of as reflecting solutions to coordination problems which are to some degree general to market-based economic systems, in particular the principal–agent/shareholder–manager conflict which is inherent in the structure of the modern business enterprise. This view holds that as barriers to trade and capital mobility are removed and more or less all systems accept the principles of market-based economic development, the rules of company and insolvency (or corporate bankruptcy) law will converge (the *formal convergence hypothesis*). In addition, the effect of this formal convergence should be to induce common outcomes in terms of increased financial development (the *functional convergence hypothesis*).

Secondly, however, it could also be the case that solutions to coordination problems take different forms in particular countries, reflecting differences in the environments within which the relevant legal rules have evolved. Where structures of share ownership, modes of financing and management style differ across countries, agency costs will take different forms, which we would expect the legal rules of a given system to respond to: thus 'it may not be accidental that codetermination in the corporate governance domain and social democratic corporatism in the polity domain coevolved in Germany, while the main bank system, the lifetime employment system, and the close alliance between industrial associations and relevant administrative bureaux coevolved in Japan, both in contrast to the so-called Anglo-American model' (Aoki, 2001: 17). This perspective gives rise to what may be called the *complementarity hypothesis*.

Thirdly, and relatedly, the presence of complementarities across institutions in a given national context limits the scope for the successful transplantation of particular institutions into other contexts, no matter how well they may have worked in their systems of origin (Pistor et al. 2003). We may call this the *transplant hypothesis*.

These hypotheses raise issues which can only be resolved through empirical inquiry. The critical variables are those relating to the nature and pace of legal change across systems and the extent of continuing diversity in market structures and patterns of business organization. While there is abundant evidence concerning the second of these, data on the first have until recently been either unobtainable or unreliable. This brings us to the second problem with the existing legal origins literature, namely the partial nature of the available data on legal systems.

10.3   Leximetric analysis: revealing the pattern of legal change

10.3.1   Identifying core shareholder and creditor rights

The anti-director right index ('ADRI') constructed by La Porta et al. (1998), in common with most of their other indices, provides a view of the state of law as it existed in the mid-1990s. Since that time, there has been considerable legal change in the area of shareholder and creditor rights. Together with colleagues at the Centre for Business Research ('CBR') at Cambridge, we have constructed datasets designed to capture the direction and extent of that change. These datasets, among other things, provide a measure of legal protection for shareholders and creditors in a sample of 25 countries over the period 1995 to 2005. The sample includes a range of developed, developing, and transition systems.[1]

Legal indices are bound to be selective. The issue is how broadly representative of the content of legal rules they are and whether bias can be avoided in their construction. The ADRI developed by La Porta et al. (1998) consisted of six indicators that were intended to capture the extent of shareholder control over the board of directors and the management of the firm more generally. These indicators related to the following matters: how far the law required companies to allow shareholders to vote by proxy; to what extent the law prevented the blocking by the board of shareholders' voting and related rights prior to a general meeting; whether companies were required to observe a 'cumulative voting' rule allowing for proportional representation of shareholders on the board; the degree to which the law provided for shareholders to have pre-emption rights in respect of new share issues, thereby preventing the dilution of stakes; and the proportion of votes required to call a shareholders' meeting. The composition of this index has been much criticized for, among other things, an apparent 'home-country bias', that is, a tendency to treat US law as the norm and, as a result, to accord unduly low scores to civil law systems which employed different legal tools to reach the same end of protecting shareholder rights (see Spamann, 2010). There are other gaps in the index; it says nothing, for example, about board composition, or about the rules governing takeover bids. These are significant omissions since the issues of board structure and takeover regulation are at the core of the international corporate governance standards, in particular the OECD *Principles of Corporate Governance* which were first issued in 1999 (see now OECD, 2004), which have been used by many countries to benchmark their corporate laws and regulations since the mid-1990s.

The CBR's longitudinal shareholder protection index ('SPI'), on which we base our analysis, contains ten variables which are intended to capture a range of legal rules relating to shareholder protection in a way which avoids 'home-country bias' while also including the more important elements of the law reform process of the past decade or so. The ten indicators include a variable for board independence and one for the mandatory bid rule in takeover law, a mechanism designed to protect minority shareholder rights during bids. Other variables cover issues relating to the powers of the general meeting, dismissal of directors, and legal support for private enforcement of rights by shareholders against directors (see Armour et al., 2009a, 2009b, 2009c).

La Porta's et al.'s 1998 'law and finance' paper also coded for creditor rights. Their creditor rights index ('CRI') contained four indicators which addressed how far the law imposed restrictions on a company entering reorganization, whether it provided for an automatic stay on claims on secured assets in insolvency, to what extent it gave priority to secured creditors rights, and whether it allowed management to initiate a stay on claims through, for example, a 'debtor in possession rule'. The CBR's creditor protection index ('CPI') contains ten indicators (Armour et al. 2009c). The range of legal data coded here is significantly wider than that contained in La Porta et al.'s CRI. The first three indicators are concerned with rules on minimum capital, dividend distribution and directors' duties which, in broad terms, determine the balance of power between creditors and shareholders while the company is a going concern. The next three relate to the protection of the rights of secured creditors, and cover the scope for creation of non-possessory security interests, the priority of creditors' rights, and the extent to which the law allows secured creditors to enforce their rights without a court order. The final four indicators code the core parts of insolvency law (that is, the law of corporate as opposed to personal bankruptcy), and cover the extent of creditors' powers to initiate insolvency proceedings, rules on the stay of secured creditors, how far the law grants creditors (as opposed to a court or the company itself) the right to close the firm down, and how far the law determines the rank order of secured creditors in the event of bankruptcy.

10.3.2 Methodological considerations in coding legal change over time

The datasets we are analysing differ from those of La Porta et al. (1998) not simply in providing a longitudinal measure of legal change, but in the approach they take to the coding of legal rules. We make three major changes from their approach. First, the choice of variables in our datasets reflects the theory of 'functional equivalents' in comparative law. This holds that a rule which takes a certain legal form in one system may be expressed in other legal systems in a different way. To respond to this, we employ coding protocols which describe the variables of interest in broad, functional terms, rather than using as a benchmark the laws in force in a particular important jurisdiction (for example, the USA). We also code for rules which, while not part of the positive law, are found in codes and other self-regulatory instruments that could nevertheless be regarded as the functional equivalent of laws in many jurisdictions. This enables us to code several variables of key concern, such as rules contained in corporate governance and takeover codes, which La Porta et al. (1998) omitted from their analyses, apparently on the grounds that they did not take the form of positive legal rules in the US system. Secondly, we use graduated variables, in order to capture more of the detail of legal variation. La Porta et al. had largely relied on binary variables, in particular in their early studies (see, for example, La Porta et al. 1998). Thirdly, we code not just for mandatory rules of law as La Porta et al. mostly did, but also for default rules and other norms which could be modified by the parties directly affected by them, adjusting the scores given in each case to allow for the ease with which the rules could be modified.

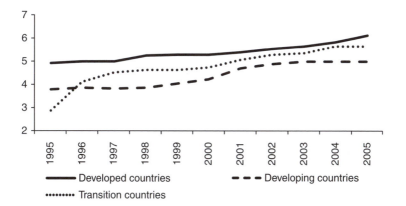

Figure 10.3   Shareholder protection 1995–2005: developed, developing and transition systems

Source: CBR Shareholder Protection Index, 25 countries, 1995–2005 (http://www.cbr.cam.ac.uk/research/programme2/project2-20.htm).

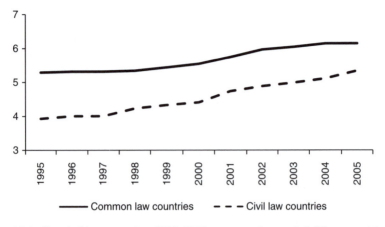

Figure 10.4 Shareholder protection 1995–2005: common law and civil law countries

Source: See Figure 10.3.

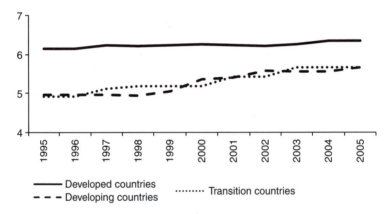

Figure 10.5 Creditor protection 1995–2005: developed, developing and transition systems

Source: See Figure 10.3.

10.3.3   Changes in the law governing shareholder and creditor rights 1995–2005

Figures 10.3–10.6 set out in graphical form the main trends in the SPI and CPI, broken down firstly by reference to countries grouped by their level of economic development and legal origin. In the case of shareholder protection, there was a steady rise in the score for all countries over the whole period. The two variables which account for most of the rise in the country scores are those relating to independent boards and the mandatory bid rule in takeover bids, both core aspects of the common law approach to corporate governance law (for further

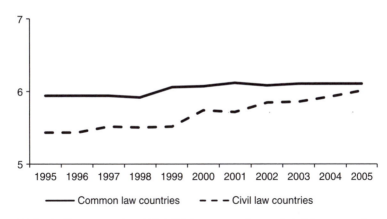

Figure 10.6   Creditor protection 1995–2005: common law and civil law countries

Source: See Figure 10.3.

details of these changes see Armour et al. 2009c). Transition systems saw a rapid jump in protection after 1995 in developing countries there was marked increase after 2000. Developed countries continued to have a higher level of protection throughout, but the gap between them and the rest had narrowed by the end of the period (Figure 10.3). When the same data are analysed by reference to legal origin, a closing of the gap between common law and civil law systems can also be seen (Figure 10.4). Thus the picture presented in La Porta et al. (1998), of strong protection for shareholder rights in the common law world, while true at the start of the period under review here which is also the point in time to which their study refers, was not true at the end of it, a finding which emphasizes the importance of having longitudinal data.

The charts tracking change in the CPI also show an increase in protection over time. Common law systems and developed systems again have the highest scores, but the gap between the common law and civil law has almost disappeared by the end of the period (Figures 10.5 and 10.6). Further analysis show that French-origin systems (a group which includes the southern European and Latin American systems) had lower scores than both English-origin and German-origin ones, but that this family of systems also experienced some of the largest increases in protection over time. This suggests that French-origin systems were converging on the more protective approaches of the other two legal families. By type of legal rule, the most significant changes across all systems involved greater protection for the rights of secured creditors, including legal measures to facilitate out-of-court enforcement of security interests (see Armour et al. 2009c for these further details).

Both datasets therefore provide strong evidence for *formal* convergence. The indices on which the data are based measure changes in the formal law, that is, the law contained in written legal texts and judicial decisions, as well as in those of certain 'soft law' measures such as corporate governance and takeover codes which are functional equivalents of state-based law in some systems. Thus we cannot interpret these findings, in isolation, as support for the claim that systems are converging at the *functional* level of the operation of legal rules. To do that we have to go to a further stage, that of econometric analysis aimed at identifying the nature of the relationship between legal change and economic change.

10.4   The relationship between legal change and financial development: econometric analysis

With longitudinal data available, it becomes possible to estimate the economic impact of legal change in new ways. The critical questions are: did the increases in shareholder protection law that we have observed in the legal datasets enhance stock market development; and did stronger creditor protection induce an expansion of private credit?

One way to address this question is to carry out country-by-country studies of the impact of the law, using time series analyses for those cases where very long runs of data are available. We have used these techniques in earlier work, using separate indices to those described above, which cover a longer period, 1970–2005, but for a smaller range of countries. Sarkar and Singh (2010) find no positive impact of increases in shareholder protection, and some negative effects, on financial development in France, Germany, India, the USA and the UK. Deakin et al. (2010) find a positive impact of changes in creditor protection on bank credit in India. A panel data analysis using a larger sample of countries may throw light on more generic properties of legal reform initiatives.

In the panel data analysis we report here for the first time, we consider two relationships: one is between the scores in the SPI and a number of measures of stock market development at national level, and the other is between the scores in the CPI and banking and credit market development, again at national level. As indicators of stock market development we employ the following four variables (used one at a time): (1) market capitalization, or the value of listed shares to GDP (*marketcap*): (2) the value of total shares traded on the stock market exchange to GDP (*sharestraded*); (3) the turnover ratio, which is the value of total shares traded over average real market capitalization (*turnoverratio*); and (4) the number of listed firms per million of population (*listed*), each in natural log. As indicators of banking and credit market development, we use the following two variables: (1) domestic credit provided by the banking sector as a percentage of GDP (*bankcredit*), and (2) domestic credit to the private sector as a percentage of GDP (*privcredit*), again in natural log.[2]

In our causality tests, we incorporate the level of economic activity in a country, which is represented by real GDP per capita in purchasing power parity constant dollars (in natural log: *gdppercap*). We also include in the regression data drawn from the Rule of Law Index (*rule*)[3] available from the WGI (World-wide Governance Indicators) project of the World Bank. Since our period of analysis is marked by the end of the dotcom bubble, we also use a dummy variable, *dot*, which takes the value zero for the period 1995–2000 and 1 for the period 2001–05.

To ascertain whether the direction of causality is from shareholder or creditor protection to financial market development or the opposite or both (reverse or cumulative causation), we use panel VAR (Vector-Autoregressive) Granger causality tests over the period, 1995–2005 (for further details, see Table 10.1). Our panel VAR causality tests first consider the overall sample of countries. We find no evidence of a causal relationship running from the SPI to stock market development (see Table 10.1a). Nor is there a causal relationship from the CPI to banking and credit market development. In short, looking at the sample of countries as a whole, legal change has not had an impact on financial development. There is also little or no evidence of reverse causation, that is to say, of changes in law caused by financial development.

However, a more nuanced picture emerges when we break the sample down by reference to countries' states of development and legal origin. When we compare developed, developing, and transition countries (Table 10.1b–10.1d), we can see that legal reform in the area of shareholder rights has had a discernible impact on financial growth in the developing country group. In their case, there is a causal relationship running from changes in the SPI to changes in stock market capitalization as a proportion of GDP. We also see evidence of reverse causation in developing countries, with a causal relationship running from the stock trading indicator to the SPI. In the case of transition systems we find evidence of an impact of legal change in the case of creditor protection, with changes in the CPI linked to domestic credit provided through the banking system. With the transition systems we also see evidence of growth in stock markets feeding into changes in the law, with causation running from the stock market listing indicator to the SPI. However, there is no discernible impact of the SPI on stock market development in transition systems.

Next we examine the impact on countries by reference to their legal origin. For the common law countries in our sample, changes in the SPI are positively linked to changes in three of the stock-market development indices, namely those relating to stock market capitalization, the value of stock trading, and stock market turnover (Table 10.1e). No such relationship can be found in the case of the civil law systems (Table 10.1f).[4]

The Granger causality tests we have just described can help to tell us whether one variable influences another, but they do not tell us whether the impact is

Table 10.1   Relationship between shareholder and creditor protection and financial development, 1995–2005: Panel VAR Granger Causality Tests

Table 10.1a   All 25 countries

Dependent variable: financial indicator	Excluded variable: legal index	Chi-square	Dependent variable: legal index	Excluded variable: financial indicator	Chi-square
marketcap lag = 2	SPI	2.3875	SPI	marketcap	3.5296
sharestraded lag = 2	SPI	1.9323	SPI	sharestraded	1.2111
turnoverratio lag = 3	SPI	3.6520	SPI	turnoverratio	1.1293
listed lag = 2	SPI	2.2775	SPI	listed	1.5507
bankcredit lag = 2	CPI	0.5377	CPI	bankcredit	0.1852
privcredit lag = 3	CPI	4.3508	CPI	privcredit	1.2799

Table 10.1b   Developed countries

Dependent variable: financial indicator	Excluded variable: legal index	Chi-square	Dependent variable: legal index	Excluded variable: financial indicator	Chi-square
marketcap lag =4	SPI	6.6875	SPI	marketcap	3.3164
sharestraded lag = 5	SPI	5.1465	SPI	sharestraded	0.8701
turnoverratio lag = 2	SPI	4.0408	SPI	turnoverratio	1.2568
listed lag = 3	SPI	0.5766	SPI	listed	4.0517
bankcredit lag = 2	CPI	0.2445	CPI	bankcredit	1.3692
privcredit lag = 5	CPI	2.1139	CP1	privcredit	2.7815

Table 10.1c Developing countries

Dependent variable: financial indicator	Excluded variable: legal index	Chi-square	Dependent variable: legal index	Excluded variable: financial indicator	Chi-square
marketcap lag =3	SPI	8.9586*	SPI	marketcap	4.8162
sharestraded lag = 5	SPI	4.5469	SPI	sharestraded	14.2443*
turnoverratio lag = 2	SPI	1.4009	SPI	turnoverratio	0.9437
listed lag = 2	SPI	0.7572	SPI	listed	0.8878
bankcredit lag = 5	CPI	6.8047	CPI	bankcredit	1.9443
privcredit lag = 5	CPI	8.6555	CPI	privcredit	26.8424*

Table 10.1d Transition countries

Dependent variable: financial indicator	Excluded variable: legal index	Chi-square	Dependent variable: legal index	Excluded variable: financial indicator	Chi-square
marketcap lag = 4	SPI	2.0098	SPI	marketcap	6.0362
sharestraded lag = 5	SPI	6.4195	SPI	sharestraded	4.9790
turnoverratio lag = 4	SPI	6.5939	SPI	turnoverratio	7.1069
listed lag = 5	SPI	4.1690	SPI	listed	24.2963*
bankcredit lag = 5	CPI	11.3119*	CPI	bankcredit	5.9692
privcredit lag = 4	CPI	5.0256	CP1	privcredit	2.9792

Table 10.1e   Common law countries

Dependent variable: financial indicator	Excluded variable: legal index	Chi-square	Dependent variable: legal index	Excluded variable: financial indicator	Chi-square
marketcap lag = 5	SPI	16.6203*	SPI	*marketcap*	0.8783
sharestraded lag = 5	SPI	16.2740*	SPI	*sharestraded*	5.6352
turnoverratio lag = 2	SPI	8.7912*	SPI	*turnoverratio*	1.2399
listed lag = 2	SPI	0.1205	SPI	*listed*	0.9630
bankcredit lag = 2	CPI	4.4378	CPI	*bankcredit*	11.7242*
privcredit lag = 4	CPI	3.2676	CP1	*privcredit*	9.0261

Table 10.1f   Civil law countries

Dependent variable: financial indicator	Excluded variable: legal index	Chi-square	Dependent variable: legal index	Excluded variable: financial indicator	Chi-square
marketcap lag = 5	SPI	8.8863	SPI	*marketcap*	6.3117
sharestraded lag = 5	SPI	6.9918	SPI	*sharestraded*	6.7643
turnoverratio lag = 5	SPI	8.2126	SPI	*turnoverratio*	4.6309
listed lag = 2	SPI	1.0952	SPI	*listed*	1.4964
marketcap lag = 5	SPI	8.8863	SPI	*marketcap*	6.3117

Table 10.1f (cont.)   Civil law countries

Dependent variable: financial indicator	Excluded variable: legal index	Chi-square	Dependent variable: legal index	Excluded variable: financial indicator	Chi-square
bankcredit lag = 2	CPI	0.1997	CPI	*bankcredit*	0.5737
privcredit lag = 3	CPI	5.0221	CP1	*privcredit*	0.4562

Notes: * Null hypothesis of no causality is rejected at 5 % level.
To ascertain whether Z (shareholder or creditor protection taken one at a time) causes X (alternative finance market variables taken one at a time), the panel VAR Granger causality test suggests fitting the following regression:

$$X_{it} = \sum_{j=1}^{p} \lambda_i X_{i,t-j} + \sum_{k=1}^{q} \psi_k Y_{i,t-k} + \sum_{l=1}^{r} \pi_l Z_{i,t-l} + \alpha + \beta.\text{rule}_{it} + \tilde{\gamma}\text{dot}_t + \varepsilon_{it} \tag{1}$$

where Y is GDP per capita (in natural log), *rule* is the rule of law index, *dot* is a dummy for dotcom bubble which takes the value zero for 1995–2000 and 1 for the period, 2001–2005, α is the fixed effect common across the panels and ε_{it} is the error term varying across time and panels. To choose the lags (p, q and r in the regression model) which indicate how many past years are to be considered, a number of possible approaches are available (such as the sequential modified LR test statistic (LRM), the final prediction error approach (FPE), the Akaike information criterion (AIC), the Schwarz information criterion (SC), and the Hannan–Quinn information criterion (HQ)). Different criteria often choose different lag lengths and we have used the maximum lag length in each case. Similarly, to test whether X causes Z we interchange the position of X and Z in the above equation.

The following abbreviations are used:
SPI is aggregate shareholder protection;
CPI is aggregate creditor protection;
bankcredit is domestic credit provided by the banking sector as a percentage of GDP (in natural log);
privcredit is domestic credit to private sector as percentage of GDP (in natural log);
marketcap is the value of listed shares to GDP (in natural log);
sharestraded is the value of total shares traded on the stock market exchange to GDP (in natural log);
turnoverratio is the ratio of the value of total shares traded to average real market capitalization (in natural log);
listed is the number of listed firms per million of population (in natural log).

In Table 10.1b the 11 developed (OECD member) countries are Canada, France, Germany, Italy, Japan, the Netherlands, Spain, Sweden, Switzerland, the UK and the USA.

In Table 10.1c the nine developing countries are Argentina, Brazil, Chile, India, Malaysia, Mexico, Pakistan, South Africa and Turkey.

In Table 10.1d the five transition countries are China, the Czech Republic, Latvia, Russia and Slovenia.

In Table 10.1e the seven common law origin countries are Canada, India, Malaysia, Pakistan, South Africa, the UK and the USA.

In Table 10.1f the 13 civil law countries are Argentina, Brazil, Chile, France, Germany, Italy, Japan, Mexico, the Netherlands, Spain, Sweden, Switzerland and Turkey.

Sources: Data on shareholder and creditor protection are derived from the CBR Shareholder Protection Index (25 countries) and Creditor Protection Index (25 countries) respectively (http://www.cbr.cam.ac.uk/research/programme2/project2-20output.htm).
Financial development indicators: World Bank Financial Structure Dataset.
Rule of law: World Bank Worldwide Governance Indicators.

Table 10.2 Relationship between shareholder and creditor protection and financial development indicators: panel-data estimation using the GMM technique

Table 10.2a Dependent variable: stock market capitalization as a proportion of GDP (*marketcap*)

Independent variable	Common law countries	Developing countries
SPI	0.333***	0.301***
	(0.107)	(0.075)
GDP per capita (*gdppercap*)	0.222***	0.348**
	(0.123)	(0.139)
dotcom dummy (*dot*)	−0.171	0.019
	(−0.198)	(0.184)
intercept (a)	0.558	−0.699
	(0.814)	(1.281)
R^2	0.659	0.329

Table 10.2b Dependent variable: value of stock trading (*sharestraded*)

Independent variable	Common law countries
SPI	0.057
	(0.108)
GDP per capita (*gdppercap*)	0.284*
	(0.123)
dotcom dummy (*dot*)	0.169
	(0.190)
intercept (a)	1.145
	(0.959)
R^2	0.368

Table 10.2c Dependent variable: turnover ratio (*turnoverratio*)

Independent variable	Common law countries
SPI	−0.359**
	(0.144)
GDP per capita (*gdppercap*)	0.246
	(0.229)
dotcom dummy (*dot*)	0.585**
	(0.236)
intercept (a)	3.385
	(1.446)
R^2	0.227

Table 10.2d Dependent variable: bank credit as a proportion of GDP (*bankcredit*)

Independent variable	Transition countries
CPI	−0.178
	(0.613)
GDP per capita (*gdppercap*)	−0.381***
	(0.153)
intercept (a)	7.414***
	(1.479)
R^2	0.189

Table 10.2e Dependent variable: shareholder protection (SPI)

Independent variable	Transition countries
listed firms per million of population (*list*)	0.535
	(0.427)
GDP per capita (*gdppercap*)	−2.721**
	(1.079)
intercept (a)	26.779*
	(8.979)
R^2	0.409

Table 10.2f Dependent variable: shareholder protection (SPI)

Independent variable	Developing countries
Value of stock trading (*sharestraded*)	0.831***
	(0.326)
GDP per capita (*gdppercap*)	−0.192
	(1.079)
intercept (a)	3.083
	(5.889)
R^2	0.160

Table 10.2g Dependent variable: creditor protection (CPI)

Independent variable	Developing countries
private credit as a percentage of GDP (*privcredit*)	0.022
	(0.031)
GDP per capita (*gdppercap*)	0.115
	(0.031)
intercept (a)	0.349
	(0.245)
R^2	0.00

Table 10.2h Dependent variable: creditor protection (CPI)

Independent variable	Common law countries
Bank credit as a percentage of GDP (*bankcredit*)	−0.038
	(0.051)
GDP per capita (*gdppercap*)	0.069***
	(0.021)
intercept (a)	0.15
	(0.089)
R^2	0.603

Notes: * significant at the 10% level.
** significant at the 5% level.
*** significant at the 10% level.
Robust standard errors are in parentheses. Our estimates are efficient for arbitrary heteroskedasticity and autocorrelation (using automatic band-width selection according to Newey-West). The Hansen-J statistic supports the proposition that all the equations are exactly specified.

Sources: See Table 10.1.

positive or negative. The next step is to ascertain whether the nature of the influence is favorable or unfavorable for those relationships where we observe statistically significant causal links. We do this by using the two-step GMM (generalized method of moment) technique. This involves using lags of the independent variables as instruments to tackle the problem of false correlation between the included (independent) variables and the error term which arises from the possible exclusion of time-variant factors in the regression. We use robust standard errors which are appropriate for dealing with the possibility of arbitrary heteroskedasticity and autocorrelation (using automatic band-width selection according to the Newey–West test).

The estimates that are reported in Table 10.2 show a significant *positive* impact of shareholder protection on stock market capitalization as a proportion of GDP in developing countries and in countries with a common law legal origin (Table 10.2a). By contrast, in common law countries, the impact of shareholder protection on the turnover ratio is *negative* (Table 10.2c). For developing countries, we find a *positive* impact of the value of stock market trading on shareholder protection (Table 10.2f). No statistically significant relationship between creditor protection laws and either bank or private credit is indicated (Tables 10.2d, 10.2g and 10.2h), and the sign in the correlation between creditor protection and bank credit in transition systems is negative. This suggests that we cannot interpret our Granger causality findings as evidence for a beneficial impact of creditor rights in transition countries.

10.5   Interpretation

In interpreting these findings, we first of all consider evidence on the causal relationship between legal change and financial development. We have seen that for the sample as a whole, no clear relationship emerges. This is evidence against the hypothesis of *functional convergence*. There is evidence of *formal convergence* of legal rules in more or less all systems, but no relationship between these legal reforms and the expected economic outcome variables, when the whole sample is considered.

However, when we look at groups of countries by reference to state of development and legal origin, a number of relationships begin to emerge. The first such finding is that increased shareholder protection leads to stock market development in the common law but not the civil law. The formal changes recorded in the SPI essentially map the worldwide diffusion of a legal model emphasizing independent boards, protection for shareholders during takeover bids, and shareholder control over key corporate decision-making processes. This model originated in the common law systems of the UK and the USA and spread out from there. Thus its positive impact on the group of common law countries as a whole is evidence in favor of the *complementarity hypothesis*. Laws originating in the two most influential common law systems appear to have worked to have had an impact in other systems which shared similar features in terms of relatively more dispersed share ownership structures and liquid capital markets. The absence of this impact on the outcome variables in the case of the civil law world is evidence for the converse proposition, namely the *transplant hypothesis*: common law institutions did not work well when adopted in the context of the civil law world's concentrated share ownership and relatively illiquid capital markets.

Our second finding is that shareholder rights matter more for financial growth in the developing world than in the developed one. At first sight this may appear a surprising finding. However, it needs to be seen in the context of evidence that firms are more, not less, reliant on stock market funding as a source of external finance in the developing world than in the developed one (Glen and Singh 2003; Gugler et al. 2004). Listed companies in developed countries make comparatively little use of the stock market to fund growth, preferring to rely on retained earnings. In the developed country context, the stock market acts principally as a mechanism of evaluation of corporate performance, rather than as a source of finance for firms. It is in developing countries that stock markets more clearly perform the function of directly supporting the growth of firms. Our finding suggests that legal reforms can usefully support this developmental role of stock markets.

The mix of positive and negative results we derived from our GMM analysis is consistent with this analysis. For common law systems, it would appear that the increase in shareholder protection led to a growth in the value of shares in listed companies as a proportion of GDP, but not to a corresponding increase in the value of shares traded. This is why the impact of increasing shareholder rights was negative in the case of the turnover ratio, which measures the value of shares traded over average real market capitalization. For developing countries, we see an increase in share values, but no fall in the turnover ratio. We also find that, in developing countries, an increase in the value of shares traded led to greater shareholder protection, suggesting a market-based demand for legal reform in those countries.

Thus for the common law world, the increase in shareholder rights contributed to a rise of share values which was not matched by a rise in the volume of trading. This is a hint, in our data, of the problem of 'irrational exuberance' in stock markets, and the resulting 'over-valuation' of equity, during this period. Our results suggest that this was a phenomenon associated with stock markets in developed, common law countries. For the developing world, by contrast, we see an increase in the volume of stock market activity, as measured by the values of shares traded, triggering demand for greater shareholder rights. Shareholder protection, in turn, helped to stimulate a growth in share values without a fall in the turnover ratio, implying that the level of stock market activity was more or less keeping up. Thus in the developing world, where growth in share values was matched by trading volumes, legal reforms were associated with financial development of a more sustainable type.

We now turn to our evidence on the question of reverse causality. We identified some influence of financial development on the law in developing countries, where growth in stock market trading was linked to an increase in shareholder rights. This is evidence of demand for legal reform in developing systems, of the kind that implies cumulative causation: legal reform is capable of stimulating financial growth which, in turn, intensifies the process of legal change.

10.6 Conclusions

As a result of the findings reported above, it is possible to obtain a clearer view of the relationship between legal change, financial development and economic growth. Shareholder-orientated corporate laws promote stock market growth in the common law world where complementary institutions, in the form of dispersed share ownership and liquid capital markets, are present. They have a greater impact, in terms of promoting financial growth, in the developing world than in developed countries. We also find evidence of reverse causation, with stock market growth triggering demand for shareholder rights, in the developing world. Our results on creditor protection are more ambivalent: we have weak evidence of a negative causal impact of creditor rights on bank credit in transition systems.

The absence of an overall correlation between law reform and financial market development indicates that the strengthening of shareholder rights and creditor rights has not had its intended effect on countries across the board. The positive impact of increased shareholder protection in common law systems, when compared to its non-impact in the civil law world, suggests the presence of complementarities between legal and financial institutions. The evidence that shareholder protection rights have stimulated financial growth in developing countries highlights the demand for external finance supplied through equity markets in those systems.

Outside these cases, however, national conditions appear to be setting limits to the effectiveness of legal transplants. Formal convergence of laws continues alongside persistent, underlying diversities. More generally, it would seem that laws work best when they are embedded in particular configurations of institutions at national level as opposed to being transplanted from outside. Thus our empirical results support the suggestion that legal rules are, to a significant degree, endogenous to the economic and political context of the systems in which they operate. Our findings question the validity of a 'one-size-fits-all' approach to law reform, and highlight the need for a more context-specific analysis of the contribution of institutions to financial development of the kind which may be appropriate for an emerging, post-Washington Consensus world.

Notes

1. The countries coded are: Argentina, Brazil, Canada, Chile, China, the Czech Republic, France, Germany, India, Italy, Japan, Latvia, Malaysia, Mexico, the Netherlands, Pakistan, Russia, Slovenia, South Africa, Spain, Sweden, Switzerland, Turkey, the UK and the USA. In addition to these datasets, described in the text, the CBR project has also produced longer time series, covering the period 1970-2005, for five countries: France, Germany, India, the UK and the USA. All the CBR datasets referred to in this paper can be consulted and downloaded on line. See http://www.cbr.cam.ac.uk/research/programme2/project2-20output.htm.
2. These are the standard measures used in analyses of stock market development and private credit at national level and are based on World Bank data. See the notes to Table 10.1 for further details.
3. This index is available for all the countries covered in the study for almost all the years, 1995–2005. For some years, no data are provided; in that case we used data for the following year. For example, where 1995 data are not available, we use 1996 data for both 1995 and 1996.
4. This analysis excludes the five transition systems which in principle have civil law origins on the grounds that, in the context of their development in the period under review, this feature was comparatively unimportant when set alongside their transition status.

Acknowledgements

We are grateful to the Economic and Social Research Council (Award reference RES-156-25-0037, 'Law, Finance and Development') and the Isaac Newton Trust for financial support, and for comments received on an earlier draft presented at the XVI Congress of the International Economic Association in Beijing, July 2011.

References

Ahlering, B. and S. Deakin (2007) 'Labour Regulation, Corporate Governance and Legal Origin: A Case of Institutional Complementarity?', *Law & Society Review*, vol. 41, no. 4, pp. 865–98.
Aoki, M. (2001) *Toward a Comparative Institutional Analysis* (Cambridge, MA: MIT Press).
Aoki, M. (2010) *Corporations in Evolving Diversity* (Oxford: Oxford University Press).
Armour, J., S. Deakin, P. Sarkar, M. Siems and A. Singh (2009a) 'Shareholder Protection and Stock Market Development: An Empirical Test of the Legal Origins Hypothesis', *Journal of Empirical Legal Studies*, vol. 6, no. 2, pp. 343–381.
Armour, J., S. Deakin, P. Lele and M. Siems (2009b) 'How Legal Norms Evolve: Evidence from a Cross-Country Comparison of Shareholder, Creditor and Worker Protection', *American Journal of Comparative Law*, vol. 57, no. 3, pp. 579–629.

Armour, J., S. Deakin, V. Mollica and M. Siems (2009c) 'Law and Financial Development: What we are Learning from Time-Series Evidence', *BYU Law Review*, vol. 2009, no. 6, pp. 1435–1500.

Deakin, S. and F. Carvalho (2011) 'System and Evolution in Corporate Governance', in P. Zumbansen and G. P. Calliess (eds), *Law, Economics and Evolutionary Theory* (Cheltenham: Edward Elgar).

Deakin, S., P. Demetriades, and G. James (2010) 'Creditor Rights and Banking System Development in India', *Economics Letters*, vol. 108, no. 1, pp. 19–21.

Glen, J. and A. Singh (2003) 'Capital Structure, Rates of Return and Financing Corporate Growth: Comparing Developed and Emerging Markets, 1994–2000', *Emerging Markets Review*, vol. 5, no. 1, pp. 161–192.

Gugler, K., D. Mueller, and B. Yurtoglu (2004) 'Corporate Governance and Globalisation', *Oxford Review of Economic Policy*, vol. 20, no. 1, pp. 129–156.

La Porta R., F. Lopez-de-Silanes, A. Shleifer and R. Vishny (1998) 'Law and Finance', *Journal of Political Economy*, vol. 106, no. 6, pp. 1113–1155.

La Porta R., F. Lopez-de-Silanes and A. Shleifer (2008) 'The Economic Consequences of Legal Origins', *Journal of Economic Literature*, vol. 46, no. 2, pp. 285–332.

Levine, R. (1999) 'Law, Finance and Economic Growth', *Journal of Financial Intermediation*, vol. 8, 36–67.

North, D. (1990) *Institutions, Institutional Change and Economic Performance* (Cambridge: Cambridge University Press).

OECD (2004) *Principles of Corporate Governance*, second edition (Paris: OECD).

Pistor, K., Y. Keinan, J. Kleinheisterkamp and M. West (2003) 'The Evolution of Corporate Law: A Cross-Country Comparison', *University of Pennsylvania Journal of International Economic Law*, vol. 23, no. 4, pp. 791–871.

Sarkar, P. and A. Singh (2010) 'Law, Finance and Development: Further Analyses of Longitudinal Data', *Cambridge Journal of Economics*, vol. 34, no. 2, pp. 325–346.

Spamann, H. (2010) 'The "Antidirector Rights Index" Revisited', *Review of Financial Studies*, vol. 23, no. 2, pp. 467–486.

11
Government Banks and Growth: Theory and Evidence*

Svetlana Andrianova
University of Leicester

Panicos Demetriades
University of Leicester

Anja Shortland
Brunel University, UK

11.1 Introduction

In their attempt to prevent financial meltdown in the Autumn of 2008, governments in many industrialized countries took large stakes in major commercial banks. While many countries in continental Europe, including Germany and France, have had a fair amount of experience with government-owned banks, the UK and the US have found themselves in unfamiliar territory. It is, therefore, perhaps unsurprising that there is deeply ingrained hostility in these countries towards the notion that governments can run banks effectively.[1] We show in this paper that such views are not well founded. Our empirical findings which utilize cross-country data for 1995–2007 suggest that, if anything, government ownership of banks has, on average, been associated with higher growth rates.

Hostility towards government-owned banks reflects the 'political view of government banks', which suggests these banks are established by politicians to shore up their power by instructing them to lend to political supporters and government-owned enterprises. In return, politicians receive votes and other favors. This hypothesis also postulates that politically motivated banks make bad lending decisions, resulting in non-performing loans, financial fragility and slower growth. The political view of government banks was purportedly backed by empirical evidence in a paper by La Porta, Lopez-de-Silanes and Shleifer (2002) (hereafter LLS). LLS predict a 0.23 percentage point increase in the annual long-run growth rate for every reduction in government ownership of banks by 10 percentage points, which is a very sizeable effect. These econometric findings have been used by the Bretton Woods institutions to back calls for privatizing banks in developing countries (see, for example, World Bank 2001).[2]

Not all previous literature is unsympathetic to the government ownership of banks. The 'developmental' view of government-owned banks, which dates back to Gerschenkron (1962), emphasizes the importance of governments in kick-starting financial and economic development. To this end, government ownership of banks can help address co-ordination problems that could prevent socially beneficial investments from being funded. A growing number of empirical studies indeed suggest that public banks in various countries have played a positive role in the process of economic growth.[3]

Although the 'developmental' view may, at first sight, appear to apply to the early stages of economic development, we argue below that it remains relevant today. The failures in corporate governance and regulation, which became apparent after the global financial crisis of 2007–2008, are not too dissimilar to the institutional weaknesses found in the early stages of development, which provide scope for government banks to play a meaningful role.[4] Many analyses of the crisis (for example, Igan, Mishra and Tressel 2009; Johnson 2009; Kane 2010) suggest that banks in developed countries behaved opportunistically by adopting excessively risky strategies aiming more at maximizing short-term trading surpluses, relying on government safety nets to cover downside risks. As a first step in our analysis, we explain how such strategies can undermine the growth-promoting role of privately owned banks.

The second step in our analysis, which is empirical in nature, is two-pronged. Firstly, we show that the LLS results, which pertain to an earlier period, are fragile to extending the set of conditioning variables to include more 'fundamental' determinants of economic growth such as institutional quality/quality of governance (Acemoglu, Johnson and Robinson 2005), which previous empirical literature has found to be significant (Knack and Keefer 1995; Hall and Jones 1999; Rodrik, Subramanian and Trebbi 2004)]. These new findings suggest that the support which the 'political' view of government banks has previously received from cross-country regressions is fragile.[5] We then proceed to main empirical contribution of this paper, which is to show that government ownership of banks has been associated with higher average growth rates during 1995–2007. Because this is such a surprising finding, we provide numerous robustness checks, including an extensive search for omitted variable bias using Extreme Bounds Analysis (EBA) and possible endogeneity bias using two alternative sets of instruments. We show that our main finding is robust, suggesting that the 'developmental' view of government owned banks remains relevant today.

Section 11.2 puts forward our theoretical contribution, which can be considered as a modern version of the 'developmental' view of government banks. Section 11.3 summarizes the two data sets we utilize and their sources. Section 11.4 contains our empirical contribution, which provides robust evidence of a positive association between government ownership of banks and economic growth. Section 11.5 summarizes and offers some ideas for further research.

11.2   A modern version of the 'developmental' view of government banks

The traditional 'developmental' view of government-owned banks emphasizes co-ordination failures and 'big-push' phenomena, which can create scope for government owned banks to play a growth-enhancing role. This view, however, predates the economics of information literature, which can provide an additional rationale for government-owned banks, particularly when the institutions that are aimed at containing moral hazard in private banking are weak.

In what follows, we put forward a new version of the 'developmental' view of government-owned banks, drawing on the implications of imperfect information for bank behavior and (the reality of) varying effectiveness of financial regulation. Specifically, we extend the model of government-owned banks in Andrianova et al (2008) in a direction that allows us to explore the effects of opportunistic behavior by banks on growth-promoting investment.

The informational problem that we focus on is the inability of depositors to observe the risks taken by banks.[6] When deposit contract enforcement is weak, banks can take excessive risks with depositors' money; at the extreme they could engage in looting behavior. This is precisely the set-up in Andrianova et al. (2008), which analyses the problems faced by depositors when deposit contract enforcement is weak and some banks behave opportunistically. Andrianova et al. (2008) assume that opportunistic banks will appropriate depositors' money if they obtain a higher expected payoff from doing so. Because that paper focuses on the implications of such behavior for savings mobilization, the investment side of the model is a very simple one. Specifically, there is no difference between an honest bank and an opportunistic bank when it comes to their investments. Thus, Andrianova et al. (2008) is silent on the implications of banks' behaving opportunistically for economic growth (other than any indirect effects through financial development).

Here we model opportunistic behavior by banks in a more natural way, by ruling out outright appropriation of depositors' money and instead allowing opportunistic banks to engage in speculation. Specifically, the opportunistic bank chooses between a 'sound' investment available to all banks and a speculative one that has a much higher payoff in the good state but fails completely in the bad state. In this setting, depositors can still lose all their money although we now introduce deposit insurance that compensates them with probability less than one. There can, therefore, be a divergence between the (expected) private and social returns of the speculative investment, as a result of which this investment can, in general, be considered growth-reducing. These assumptions accord well with many of the stylized facts surrounding the recent financial crisis, such as the compounding of agency problems by complex financial products, the lack of transparency and unreliable risk assessments by rating agencies. The assumption that some banks can engage in speculative investments that can enrich bankers in the good state but would impose a burden on the rest of society in the bad state is plausible. The anatomy of the recent crisis suggests that some investments by banks were opaque and complex by design, in order to effectively deceive investors who lacked the information and skills to evaluate them. It is, therefore, not unreasonable to postulate that such uncontained moral hazard will be growth-reducing. In addition to the gross expected social return being low or even negative once the costs in the bad state of the world are taken into account, there is the additional cost that moral hazard induced financial innovation requires talented individuals to implement it; in itself this represents an additional important distortion that is likely to reduce long-run growth rates.[7]

We introduce a risky investment as a reason for deposit contract breach in the theoretical setting of Andrianova et al. (2008) which in itself is an extended version of the 'circular city' model of product differentiation in banking.[8] As in Andrianova et al. (2008), we have private banks and a continuum of risk-neutral depositors located along a circle of unitary length. Depositors are uniformly distributed with unitary distribution density. A depositor incurs a positive transportation cost α which is proportional to the distance between the depositor and the bank. In the centre of the circle, a single government-owned and -operated bank is assumed to have been in existence for some time, and as a result has equal appeal to all depositors.[9]

The depositors are endowed with 1 unit of cash but do not have direct access to this technology: they could choose to put their cash holdings in a bank in order to earn a return. The money collected from private depositors can be invested into a safe technology with a constant rate of return r. All banks, private and government-owned, have access to this 'sound banking' technology. A proportion $\gamma \in (0, 1)$ of private banks have, in addition, access to a risky technology which returns R with probability $\rho \in (0, 1)$ or zero with probability $1 - \rho$. We call these private banks 'opportunistic' to distinguish them from the banks that do not have access to the gambling technology (the latter are called 'honest'): an opportunistic bank chooses whether to invest safely or to gamble with depositors' money. The type of private bank is its private information, while the value of γ is common knowledge. Because of the riskiness of the gambling technology, an opportunistic bank fails to honor its deposit contract whenever the return on the investment is zero. We think of this investment as speculative and socially unproductive. As such, it is outlawed by the regulator: a private bank that chose to gamble is found out with probability λ and if additionally the positive return from gambling is realized, the bank is fined by the amount $f > 0$ per depositor contract. Investments in the risky technology that return zero are sunk and in such case, depositors lose their deposit but with probability $\lambda \in (0,1)$ are compensated by the amount $0 < d \leq 1$ through a deposit insurance scheme.[10] We interpret λ as the index of institutional quality.

The government bank offers a net deposit rate of $r_s = r_s^0 - \alpha/(2\pi) > 0$ to all depositors. Private banks are located anywhere along the circle with bank i offering deposit rate r_i $(i = 1,\ldots,n)$ which is set up so as to maximize profits. There are potentially many identical private banks that can enter the industry at a positive fixed cost, F, and with free entry n banks will enter.

The timing of events is as follows:

(1) Private banks decide whether to enter; n banks enter.
(2) Private bank i $(i = 1,\ldots,n)$ sets its deposit rate r_i.
(3) Each depositor chooses the bank in which to place the deposit of 1 monetary unit.
(4) Opportunistic banks choose whether to invest in a safe or risky technology.
(5) Risky investments are discovered with probability λ.
(6) Returns on investments are realized. Payoffs are realized.

The model is solved by backward induction. Firstly, for a given strategy of opportunistic banks (namely, safe or risky investment), depositors choose which bank (private or government-owned) to deposit their money. Secondly, given the realized deposit demand, each bank sets the deposit rate at the level which maximizes its profits. Finally, for a given level of demand and profit-maximizing deposit rate, each private bank decides whether to enter.

Let $\kappa \in \{0,1\}$ represent an opportunistic bank's decision to invest into the safe technology $(\kappa = 0)$ or invest in the risky technology $(\kappa = 1)$. The expected payoffs of the depositor located at distance x_i from a private bank i and depositing his money in bank i is

$$U_i^{pb}(\kappa) = [1 - \gamma\kappa(1 - \rho)] \cdot (1 + r_i) + \gamma\kappa(1 - \rho)\lambda d - \alpha x_i, \tag{1}$$

where κ is set by the bank to maximize its profits. If the depositor, instead, puts his money into the government bank, then his payoff is

$$U^{sb} = 1 + r_s \tag{2}$$

because every depositor is one radius away from the state bank and $r_s = r_s^0 - \alpha/(2\pi)$. The expected payoffs of an honest bank and an opportunistic bank are, respectively:

$$V^{1-\gamma} = (r - r_i) \cdot D_i, \tag{3}$$

$$V^\gamma(\kappa, \lambda, d) = (1 - \kappa)(r - r_i) \cdot D_i + \kappa\rho \cdot [R - r_i - \lambda f] \cdot D_i, \tag{4}$$

where D_i is bank i's deposit demand. The government bank's expected payoff is $V^s = (r - r_s^0) \cdot D_s$, where D_s is the state bank's deposit demand. There is an assumed bias against the government-owned bank:

Assumption 1

$$r_s \leq r - 3/2 \cdot \sqrt{\alpha F} \tag{A1}$$

(A1) states that in the absence of speculative investments, private banking is more efficient than government banking.

Assumption 2

$$\alpha F > 1 \quad \text{and} \quad f \geq R - r \tag{A2}$$

(A2) states that the costs borne by private banks and depositors (set up and transportation) are higher than an individual deposit, and also that the punishment of a bank found by the regulator to have invested in the risky technology is higher than the excess return from the risky technology. The assumption is a technical one and makes the model set up interesting.

Three types of (pure strategy) equilibria are possible in this model. 'High' equilibrium (HE), where there is no demand for the government bank and no speculative investment by the private banks; 'intermediate' equilibrium (IE), with both the government and private banks having positive demand for deposit contracts; and 'low' equilibrium (LE), where there is positive demand only for the government bank and no private bank enters. For expositional convenience, define the following bounds:

$$\lambda_g \equiv \frac{\rho(R-r) - (1-\rho)\sqrt{\alpha F}}{\rho f}, \tag{5}$$

$$\lambda_x \equiv \frac{\gamma(1-\rho)(1+r) - (r-r_s)}{d(1-\rho)} \tag{6}$$

$$\tilde{n} \equiv \frac{1}{2F}\left(r - \frac{(1-\rho)(1-\lambda d)\gamma r_s}{1 - \gamma(1-\rho)}\right) \tag{7}$$

Proposition 1 *Assume (A1) and (A2). A unique (pure strategy) equilibrium exists and it is of type:*

(i) *HE, if $\lambda \geq \lambda_g$. Then $r_i = r - \sqrt{\alpha F}$, $D_i = \sqrt{F/\alpha}$, and $n = \sqrt{\alpha/F}$ $(i = 1, \ldots, n)$;*

(ii) *IE, if $\lambda_x \leq \lambda < \lambda_g$. Then $r_i = \frac{1}{2}[r + \frac{r_s + \gamma(1-\rho)(1-\lambda d)}{2(1-\gamma(1-\rho))}]$, $D_i = [r - r_s - \gamma(1-\rho)(1 + r - \lambda d)]/\alpha$ and $n < \tilde{n}$ $(i = 1, \ldots, n)$;*

(iii) *LE, if $\lambda < \min\{\lambda_x, \lambda_g\}$. Then $D_i = 0$ $(i = 1, \ldots, n)$, and $n = 0$.*

Remark 1 *The depositors' demand for private banking is greater when the institutional quality is higher and the proportion of opportunistic banks is lower.*

This is easily verified by noting that in IE the demand for a private bank i, D_i, is an increasing function of λ and a decreasing function of γ.

Remark 2   *When private and government banking coexist, the productivity of capital is increasing with institutional quality, decreasing with the proportion of opportunistic banks and (consequently) increasing with the share of deposits in the government bank.*

This immediately follows from the observation that in IE, the only equilibrium in which there is positive demand for both private and government deposit contracts, the productivity of capital is inversely related to the total capital invested in the speculative activity. The latter happens to be $\gamma \cdot n(\gamma, \lambda) \cdot D_i(\gamma, \lambda)$, and it is rising with λ and falling with γ.

11.3   Data and sources

For the first set of regressions aimed at examining the robustness of the LLS results we use the original database from LLS. We first reproduce results from Table V and Table VI in LLS; we then add two additional conditioning variables from the LLS database, which capture 'institutional quality': the index measuring bureaucratic quality and its insulation from political intervention (*bqualitt*) and the index of property rights (*prop_hf9*), which measures how well private property rights are protected.

For the new results we utilize annual GDP growth, GDP per capita and inflation rates from the World Economic Outlook database. Annual GDP per capita growth (in 2005 US$) is from the ERS. Data on institutional quality are from Kaufmann, Kraay and Mastruzzi (2005) Quality of Governance dataset. We create the average value of each institutional quality variable from all the available databases spanning 1998–2005.[11] Both transition economies and many oil-exporting countries have seen above-average growth during the period. We therefore include two dummy variables in the regressions. The first is a 'transition dummy' for all former members of the Warsaw Pact and the former Soviet republics.[12] The second is a dummy for all net oil exporters: we use the Fearon (2005) pirmary commodity export measure and construct a dummy for all countries were on average oil exports exceed 20 per cent of exports. This is to control for countries which have grown fast after their transitional recessions or on the basis of oil exploitation over the period, regardless of economic instability, institutional quality or regulatory structures.

The government ownership of banks variables are from the various World Bank datasets on banking regulation and financial structure (Caprio, Levine and Barth (2008) – henceforth, CLB). We supplement the CLB dataset with Cambodia, China, Vietnam, Myanmar, Iran, Iraq and Yemen. These countries did not respond to the World Bank questionnaire on government ownership, but we assume due to the political situation that 100 per cent of banks in these countries take political orders. These variables measure the 'percentage of (the) banking system's assets in banks that are 50% or more owned by government.'

The data are available for 1999, 2001 and 2005. We also include the LLS variable for government ownership of banks in 1995 (with government ownership at 50 per cent for compatibility) for robustness checks. Correlation between the CLB 2001 and 2005 variables is high (.866) and the correlation between the CLB 1999 and 2001 observations slightly lower (0.721). The correlation between the LLS 1995 variable and the CLB 2001 and 2005 variable is 0.654 and 0.572 respectively. Data availability is best in the 2001 dataset with 134 observations, compared to 110 in 2005, 103 in 1999 and 92 in the LLS dataset. Figure 11.1 shows the distribution of the 2001 CLB government ownership variable. Even after a decade of determined privatization under the 'Washington Consensus' a number of countries have preserved often significant shares of government ownership of banks.

The LLS regressions include a variable for the average years of secondary schooling in the labor force. We collect data on educational attainment from the World Development Report, which records the percentage of the labor force with at least secondary education. We use the first available entry for secondary and tertiary education between 1995 and 2007 to maximize data availability. The series is highly correlated with the Barro and Lee (2000) dataset on the average number of years of schooling. For both variables the number of observations for the final regression specification is low (80 observations or below) and there are no statistically significant effects for the education variable. The results reported below therefore mostly exclude this variable.

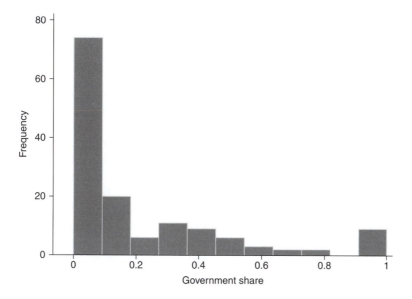

Figure 11.1 Government ownership of banks, 2001

More details on the variables we utilize and their sources, as well as summary statistics and the list of countries on which the reported results are based are provided in the Data Appendix.

11.4   Empirical analysis

11.4.1   Fragility of LLS results

Table 11.1 demonstrates the fragility of the LLS results when (their own) institutional controls are introduced in the equations. The first and second columns are the original LLS regressions (from LLS Table V and Table VI respectively) that we replicated and are reporting for comparison purposes. Columns 3 and 4 introduce bureaucratic quality and the index of property rights simultaneously in the equations, both of which enter with positive coefficients and are significant at the 5% level. The consequence of this is that the government ownership variable loses significance. In the third column – which contains few other controls– its sign remains negative but the magnitude of its coefficient declines by more than three quarters. Specifically, it decreases from just under 2.0 percentage points to under half a percentage point. In the fourth column which contains additional controls the LLS coefficient changes sign i.e. it is now positive. It is also noteworthy, that the introduction of the institutional variables increases the adjusted R-squared of the regressions from 0.34 to 0.54 in the first instance and from 0.50 to 0.64 in the second instance. Besides the results reported in Table 11.1, we have ran numerous other models that are not reported here for brevity but which confirm the fragility of the LLS results. These include running the regression with one institutional quality indicator at a time and using alternative institutional variables.[13]

To summarize, government ownership of banking in LLS had a negative and almost always statistically significant coefficient in the published model specifications. However, the LLS models excluded institutional quality indicators which are widely considered the more fundamental determinants of long-run growth. As argued in Andrianova et al. (2008), government ownership of banks is a symptom of weak institutions. If institutional quality is omitted from growth regressions, government ownership acts as a proxy for the missing fundamental variable. This explains the LLS results. Once, however, institutional quality indicators are added alongside government ownership of banking, government ownership of banks is no longer significant and the main LLS finding evaporates. 'Governance' matters, while bank ownership does not. The widely publicized negative effect of government ownership of banks was clearly the result of omitted variable bias, rather than the true effect of government owned banks on the long-run average growth rate.

Table 11.1 Robustness checks of LLS

Ordinary least squares regressions of the cross-section of countries

The dependent variable is the average annual growth rate of per capita GDP, 1960–95

	LLS Table V 'Simple Growth" Regressions'	LLS Table VI 'Growth Results with Different Combinations of Controls'	LLS Models with Institutional Variables	
	Ia	IIa	Ib	IIb
GB70 [gbbp_70]	-0.0199***	-0.0152*	-0.0045	0.0012
	(0.0071)	(0.0091)	(0.0064)	(0.0083)
Log of initial GDP per capita [logy60f]	-0.0160***	-0.0157***	-0.0211***	-0.0204***
	(0.0033)	(0.0042)	(0.0028)	(0.0037)
Average years of schooling [ysch av]	0.0061***	0.0044**	0.0028***	0.0021
	(0.0013)	(0.0018)	(0.0011)	(0.0018)
High inflation dummy [infl d20]		-0.0073		-0.0093
		(0.0070)		(0.0060)
Latitude [lat_abst]		-0.0039		-0.0004
		(0.0184)		(0.0157)
Private credit / GDP in 1960 [prif i60]		0.0217**		0.01467*
		(0.0102)		(0.0088)
Bureaucratic quality [bqualitt]	omitted	omitted	0.0040***	0.0043***
			(0.0010)	(0.0011)
Property rights [prop_hf9]	omitted	omitted	0.0081***	0.0066**
			(0.0029)	(0.0031)
Intercept	0.0911***	0.1019***	0.0764***	0.0808***
	(0.0171)	(0.0212)	(0.0137)	(0.0176)
Regional dummies	No	Yes	No	Yes
R^2	0.3403	0.5012	0.5416	0.6390
Observations	85	82	83	80

Notes: All variables are defined in La Porta et al. (2002) and taken from La Porta et al database available at http://mba.tuck.dartmouth.edu/pages/faculty/rafael.laporta/publications.html.
*denotes significance at the 10% level; **denotes significance at the 5% level; ***denotes significance at the 1% level. Figures in parentheses are robust standard errors.

11.4.2 Government ownership of banks and economic growth, 1995–2007

Table 11.2 presents the estimation results of the baseline model with different samples of countries. The first column provides the estimates using the entire dataset of 128 countries. The coefficient on government ownership is positive and significant at the 1% level. Its magnitude of 0.036 is quite large, suggesting that countries with 50 per cent government ownership grew by 1.8 per cent per annum more than countries without government owned banks, all other things equal. Moreover, the remaining coefficients have the expected signs and are statistically significant. The second column excludes seven countries with 100 per cent government ownership of banks (China, Vietnam, Cambodia, Myanmar, Iran, Iraq and Yemen) to check whether the main result is driven by these countries. While the coefficient on government ownership declines to 0.029, it remains sizeable and highly significant, suggesting that a 50 per cent government share in the banking system resulted in nearly 1.5 per cent higher growth p.a. The third column excludes countries with population less than four million, which results in a reduction in the number of countries to 92. Nonethelss, the coefficient of interest, if anything rises slightly compared to the first column, suggesting that small countries are not driving the results.

Column 4 restricts the sample to the LLS countries in order to examine whether the difference between our results and the LLS ones is due to the addition of 'new' countries in the later period. Once again, the coefficient of interest remains positive and significant at the 1% level. If anything, it rises slightly compared to the baseline sample. Column 5 utilizes the LLS measure of government ownership of banks (which is not available for the larger group of countries). This time the coefficient of interest declines to about half its size but remains positive and highly significant. Even with this smaller coefficient, the effect of a 50 per cent government share is economically larger: it is associated with a nearly 0.9 per cent higher growth rate during the sample period.

Table 11.3 reports regression results with additional control variables as a first check for possible omitted variable bias. These variables include an oil dummy, inflation, banking concentration, FDI and bank privatization, added one at a time. Of these additional control variables, only two appear significant: FDI and the oil dummy, although the latter is significant only at the 10% level. Notwithstanding the significance or not of these additional controls, the coefficient on government ownership remains positive and significant throughout. Its estimated coefficient is rather large suggesting that 50 per cent government ownership of banks is associated with 1.6–1.9 per cent higher growth p.a.

11.4.3 Extreme Bounds Analysis

Additional robustness checks are reported in Table 11.4, which summarizes the results of an Extreme Bounds Analysis (EBA), designed to check whether the

Table 11.2 Baseline model with different samples

Ordinary least squares regressions of the cross-section of countries
The dependent variable is the average annual growth rate of per capita GDP, 1995–2007

Sample	Model III Baseline sample	Model IV Excluding 100% government ownership	Model V LLS countries	Model VI LLS countries	Model VII Excluding small countries
Government owned banks in 2001	0.0359***	0.0289***		0.0365***	0.0370***
	(0.0072)	(0.0089)		(0.0093)	(0.0080)
Government owned banks in 1995 (LLS)			0.0172***		
			(0.0065)		
Log of initial per capita GDP	−0.0046***	−0.0041***	−0.0036*	−0.0044**	−0.0020
	(0.0015)	(0.0018)	(0.0020)	(0.0018)	(0.0015)
Regulatory quality	0.0112***	0.0103***	0.0089***	0.0136***	0.0071**
	(0.0025)	(0.0030)	(0.0029)	(0.0029)	(0.0030)
Transition	0.0324***	0.0332***	0.0169***	0.0234***	0.0271***
	(0.0063)	(0.0064)	(0.0043)	(0.0044)	(0.0059)
Intercept	0.0519***	0.0488***	0.0447***	0.0479***	0.0299***
	(0.0128)	(0.0146)	(0.0174)	(0.0159)	(0.0119)
R^2	0.4265	0.4031	0.2496	0.4714	0.4497
Observations	128	121	90	80	92

Notes: *denotes significance at the 10% level; **denotes significance at the 5% level; ***denotes significance at the 1% level. Figures in parentheses are robust standard errors.

Table 11.3 Robustness checks with additional control variables

Ordinary least squares regressions of the cross section of countries
The dependent variable is the average annual growth rate of per capita GDP, 1995–2007

	Model VIII	Model IX	Model X	Model XI	Model XII
Government owned banks in 2001	0.0362***	0.0382***	0.0326***	0.0326***	0.0370***
	(0.0079)	(0.0072)	(0.0101)	(0.0074)	(0.0098)
Log of initial per capita GDP	−0.0059***	−0.0040***	−0.0066*	−0.0045**	−0.0044***
	(0.0017)	(0.0017)	(0.0018)	(0.0017)	(0.0018)
Regulatory quality	0.0147***	0.0113***	0.0167***	0.0096***	0.0137***
	(0.0039)	(0.0030)	(0.0034)	(0.0028)	(0.0029)
Transition	0.0310***	0.0282***	0.0325***	0.0321***	0.0220***
	(0.0051)	(0.0059)	(0.0076)	(0.0062)	(0.0046)
Oil exporter oil > 20% of exports	0.0090*				
	(0.0054)				
Inflation average 1995–2005		0.0000			
		(0.0051)			
Concentration			0.0025		
			(0.0075)		
FDI/GDP average				0.0011***	
				(0.0004)	
Privatisation					0.0043
					(0.0067)
Intercept	0.0592***	0.0471***	0.0640***	0.0467***	0.0471***
	(0.0132)	(0.0135)	(0.0159)	(0.0145)	(0.0159)
R^2	0.4983	0.4605	0.4363	0.4669	0.4750
Observations	103	124	95	116	80

Notes: * denotes significance at the 10% level; ** denotes significance at the 5% level; *** denotes significance at the 1% level. Figures in parentheses are robust standard errors.

main result is robust to the inclusion of all possible linear combinations of an additional group of conditioning variables.[14] The baseline regression includes the variable of interest and a group of 'focus' variables which in our case include initial GDP per capita, regulatory quality and a transition dummy. Initial GDP per capita is an uncontroversial variable to include in the focus group as it is intended to capture convergence. The inclusion of the transition dummy in the focus group is intended to avoid potential upward bias of the coefficient of the variable of interest. Most transition countries experienced fast growth during the period under investigation while their banking systems remained at least partially under government control; not including a transition dummy could bias the coefficient of interest upwards as government ownership of banks may then act to some extent as a proxy for transition. Including regulatory quality in the focus group can be rationalized by alluding to the literature that emphasizes institutions as a fundamental determinant of economic growth, and is consistent with the uniformly highly significant coefficients found for institutional quality in Tables 11.1, 11.2 and 11.3. The group of 'doubtful' variables that we include in our EBA comprises: (i) the average inflation rate; (ii) trade openness, defined as the ratio of exports plus imports to GDP; (iii) liquid liabilities as a ratio of GDP; (iv) Foreign Direct Investment as a ratio of GDP; (v) banking concentration; (vi) small country dummy; and (vii) oil exporter dummy. Thus, the results presented in Table 11.4 are the summary outcome of running 256 regressions in the EBA (our fixed set and 7 additional variables). The extreme bounds reported in Table 11.4 are the upper and lower bounds of the estimated coefficient of the variable of interest, plus or minus two standard errors, respectively. As can be seen, the range between the lower and upper bounds does not include zero, which suggests that the main result is robust.

11.4.4 Instrumental variable estimation

Considerable caution needs to be exercised when deriving policy implications from findings obtained from cross-country regressions. The implicit assumption that is frequently made when interpreting such results is that the long-run relationship between the variables of interest is homogeneous across countries. This need not be the case if, for example, countries have differential access to technology. If the relationship is heterogeneous across countries, the average relationship estimated from cross-country regressions cannot be used to carry out policy experiments such as 'What is the effect on country X's long-run growth if country X's share of government ownership increased by Z per cent?' Even if the long-run relationship is homogenous across countries, it does not necessarily follow that the direction of causality is the same across countries.[15] Hence, while government ownership of banks appears to have been associated with higher long-run growth in a cross-country setting during 1995–2007, our results should not be taken to imply that increasing the degree of government

Table 11.4 Extreme Bounds Analysis

Dependent variable: average annual growth rate of per capita GDP for 1995–2007

	$\beta_{\text{government-owned banks}}$	Observations	R^2	Additional Z variables	Result
Upper Bound	0.0602	87	0.5836	Inflation, Concentration, Liquid Liabilites	
Baseline	0.0359	128	0.4265	None	Robust
	(0.0072)				
Lower Bound	0.0044	85	0.5831	Inflation, FDI, Liquid Liabilities, Small country dummy	

Notes: Variables included in every specification: Government-owned banks in 2001, initial GDP per capita, regulatory quality, transition. Doubtful (Z) variables: Liquid liabilities/GDP, openness, FDI, inflation rate, concentration, small country, oil exporter. The upper bound estimate is the largest estimated coefficient + 2 (robust) standard errors; the lower bound estimate is the smallest estimated coefficient –2 (robust) standard errors; the baseline is coefficient estimate and robust standard error in parentheses.

ownership in countries with little or no government ownership will result in higher long-run growth rates. Although reverse causality would be hard to rationalize in this particular case – there is no obvious reason why high growth rates should result in greater government ownership of banking – the relationship, if homogeneous across countries, could reflect common unobserved driving factors. Likely unobservable factors that may result in greater government ownership of banks and have an impact on GDP growth include various forms of financial market failures. If such failures abound and if, also, institutions designed to contain them are weak, governments may choose to nationalize banks. Such failures would, of course, correlate negatively with GDP growth, so arguably the coefficients of government ownership of banks on growth in OLS regressions may display downward bias.

The above analysis suggests that an important final check of robustness of our results would be to isolate the effect of the 'exogenous' component of government ownership of banks on economic growth in so far as this is feasible. To this end, Table 11.5 reports results from Instrumental Variable regressions designed to shed further light on this issue. We utilize two alternative instrument sets for the government ownership of banks. This is partly because our preferred instrument set results in a much smaller group of countries due to data availability. The second set of instruments enables us to estimate the model on the entire dataset, although the trade-off is a less than ideal instrument set.

Our preferred instrument for government ownership of banks is the black market premium which is, by definition, a good indicator of the extent of market failure and/or institutional weakness. This variable correlates well with government ownership of banks and much less so with economic growth, making it an ideal instrument for government ownership.[16] As an additional instrument we also use bank failures at the beginning of the estimation period, which provide another form of evidence on financial market failure which frequently necessitates takeovers of banks by government. In the regressions in which regulatory quality is treated as endogenous, we additionally utilize latitude and regional dummies as additional instruments. The first instrument is in line with a large literature searching instruments for institutional quality which emphasizes the disease environment encountered by settlers from colonizing powers as one of the primary determinants that shaped the nature of a country's institutions (Acemoglu et al. 2005). In similar vein, regional dummies can proxy different cultural attitudes toward institutions that govern economic interactions such as, for example, property rights or economic and financial regulation.

The downside of using the aforementioned instruments is that the sample is reduced to 58 countries, because the black market premium is missing for many countries. For this reason, in order to check robustness further, we also utilize legal origin dummies as an alternative set of instruments for government ownership of banks. These variables, which are available for the entire dataset,

Table 11.5 Government ownership of banks and growth

Average annual per capita GDP growth rate 1995–2007	IV regressions of the cross section of countries			
	Model I	Model II	Model III	Model IV
Instrumental Variables				
Government owned banks in 2001	0.0404***	0.0274**	0.0478**	0.0424***
	(0.0067)	(0.0124)	(0.0219)	(0.0133)
Regulatory Quality		0.0194**		0.0218***
		(0.0086)		(0.0087)
Exogenous Variables				
Log of initial GDP per capita	−0.0040*	−0.0081	−0.0050***	−0.0094***
	(0.0022)	(0.0053)	(0.0018)	(0.0046)
Regulatory Quality	0.0123**		0.0134***	
	(0.0051)		(0.0052)	
Transition			0.0328***	0.0326***
			(0.0064)	(0.0065)
Intercept	0.0445*	0.0786	0.0523***	0.0875**
	(0.0169)	(0.0429)	(0.0125)	(0.0370)
ψ^2 test of over-identifying restrictions [p-value]	0.14 [0.70]	4.95 [0.08]	4.02 [0.13]	5.89 [0.21]
F-test for weak instruments	36.09 [0.00]		12.37 [0.00]	
R^2 (first stage regressions)				
Gov. ownership	0.3137	0.3722	0.2723	0.2377
Regulatory Quality		0.2504		0.1337
Observations	58	58	128	128
Instruments: all exogenous variables plus	Black market premium, bank failures 1995	Black market premium, bank failures 1995, latitude, Sub-Saharan Africa, East Asia	Anglo-Saxon legal origin, French legal origin, Socialist legal origin	Anglo-Saxon legal origin, French legal origin, Socialist legal origin, latitude, Sub-Saharan Africa, East Asia

Notes: *denotes significance at the 10% level; **denotes significance at the 5% level; ***denotes significance at the 1% level. Figures in parentheses are robust standard errors.

are plausible instruments for government ownership of banks since legal origin is widely believed to be a good predictor of financial structure.[17] Countries of Anglo-Saxon legal origin are less likely to have government-owned banks than countries of French legal origin. Similarly, countries with socialist legal origin are more likely to have retained some government-owned banks than others, for historical reasons. However, pair-wise correlations between legal origin dummies and government ownership of banks show that these variables are less strongly correlated with government ownership than the black market premium. Moreover, they are not uncorrelated with GDP growth, which suggests that they may be weaker instruments than the black market premium.

The results of fitting the baseline model to the data using the first set of instruments are presented in the first and second columns of Table 11.5. The third and fourth columns show the results using the instrument set that contains the legal origin dummies. The table reports a test of the over-identifying restrictions – a significant test statistic indicates that the instruments may not be valid. The table also reports a test of weak instruments, which is, however, available only when the model contains one endogenous regressor. We also report some first-stage goodness of fit statistics to shed light on instrument strength. In the cases of more than one endogenous regressor (columns 2 and 4), we report Shea's partial R-squared.

Starting with column 1 in Table 11.5, it can be noted the coefficient of interest remains positive and highly significant. If anything, it is slightly higher than in the corresponding OLS estimate. This is, of course, not very surprising because, as explained above, endogeneity is more likely to bias the coefficient on government ownership downwards. Regulatory quality remains significant at the 5% level, while initial income remains negative but is significant at only the 10% level. The estimated coefficients of both these variables are very similar to those obtained with OLS. Importantly, the over-identifying restrictions cannot be rejected, suggesting that the instruments are not invalid. Moreover, the hypothesis of weak instruments is strongly rejected. The results in column 2, in which regulatory quality is also treated as an endogenous variable, are very similar to those reported in column 1. Both the endogenous variables remain positive and are significant at the 5% level. Although their coefficients change somewhat, the estimates are not too dissimilar from those obtained with OLS. Moreover, the over-identifying restrictions cannot be rejected at the 5% level and the diagnostics from both the first stage regressions indicate that the instruments are not weak.

In the third column, in which government ownership is instrumented with legal origin dummies, the coefficient of interest remains positive and significant; its magnitude is about 1.0 percentage point higher than the corresponding OLS estimates. The remaining variables remain significant and have the expected signs. Moreover, the over-identifying restrictions cannot be rejected suggesting that the instruments are valid, while the hypothesis of weak instruments can once again be rejected. Finally, the results in column 4, in which regulatory quality is also treated as an endogenous variable, reveal that both the endogenous regressors retain their positive coefficients and are now sigtnificant at the 1% level. The coefficient of government ownership is somewhat higher than the one obtained with OLS while the coefficient on regulatory quality doubles compared to the corresponding OLS estimate. The remaining coefficients have the expected signs and are statistically significant. Furthermore, the over-identifying restrictions cannot be rejected and the diagnostic statistics do not indicate that the instruments are weak.

11.4.5   The trade-off between regulation and government ownership

If government ownership of banks is indeed an answer to weak regulation, its positive effects on growth may well diminish as the quality of regulation improves. We test this corollary of our analysis by introducing an interaction term between regulatory quality and government ownership of banks in the baseline regression.

The results, which are obtained using both OLS and IV estimation, are reported in Table 11.6 Panel A. We also report the corresponding estimates of the baseline model without the interaction term for comparison purposes. The OLS estimates suggest that the interaction term is negative and highly significant. The level terms remain positive and significant, although with slightly changed coefficients. Government ownership has a slightly smaller coefficient of 0.0287 compared to 0.0359 in the baseline model, while regulatory quality has a slightly higher coefficient of 0.0153 compared to 0.0112 in the baseline. These results suggest that at the world average of regulatory quality (which is standardized at 0), a 50 per cent government ownership of banks is associated with 1.4 percentage points of higher growth per year.

Panel B in Table 11.6 uses the OLS estimates to report the partial derivatives of growth with respect to government ownership of banks at different levels of regulatory quality. These derivatives decrease in regulatory quality. At the 10th percentile of regulatory quality the derivative is 0.0448 and is significant at the 1% level. It declines to 0.0371 at the 25th percentile and then to 0.0309 at the median level, remaining significant at the 1% level. At the 75th percentile, the derivative declines to 0.0189 and is significant at the 5% level. At the 90th percentile of regulatory quality it declines to 0.01 and is no longer significant. These results, therefore, suggest that government ownership of banks has its greatest impact in countries with weak regulation. They also indicate that even in countries with above-average regulation, government ownership of banks is associated with higher growth. It ceases to have an impact on growth when regulation reaches one standard deviation above the mean.

Table 11.6 Regulation-government ownership trade-off

Panel A: Cross-country growth regressions

	Method of estimation OLS		Instrumental Variables	
	Baseline Model	Model with Interaction Term	Baseline Model	Model with Interaction Term
Government owned banks in 2001	0.0359***	0.0287***	0.0424***	0.0385**
	(0.0072)	(0.0075)	(0.0133)	(0.0192)
Log of initial per capita GDP	-0.0046***	-0.0059***	-0.0094**	-0.0095**
	(0.0015)	(0.0015)	(0.0046)	(0.0039)
Regulatory quality	0.0112***	0.0153***	0.0218***	0.0222***
	(0.0025)	(0.0028)	(0.0087)	(0.0073)
Transition	0.0324***	0.0315***	0.0326***	0.0328***
	(0.0063)	(0.0062)	(0.0065)	(0.0065)
Interaction Term		-0.0132***		-0.0048
		(0.0041)		(0.0121)
R^2	0.4265	0.4445		
Test of over-identifying restriction [p-value]			5.89 [0.21]	7.58 [0.18]
Observations	128	128	128	128

Panel B: Partial derivatives of growth with respect to government ownership of banks (using OLS estimates)

Level of Regulatory Quality				
10th percentile	25th percentile	Median	75th percentile	90th percentile
0.0448***	0.0371***	0.0309***	0.0189***	0.0100
(0.0076)	(0.0072)	(0.0070)	(0.0090)	(0.0110)

Notes: *denotes significance at the 10% level; **denotes significance at the 5% level; ***denotes significance at the 1% level. Figures in parentheses are robust standard errors.

However, these conclusions must be treated with some caution because the IV estimates reported in panel A indicate that the interaction term is not significant. These estimates have, however, been obtained treating not only government ownership as endogenous but also regulatory quality and the interaction term. To obtain these estimates we used the legal origin instruments and regional dummies and latitude set to start with, adding interactions between the legal origins and latitude to instrument the interaction term. The results are not sensitive to adding additional interaction terms to the instrument set. They do nevertheless continue to provide strong support to the hypothesis that government ownership of banks and regulatory quality are drivers of economic growth during 1995–2007, since both these variables enter with positive and highly significant coefficients. We cannot therefore be confident that the positive association between government-owned banks and growth weakens with better regulation.

11.4.6 Summary

To sum up, the evidence we have presented in this section suggests that government ownership of banks during 1995–2007 has been robustly associated with higher economic growth. Extreme Bounds Analysis shows that this finding does not appear to be the result of omitting other potentially important determinants of growth, such as openness, inflation, overall financial development or FDI. Moreover, we have shown that it is not the result of omitting bank privatization from the regressions.[18] IV estimations show that the main result does not reflect reverse causality or common driving factors, although the latter, if important, would likely have biased the relevant OLS coefficient downwards. Finally, we have explored the possibility that the effect of government ownership on growth declines with the degree of regulation. We have found strong support to this hypothesis from OLS regressions, which suggest that the effect is very sizeable in weak regulatory environments but becomes insignificant when regulation reaches the top 10 per cent international standard. If true, this result suggests that government-owned banks could be an effective substitute for good regulation.

11.5 Concluding remarks

Our empirical findings suggest that government ownership of banks has, if anything, been associated with faster long-run growth. Specifically, we have found that, conditioning on other determinants of growth, countries with government-owned banks have, on average, grown faster than countries with no or little government ownership of banks. It is therefore clear that, on balance, government ownership of banks, where it prevailed, has not been harmful to economic growth.[19] This is, of course, a surprising result, especially in light of the widespread belief – typically supported by anecdotal evidence – that '... bureaucrats are generally bad bankers' (see, for example, World Bank 2001, p. 127). Our results certainly suggest that such anecdotal evidence cannot and should not be generalized. Indeed, a growing body of evidence suggests that publically owned banks are no less efficient than privately owned banks and have helped to promote economic growth (Altunbas et al. 2001; Karas et al. 2008; Demetriades et al. 2008; Rousseau and Xiao 2007).[20]

There are a number of avenues for future research emanating from this paper. It could be fruitful to re-examine the political view of government-owned banks in light of our results. Our conjecture is that the view can be turned on its head because corrupt politicians in democracies might find it easier to extract rents from poorly regulated private banks than from government-owned ones. New empirical research could be fruitful if longitudinal data on government ownership of banks could be made available. Such data would allow exploiting the time dimension to arrive at more precise estimates of the parameters of interest and could provide the basis for more in-depth policy analysis.

Notes

* We would like to thank Badi Baltagi, George Chortareas, John Driffill, Jake Kendall, Alan Morrison, Dimitris Moschos, Alex Michaelides, Andreas Papandreou, Peter Rousseau, Andrei Schleifer and Yanis Varoufakis for useful comments. We acknowledge financial support from the Economic and Social Research Council (Award reference RES-000-22-2774). We gratefully acknowledge permission by John Wiley & Sons to reproduce material from S. Andrianova, P. Demetriades and A. Shortland (2011) 'Government Ownership of Banks, Institutions and Economic Growth', Economica, DOI: 10.1111/j.1468-0335.2011.00904.x.
1. See, for example, the article by Martin Wolf in the 16 October 2008 edition of the *Financial Times* which aptly summarizes these views in its conclusion: '...Crisis-prone private banking is bad; government monopoly banking is still worse.'
2. World Bank (2001: 127) elaborates on the LLS results as follows: '... the fitted regression line suggests that had the share of government ownership in Bangladesh been at the sample mean (57 percent) throughout the period from 1970 instead of at 100 percent, annual average growth would have risen by about 1.4 percent, cumulating to a standard of living more than 50 percent higher than it is today.'
3. Specifically, bank-level studies suggest that in Germany and Russia public banks are more efficient than private banks (Altunbas, Evans and Molyneux 2001; Karas, Schoors and Weill 2008). There is also evidence from China, where government-owned banks dominate the banking system, which suggests that banks there helped to promote economic growth, by boosting the productivity and value-added growth of firms they financed (Demetriades, Du, Girma and Xu 2008; Rousseau and Xiao 2007).
4. See, for example, Diaz-Alejandro (1985) for a classic analysis of the institutional weaknesses in Latin America that led to the failures of bank privatizations in the 1970s and 1980s. Zhang and Underhill (2003) provide a similar analysis of East Asian liberalizations that led to crises in the late 1990s.

5. We hasten to add that this does not necessarily invalidate case studies which provide support for this view (World Bank 2001), although one must also acknowledge case studies which provide support for the developmental view.

6. There are, of course, many other informational failures in banking that can provide a rationale for other forms of government intervention including financial regulation, deposit insurance, lender of last resort services and even deposit rate ceilings. See, for example, Stiglitz (1993).

7. See, for example, Hakenes and Schnabel (2006) for a similar argument. Recent evidence utilizing data from 44 countries during 1973–2005 in fact shows that wages in the financial sector relative to the technology sector had a negative and strongly significant impact on technological innovation measured by the stock of patents (Aug 2011), providing empirical support for our conjecture.

8. See Salop (1979).

9. This implies, in particular, a zero fixed cost of the government bank.

10. The depositor compensation probability does not have to be the same as the bank punishment probability. Nevertheless, as the two measure different aspects of government effectiveness, they are likely to be highly correlated and in the model we treat both as λ for expositional convenience.

11. The table of pair-wise correlations in the Data Appendix shows a correlation of average regulatory quality and government ownership of banks of -0.325. As in our previous paper, better regulatory quality is associated with a lower share of government-owned banks.

12. The table of pair-wise correlations in the Data Appendix shows that transition has been strongly associated with a strong growth performance in the period 1995–2007.

13. Some of these can be found in the discussion paper version of our paper (Andrianova, Demetriades and Shortland 2009).

14. Extreme Bounds Analysis has its origins in the pioneering work of Leamer (1983) and has been applied extensively in the growth literature.

15. For example, although cross-country regressions show that finance and growth are positively correlated, it does not follow that finance leads growth in all countries; indeed time-series evidence suggests that causality between finance and growth varies across countries. See, for example, Demetriades and Hussein (1996).

16. The correlation coefficient between the black market premium and government ownership of banks is 0.48; the same variable has a correlation coefficient with GDP per capita growth of 0.17.

17. There is, however, some recent literature by legal scholars that questions widely held views in economics about the relationship between legal origins and financial market structure (Armour, Deakin, Lele and Siems 2009), which is the main reason we are slightly skeptical of its ability to predict financial structure.

18. In the discussion paper version of the paper we show that privatization has a positive effect only when the transition dummy is omitted when it acts as a rather crude proxy for transition.

19. In the sense that, all other things equal, these countries did not have lower growth rates than countries without government-owned banks. It can, of course, be argued that countries with government-owned banks and high growth rates, like China, India and Taiwan, could have grown even faster if they had privatized their banking systems. This is, of course, something that cannot be tested directly, although the evidence presented in this paper and elsewhere (Demetriades et al. 2008, Rousseau and Xiao 2007) does not provide much support to this view.

20. See also Ang (2011) who finds that financial liberalization measures that include bank privatization have a negative and significant effect on technological innovation.

References

Acemoglu, D., S. Johnson and J.A. Robinson (2005) 'Institutions as a Fundamental Cause of Long-run Growth', in Philippe Aghion and Steven N. Durlauf (eds), *Handbook of Economic Growth*, vol. 1(1) (Amsterdam: Elsevier, North-Holland), pp. 385–472.

Altunbas, Y., L. Evans and P. Molyneux (2001) 'Bank Ownership and Efficiency', *Journal of Money, Credit and Banking*, vol. 33, no. 4, pp. 926–954.

Andrianova, S., P. Demetriades and A. Shortland (2008) 'Government Ownership of Banks, Institutions, and Financial Development', *Journal of Development Economics*, vol. 85, 218–252.

Andrianova, S., P. Demetriades and A. Shortland (2009) 'Is Government Ownership of Banks Really Harmful to Growth?', University of Leicester, Discussion Paper 09/11.

Ang, J. (2011) 'Financial Development, Liberalization and Technological Deepening', *European Economic Review*, vol. 55, pp. 688–701.

Armour, J., S. Deakin, P. Lele and M. Siems (2009) 'How Do Legal Rules Evolve? Evidence from a Cross-country Comparison of Shareholder, Worker and Creditor Protection', *American Journal of Comparative Law*, vol. 57, pp. 579–629.

Barro, R.J. and J.W. Lee (2000) 'International Data on Educational Attainment: Updates and Implications', CID Working Paper no. 42.

Beck, T., Demirgüç-Kunt, A. and Levine, R. (2000) 'A New Database on Financial Development and Structure', *World Bank Economic Review*, vol. 14, pp. 597–605. Updated November 2008.

Caprio, G., R. Levine and J. Barth (2008) 'Bank Regulation and Supervision', Permanent URL: http://go.worldbank.org/SNSUSW978PO.

Demetriades, P.O. and K.A. Hussein (1996) 'Does Financial Development Cause Financial Growth? Time-series Evidence from 16 Countries', *Journal of Development Economics*, vol. 51, pp. 387–411.

Demetriades, P.O., J. Du, S. Girma and C. Xu (2008) 'Does the Chinese Banking System Promote the Growth of Firms?', University of Leicester Discussion Paper in Economics, 08/6.

Diaz-Alejandro, C. (1985) 'Good-bye Financial Repression, Hello Financial Crash', *Journal of Development Economics*, vol. 19, pp. 1–24.

Fearon, J. (2009) 'Primary Commodity Exports and Civil War', *Journal of Conflict Resolution*, vol. 49, pp. 483–507. data (zipped in Strata format): sxprepdata.zip.

Gerschenkron, A. (1962) *Economic Backwardness in Historical Perspective: A Book of Essays* (Cambridge, MA: Harvard University Press).

Hakenes, H. and I. Schnabel (2006) 'The Threat of the Capital Drain: A Rationale for Public Health', GESY Discussion Paper no. 107, University of Mannheim.

Hall, R.E. and C. Jones (1999) 'Why Do Some Countries Produce So Much More Output per Worker than Others?', *Quarterly Journal of Economics*, vol. 114, no. 1, pp. 83–116.

Igan, D., P. Mishra and T. Tressel (2009) 'A Fistful of Dollars: Lobbying and the Finacial Crisis', IMF Research Department.

Johnson, S. (2009) 'The Quiet Coup', *The Atlantic Online*.

Kane, E.J. (2000) 'The Importance of Monitoring and Mitigating the Safety-net Consequences of Regulation-induced Innovation', *Review of Social Economy*, vol. 68, no. 2, pp. 145–161.

Karas, A., K. Schoors and L. Weill (2008) 'Are Private Banks More Efficient than Public Banks? Evidence from Russia', BOFIT Discussion Papers 3/2008, Bank of Finland.

Kaufmann, D., A. Kraay and M. Mastruzzi (2005) 'Governance Matters IV: Governance Indicators 1996–2004', World Bank.

Knack, S. and P. Keefer (1995) 'Institutions and Economic Performance: Cross-Country Tests Using Alternative Institutional Measures', *Economics and Politics*, vol. 7, pp. 207–227.

La Porta, R., F. Lopez-de-Silanes and A. Shleifer (2002) 'Government Ownership of Banks', *Journal of Finance*, vol. 57, no. 1, pp. 265–301.

Leamer, E.E. (1983) 'Let's Take the Con out of Econometrics', *American Economic Review*, vol. 74, no. 1, pp. 31–43.

Rodrik, D., A. Subramanian and F. Trebbi (2004) 'Institutions Rule: The Primacy of Institutions Over Geography and Integration in Economic Development', *Journal of Economic Growth*, vol. 9, pp. 131–165.

Rousseau, P.L. and S. Xiao (2007) 'Banks, Stock Markets, and China's Great Leap Forward', *Emerging Markets Review*, vol. 8. pp. 206–217.

Salop, S. (1979) 'Monopolistic Competition With Outside Goods', *Bell Journal of Economics*, vol. 10, no. 1, pp. 141–156.

Stiglitz, J.E. (1993) 'The Role of the State in Financial Markets', in *Proceedings of the World Bank Annual Conference on Development Economics* (Washington, DC: World Bank), pp. 19–52.

World Bank (2001) *Finance for Growth: Policy Choices in a Volatile World* (Oxford: Oxford University Press).

Zhang, X. and G. Underhill (2003) 'Private Capture, Policy Failures and Financial Crisis: Evidence from South Korea and Thailand', in G. Underhill and X. Zhang (eds), *International Financial Governance Under Stress* (Cambridge: Cambridge University Press).

Data Appendix

Description of variables and data sources

Variable	Dates	Number of obser- vations	Definition/Source
Average annual GDP per capita growth rate	1995–2007 2000–2007	177	In 2005 US$, http://ww.ers.usda.gov/Data/
Average annual GDP growth rate	1995–2007 2000–2007	173 177	World Economic Outlook database
Inflation average	1995–2005	177	World Economic Outlook database
Initial GDP per capita	1999	177	World Economic Outlook database
Initial GDP per capita	1995	173	In 2005 US$, http://www.ers.usda.gov/Data/

(Continued)

Continued

Variable	Dates	Number of obser-vations	Definition/Source
Government owned banks	1995	92	Share of assets of the top ten banks controlled by the government at the 50% level: LLS dataset available from http://mba.tuck.dartmouth.edu/pages/faculty/rafael.laporta/publications
Government owned banks	1999 2001 2005	103 134 110	"What fraction of the banking system's assets is in banks that are 50% or more government owned as of yearend". caprioetal2008 , permanent URL: http://go.worldbank.org/SNUSW978P0. 1999 data from original database, 2001 data from 2003 database; 2005 data from 2007 database
Regulatory Quality (Rule of Law and Corruption for robustness checks)	Average of 1998, 2000, 2002–2005	185	Measures whether regulation aids the functioning of private markets (including banking supervision). It also measures whether the regulatory burden is perceived to be excessive, undermining private business. kauf05, permanent URL: http://go.worldbank.org/V9IMLWZ4C1
Secondary education	First post-1995 observation	95	Percentage of labor force with completed secondary education (% secondary education + % tertiary education). World Development Indicators, December 2008
Openness	Average 1995–2005	165	Export Share / GDP + Import Share / GDP. World Development Indicators, December 2008
FDI	Average 1995–2005	160	Net Foreign Direct Investment / GDP. World Development Indicators, December 2008
Privatization	1970, 1995	92	(Government ownership of banks in 1970) - (Government ownership of banks in 1995): LLS dataset available from http://mba.tuck.dartmouth.edu/pages/faculty/rafael.laporta/publications

Continued

Variable	Dates	Number of observations	Definition/Source
Financial Development (Liquid liabilities/GDP)	1995	147	Beck, Demirguç-Kunt and Levine (2000)
Oil Exporters Dummy	1980–1999	138	Countries in which average oil exports exceed 20% of exports. Calculated from Fearon (2005).
Transition Countries Dummy	1988	185	Countries of the Former Soviet Union and the Central and Eastern European members of the former Warsaw Pact

List of countries

Albania, Algeria, Antigua and Barbuda, Argentina, Armenia, Australia, Austria, Azerbaijan, Bahrain, Belarus, Belgium, Belize, Benin, Bhutan, Bolivia, Bosnia and Herzegovina, Botswana, Brazil, Bulgaria, Burkina Faso, Cambodia, Canada, Chile, China, Colombia, Costa Rica, Cote d'Ivoire, Croatia, Cyprus, Czech Republic, Denmark, Dominica, Ecuador, Egypt, El Salvador, Estonia, Fiji, Finland, France, Germany, Ghana, Greece, Grenada, Guatemala, Guinea, Hong Kong SAR, Hungary, Iceland, India, Indonesia, Iran, Iraq, Israel, Italy, Japan, Jordan, Kazakhstan, Kenya, Korea, Kuwait, Kyrgyzstan, Latvia, Lebanon, Lesotho, Lithuania, Luxembourg, Macau, Macedonia, Madagascar, Malaysia, Mali, Malta, Mauritius, Mexico, Moldova, Morocco, Myanmar, Namibia, Netherlands, New Zealand, Niger, Nigeria, Norway, Oman, Pakistan, Panama, Paraguay, Peru, Philippines, Poland, Portugal, Puerto Rico, Russia, Rwanda, Saudi Arabia, Senegal, Seychelles, Singapore, Slovakia, Slovenia, South Africa, Spain, St. Kitts and Nevis, St. Lucia, St. Vincent and the Grenadines, Sudan, Suriname, Swaziland, Sweden, Switzerland, Taiwan Province of China, Tajikistan, Thailand, Togo, Tonga, Trinidad and Tobago, Tunisia, Turkey, Turkmenistan, Ukraine, United Arab Emirates, United Kingdom, United States, Uruguay, Vanuatu, Venezuela, Vietnam, Yemen, Zimbabwe.

Summary statistics of key variables

Variable	Observations	Mean	Std. deviation	Minimum	Maximum
GDP per cap growth average 1995–2007	123	2.938	2.307	−2.857	15.150
GDP per cap growth average 2000–2007	123	3.330	2.931	−5.477	16.676
Government ownership of banks 2001	142	0.202	0.280	0.000	1.000
ln GDP 1995	124	8.196	1.525	3.918	10.907
ln GDP 2000	124	8.315	1.539	3.895	11.141
Inflation average 1995–2005	121	13.884	29.097	−0.070	197.474
Regulatory quality	123	0.293	0.885	−1.987	1.889
Liquid liabilities	108	0.536	0.421	0.063	2.887
Openness	121	88.257	44.890	21.128	296.321
Foreign Direct Investment	113	4.195	4.143	0.063	22.099

Pairwise correlation of key variables

	[2]	[3]	[4]	[5]	[6]	[7]	[8]	[9]	[10]
[1] GDP per cap growth average 1995–2007	0.2341	−0.0522	0.2035	−0.0124	0.0758	0.4169	−0.0578	0.1194	0.4877
[2] Government ownership of banks 2001		−0.2894	0.2424	−0.4468	0.2383	0.0023	−0.1633	−0.1185	−0.0480
[3] Log GDP 1995			−0.1283	0.8116	0.1279	−0.0710	0.5721	0.2665	0.0503
[4] Inflation average 1995–2005				−0.2674	0.2257	0.1527	−0.2236	0.0119	0.0970
[5] Regulatory quality					−0.2232	−0.0617	0.5465	0.2643	0.0042
[6] Oil						0.0072	−0.0277	0.0018	0.0320
[7] Transition							−0.1740	0.1379	0.0206
[8] Liquid liabilities								0.4569	0.0899
[9] Openness									0.4191
[10] FDI									

Index